Bristol Radical Pamphleteer #48

God's Beautiful Sunshine

The 1921 Miners' Lockout in the Forest of Dean

W0007978

Ian Wright

ISBN 978-1-911522-54-6

Bristol Radical History Group. 2020.
www.brh.org.uk
brh@brh.org.uk

Contents

Acknowledgements iv

Glossary v

Introduction 1

Chapter One: Miners and Colliery Owners 21

Chapter Two: Labour and Capital 43

Chapter Three: Direct Action or Constitutional Reform? 68

Chapter Four: The Lockout 131

Chapter Five: A Glimpse of the Knife 191

Conclusion 219

Appendix One: Timeline of 1921 Lockout in the
    Forest of Dean 225

Appendix Two: FDMA Executive Committees 229

Appendix Three: MFGB Executive Committees 232

Appendix Four: Forest of Dean Colliery Companies 234

Appendix Five: Forest of Dean Collieries employing less
    than 120 men in 1918 238

Appendix Six: The Government 244

Appendix Seven: Booth in Nottingham 245

Appendix Eight: Labour Unrest in the 1919 Miners' Strike . 250

Bibliography 252

Acknowledgements

Many thanks to all those who have helped me with this project. I thank all those members of Bristol Radical History Group and friends who offered help and encouragement. Thanks to Mike Richardson who offered valuable advice and criticism and to Barbara Segal and Richard Musgrove for their copy editing, proof reading and comments, and Rich Grove for the design. Also, thanks to Lynda Mansell and Ewan Wright for help and encouragement. Thanks to the Forest of Dean Local History Society for allowing me use materials from their publications and CDs. Thanks to Nicola Wynn from the Dean Heritage Centre for providing diaries and memoirs from the Gage Library. Thanks to the staff at the Richard Burton Archives at Swansea University and Cinderford library. Thanks to Geoff Davies from Sungreen in Bream for allowing me to use photos from his website. Thanks to Dave Chapple for sending me information on the Forest miners he discovered while carrying out his research on the Somerset miners, and to Philip Kuhn who provided me with information about the 1919 railway strike. Thanks to Dave Tuffley for sending his research findings on the tragic deaths of miners in the Forest pits during this period. Thanks to David M Organ, Barbara Allen, Andrew Davies-Hoare, Averil and Alec Kear, Robert Toomer, Sheila Bowker, Graham Morgan and Dave Morris for allowing me to use quotes, pictures or biographical details of their relatives. Also, thanks for information supplied by Steven Carter and Jonathan Wright. The interpretations of events in this book are mine alone. I would be interested in hearing from any relatives of the people mentioned or from anyone who can provide more information for further research. Please contact iankwright1953@gmail.com

Glossary

Throughout the text monetary sums are given in the old imperial coinage:
d is a penny; s is a shilling and £ is a pound
12d = 1s and 20s = £1
Decimal equivalents: 1s =5p and £1 = 100p

CLC: Central Labour College
DWRGLU: Dock, Wharf, Riverside and General Labourers' Union
FDMA: Forest of Dean Miners' Association
FDCOA: Forest of Dean Colliery Owners' Association
MAGB: Mining Association of Great Britain
MFGB: Miners' Federation of Great Britain
MP: Member of Parliament
NADSS: National Association of Discharged Sailors and Soldiers
NFDDS: National Federation of Discharged and Demobilized Sailors
      and Soldiers
NMA: Nottinghamshire Miners' Association
NTWF: National Transport Workers' Federation
NUC: National Union of Clerks
NUR: National Union of Railwaymen
NUM: National Union of Miners
NUX: National Union of Ex-Servicemen
SSAU: Soldiers, Sailors and Airmen's Union
SWMF: South Wales Miners' Federation
TUC: Trades Union Congress
URC: United Reform Committee
YMA: Yorkshire Miners' Association

We have not entered upon the struggle without counting the cost; we know all about the depleted funds of our Union caused largely through unemployment, and we realise what it will mean to our families; but better die of starvation in God's beautiful sunshine than to go back to servile labour and semi-starvation caused by a wage that is not sufficient to keep a man, to say nothing about a family and a respectable home which the law expects us to do.

Letter to the *Gloucester Citizen* 9 April 1921
from a locked-out Forest of Dean miner.

Introduction

It is easy to see now that the decline of the past two years, far more than the apparent prosperity of the preceding period, is the real outcome of war, and to trace the decline of the coal industry to its fundamental causes in war exhaustion and economic dislocation perpetuated under peace. The history of the coal industry reveals, as clearly as anything, the true economic consequences of war, and therein lies the heart of the tragedy. Opinions differ in apportioning blame for this or that incident of the calamity, but the calamity as a whole is the fruit of war. A different policy in relation to the industry might have made its effects less terrible: none under the economic conditions of the post-war period could have prevented it altogether. Every man can make, in the light of facts, his own estimate of the relative importance of the various causes of disaster: the fact that it is a war disaster admits no dispute. The tragedy is felt, day in and day out, in many thousand homes.[1]

G.D.H. Cole, 1923

In 1918, the day after the armistice, Lloyd George promised returning servicemen a land fit for heroes.[2] However, in 1919 the government faced a developing economic and social crisis and cut back on its plans to invest in industry, housing, public works and public services.[3] Two years later, a severe economic depression had a devastating impact on the Forest of Dean mining community which led to the 1921 miners' lockout.

The thirty years leading up to the war witnessed unrivalled expansion in the coal industry as an ever-increasing workforce produced a record output of nearly fifty-seven million tons of coal in 1913. Coal had laid the foundations for British industrial supremacy and coal exports paid for the country's imports of cheap food. The continued prosperity of the industry and the society that was dependent upon it appeared certain. Up to 1914, the political affairs of the Forest coalfield community were largely entrusted to those local notables who symbolised the combination of the

---

1 G. D. H. Cole, *Labour in the Coal Mining Industry* (Oxford: Clarendon Press, 1923) 244
2 Lloyd George's actual words were homes "fit for the heroes who have won the war."
3 The Ministry of Reconstruction was formed by Lloyd George in 1916 with the aim of investing in labour, industry, transport, housing, education and health in the post-war years. But when the Ministry should have been in full swing in June 1919, it was disbanded along with other wartime committees.

values of commercial success, the idealised notion of an undifferentiated community and non-conformist and Liberal political identification.

However, in the years leading up to 1921, miners had become more and more dissatisfied with their remuneration and conditions of work, while becoming conscious of the importance of their contribution to the economy and the contrast between their living conditions and those of many others. In the years from its formation in 1888, British miners had, by 1919, built up their trade union, the Miners' Federation of Great Britain (MFGB), to be probably the most powerful trade union in the world, with the ability to challenge the colliery owners and their backers in the government. As a result, in this period, the industry was characterised by bitter struggles between the employers and the increasingly powerful MFGB.

World War One exacerbated the divergence of class interests in the Forest of Dean coalfield and eroded the prevailing pre-war purchase of liberal notions of a classless society and a commonality of interest among those who sought to represent the interests of the miners. Ultimately it was the challenge made by Forest miners in their struggles with the employers, combined with a more class-conscious approach to industrial and social problems, that was the legacy of the domestic and industrial experience of the war in the Forest of Dean. It was this legacy that accounted for the aggressive and militant post-war mood of labour in the coalfield, which the ruling class desperately sought to control and which laid the foundations for the confrontation in 1921.

Post-World War One Britain witnessed a wave of social unrest as workers demanded a more just way to organise society in response to aspirations raised by the war. At the forefront of this movement were the coal miners, many of whom had either fought in the war itself or worked flat out in the mines to produce coal for the war effort. However, in the post-war period, miners faced a developing economic crisis in their industry as demand for coal dropped away. In spite of this, there was no attempt by the government or colliery owners to introduce greater resilience in organisation, attitudes, and techniques or to reduce the pace of economic decline and absorb some of its stresses.[4]

In 1921, the response from the government and the owners to the depression in trade was to allow ruthless competition to take its toll. They argued they had no alternative but to resolve the economic crisis in the coal industry by radically reducing labour costs, translated into wage cuts

4 Barry Supple, *The History of the British Coal Industry*, Volume 4 (Oxford: Clarendon, 1987) 4-5.

of up to 50 per cent. The miners refused to go to work under these new terms and downed tools. As a result, on 31 March 1921, one million British miners, including many war veterans, were locked out of their pits; this included over 6,000 miners from the Forest of Dean. The consequences for miners, their families and the whole community in the Forest were brutal. However, the Forest miners fought a determined battle against this brutality and showed extraordinary resilience in their struggle for an alternative which they passionately believed was possible.

The shadow of the sacrifices many of these men had made during World War One hung over the whole conflict, as it became clear there would be no land fit for heroes. During the war, about 6,000 Forest miners worked long hours, including during holidays, to sustain the supply of coal; 22 were killed and many injured in the pits. At least 6,200 men from the Forest of Dean local authority area fought in the war, hundreds had died and many more had been injured and permanently disabled.[5] At Cannop colliery, 227 employees volunteered or were conscripted and 21 were killed out of a workforce of about 670. At Eastern United and Lightmoor collieries, 64 employees were killed out of a workforce of about 1200.[6] Some were so badly injured they no longer could work in the mines on their return.

In addition, the sacrifice experienced by the Forest working-class community shattered existing liberal notions of civil equality, particularly when it became apparent that the colliery owners had made huge profits out of the war. As a result, the majority of the Forest of Dean working class, from tradesmen to miners' wives, sided with the miners in a struggle many viewed as fundamental to the very existence of their community which was so dependent on mining.

The post-war stagnation in the British coal industry was compounded by competition from abroad, changes in the pattern of demand and a reduction in the levels of consumption. Despite the role of the state in developing the war economy, the post-war government refused to accept it could have a role in intervening and regulating the post-war capitalist economy. One of the consequences of this was that it failed to modernise the coal industry to enable it to compete with its foreign competitors.

The ownership of the British coal industry at the time was highly fragmented, consisting of 3000 coal mines and 1500 mining companies.

5 Forest of Dean Family History Society, https://forest-of-dean.net (Last accessed on 18 November 2019).
6 Sungreen, https://www.sungreen.co.uk/cinderford_east_dean/crawshay_employees.html (Last accessed on 18 November 2019).

After World War One, the colliery owners refused any attempt to re-organise their industry and did little to improve productivity, partly due to fears of nationalisation. The industry lacked investment and was dominated by the short-term seeking of profits and competition between the colliery owners who pursued their sectional interests. Slow modernisation of production methods, decrepit haulage systems, inadequate underground layout and poor and costly distribution contributed to the stagnation and low productivity. Inadequate training and conservatism of managers combined with poor industrial relations made the situation worse.[7]

This was particularly the case in the Forest of Dean where the eleven large deep collieries were owned by eight separate companies whose shareholders—a mixture of wealthy industrialists, aristocrats and local gentry—were primarily concerned with short-term returns from their investments. They made little attempt to modernise the mines and much of the machinery was ancient and dangerous. After the war, miners complained of the lack of drams to transport coal underground and timber to make the workplace safe.[8] This slowed up production, reduced earnings and often forced the men to work in dangerous conditions.

It might appear that British miners were simply victims of powerful economic forces which were beyond their control and that mining communities had little chance of resisting the attack by the government and colliery owners on their living and working conditions. However, such a view gives little agency to the miners themselves in terms of the tactics they adopted and the degree of solidarity within the wider working-class communities. Nor does it recognise the unique nature of the British coal mining industry and the insidious relationship which existed between the British colliery owners and the British state.[9]

This book describes the 1921 Lockout in the Forest of Dean by considering the personalities involved, the lost opportunities and the events leading up to defeat. It will discuss how events which took place nationally and in other districts influenced government policy and how this impacted on the whole Forest of Dean community. In particular, the book will discuss how unrest in the armed forces, civil disorder and industrial conflict created a climate which led many within the ruling class to believe that mining communities such as the Forest of Dean were

7 Supple, *The History of the British Coal Industry*, 32-33.
8 Ibid.
9 Patrick Renshaw, *The General Strike* (London: Eyre Methuen, 1975) and R. H. Desmarais, The British Government's Strikebreaking Organization and Black Friday, *Journal of Contemporary History*, Vol. 6, No. 2 (1971).

a dangerous threat to the existing social order and had to be defeated whatever the costs.

Chapter one provides background information on the Forest of Dean Miners Association (FDMA) which was the main trade union representing miners in the Forest of Dean and describes the particular characteristics of the Forest of Dean mining industry. It will then give an account of the living and working conditions in the Forest of Dean coalfield.

Chapter two places the 1921 Lockout within the context of a momentous confrontation between the forces of labour and capital. It will outline the competing ideologies within the labour movement which sought to represent the interests of the working class and how these were represented in the Forest of Dean. Secondly, it will briefly describe the forces of capital and its representatives in government.

Chapter three outlines the crisis facing the British government in 1919 and provides information on national and regional events which impacted on government policy. In this context, the chapter considers the tactical debate within the MFGB over constitutional reform or industrial action as the miners fought for the nationalisation of the coal industry and describes how this played out in the Forest of Dean.

Chapter four provides an account of the lockout in the Forest of Dean in relation to tactics and decisions that were taken nationally and locally.

Chapter five describes how the miners came to terms with the devastating impact of their defeat and how they organised in response. The final chapter attempts to draw some general conclusions.

Main Characters On The Side Of Labour

The biographies in this section describe the background and political careers, up to the end of 1921, of the main characters who were known to have been involved locally and nationally in the events surrounding the 1921 Lockout. The subsequent careers of some of the characters are described in the conclusion.

Forest of Dean Miners' Association

Ambrose Adams (1859–1930) was born in Ruspidge, the son of a coal miner. He started work as a coal miner on leaving school and became involved in the FDMA. He married Annie Wood in 1885 and had five children. In about 1897, he was elected checkweighman at Crump Meadow colliery, a role he held for the rest of his working life. In 1921, he was an auditor on the FDMA Executive. He was also Treasurer of Cinderford Co-operative Society and a magistrate.

Frank Ashmead (1856–1930) was born in Upton St Leonards, the son of a farmworker who died as a result of an accident at work at an early age. Frank Ashmead was brought up by his mother and started work as a farm labourer at the age of eleven. He then migrated to the Forest of Dean, first working as a farm labourer, then for the Bowson Colliery company and then as a hodder at Crump Meadow. He worked his way up to be a hewer and became an active member of the FDMA. He married Mary Baker in 1878 and went on to have seven children. In 1904 he obtained work in the Cinderford Co-operative Society as a baker's clerk but continued to be involved with the FDMA as one of its auditors. He was also a member of the Amalgamated Union of Co-operative Employees. He held many public positions including being a member of the Westbury Board of Guardians, Chairman of East Dean Parish Council, a member of East Dean District Council and a magistrate.

Herbert Booth (1886–1978) was born in Hucknall, the son of a labourer. Shortly after his birth, the family moved from Hucknall and lived at various other locations in the Nottingham area. When he was 11, Booth left school and started work on a farm, followed by a spell working at a brewery.[10] At 14, Booth started work at the Hucknall No 1 colliery where he became active in the Nottinghamshire Miners' Association (NMA) which was affiliated to the MFGB.

In September 1912, Booth was the first Nottinghamshire miner to win a Nottinghamshire Miners' Association (NMA) scholarship to attend the Central Labour College (CLC) which was established in August 1909 by a group of working class students and former students of Ruskin College, Oxford.[11] Booth returned to Nottinghamshire in August 1914 and joined the Independent Labour Party (ILP).[12] In addition, he became an active member of the NMA, campaigning for a left-wing programme.[13]

---

10 *Dean Forest Mercury* 29 March 1918.
11 In fact, Booth had planned to emigrate to Australia but cancelled his ticket after receiving the news that he had a scholarship at the CLC.
12 The Independent Labour Party (ILP) was established in 1893 in an attempt to create a working class organisation politically independent of the Liberal Party. It went on to provide much of the activist base of the Labour Party which did not have individual membership until 1918.
13 Alan R. Griffin, *The Miners of Nottinghamshire* 1914–1944, (London: George Allen and Unwin, 1962) 40.

In July 1915, Booth married Kate Wheat, the daughter of a greengrocer and they had four children. In March 1918, Booth was successful in his application to become the agent[14] for the Forest of Dean Miners' Association (FDMA).[15] He remained in this post during the 1921 Lockout but returned to Nottingham in 1922.

Harold Craddock (1895–1953) was born in New Road, Whitecroft. His father worked in the mines as a road repairer. Harold Craddock started work at 14 at the Princess Royal Colliery as a hodder. He was sponsored by the FDMA to attend a two-year course at the Central Labour College in London from September 1920.

Thomas Etheridge (1896–1969) was born in Cinderford, the son of a miner. On leaving school, he started work as an office boy in the FDMA office under George Rowlinson. He continued in a paid role as a clerk and then was appointed to the full-time role of FDMA Secretary and Financial Secretary in 1920.

William Hoare (1883–1959) was born in Bream, the son of Thomas Hoare, a stone cutter, and Sarah Pace. They together had eight children including William. Sarah Pace had two other children, born in the Monmouth workhouse before marrying Thomas Hoare in 1873. Two of William's siblings died as children. Thomas Hoare died in 1888 and in 1890 Sarah married Joseph James, a hewer, and temporarily moved to Drybrook. She went on to have three more children and moved back to Bream.

In 1901 Hoare, at the age of 17, was living with his family in Bream and working as a hewer. He then moved to work in the South Wales coalfield, and, in October 1907, he married Ann Jones from Pontypool. In April 1908 Ann died, possibly in childbirth. Hoare then moved back to live with his mother's family in Bream and worked as a hewer at Princess Royal colliery. In July 1918, he married Beatrice Morgan and by this time was working at Norchard colliery. He had seven children.[16] In 1919, he was sponsored by the FDMA to attend a two-year course at the Central Labour College in London.

---

14 See the discussion of the role of the agent on pages 21–22.
15 *Dean Forest Mercury* 29 March 1918.
16 Thanks to Andrew Davies-Hoare, William Hoare's grandson, for providing additional information.

Flour Mills Colliery, Forest of Dean, Glos.

Princess Royal (Flour Mill) Colliery.

Jesse Hodges (1880–1964) was born in Nailbridge, near Cinderford, and was a son of a miner. He married Annie Matthews in 1901 and continued to live at Nailbridge. They had nine children, one of whom died from laryngitis. He started work in an iron mine as a boy and then moved to Crump Meadow colliery where he worked his way up to be a buttyman and then to the post of checkweighman.[17] He represented Crump Meadow on the FDMA Executive during the lockout. His son, Jesse Hodges (Jnr), born in 1907, also became an active member of the FDMA. He worked for his father as a hodder at Crump Meadow in the early 1920s.

Reuben James (1870–1948) was born in Pillowell, the son of a miner. He started work in the mines at fourteen. He married Alice Charles in 1890 and went on to have six children and worked for a while as a haulier and then a hewer at Princess Royal Colliery. He soon became active in the FDMA and joined a group of miners from West Dean who opposed the existing policies of conciliation and moderation. He was elected President of the FDMA from February 1918 to February 1919 and then represented Princess Royal Colliery on the FDMA Executive during the lockout. Reuben James was related to Warren James, the free miner who was the leader of the 1831 Forest of Dean uprising against enclosure and the attack on free mining rights.[18]

Horace Jones (1874–1967) was born in Yorkley, the son of a miner. He started work at one of the Parkend pits as a teenager. In February 1889, he helped found the Pillowell brass band and was a playing member until 1903 when he helped found the Yorkley Onward band. He married Cora Biddington in 1901; however, she died two years later. In 1904, he married Florence Nelmes and went on to have six children. He lived in Yorkley Wood and by 1911 was working as a checkweighman in one of the Parkend pits. He represented the Parkend collieries on the FDMA Executive during the lockout. At this time, Jones was the conductor of the Yorkley Onward Band which led some of the demonstrations during the lockout. The band sometimes shared members with the Pillowell brass band who also led some of the demonstrations. Wallace Watkins, who represented Crown colliery on the FDMA Executive in 1919 and 1920, also played in these bands.

---

17 Interview with Jesse Hodges' son, also Jesse Hodges (born 1907), by Elsie Olivey on 16 May 1983, Gage library.
18 Ralph Anstis, *Warren James and Dean Forest Riots* (London: Breviary, 2014).

Wallace Jones (1894–1971) was born in Cinderford, the son of a grocer. He left school at the age of thirteen to become an apprentice baker and by 1911 was working as a woodman. Soon after, he moved to Aberdare to work in one of the Powell Duffryn collieries. In 1914, Jones joined the Royal Welsh Fusiliers and served with them in France and Belgium. In December 1916, he was with a group of six others who were buried by a shell explosion and was the only one to survive. He was invalided home to England and then was billeted to the Labour Corps where he was promoted to the rank of corporal. Jones married Hilda Merriman on 10 October 1918 and would go on to have four children: Evelyn, Iris, Cyril and Helen. After his discharge, in May 1919, Jones worked for a short time in a local timber yard before joining the Eastern United Colliery where he became an active member of the FDMA, eventually representing the pit on the FDMA Executive.[19]

Richard Kear (1876–1949) was born in Oldcroft, West Dean, the son of a miner. In 1891, at the age of 15, he was working as a general labourer and then started work at New Fancy as a hewer. He married Martha James in 1900 and went on to have six children. Kear represented New Fancy Colliery on the Executive of the FDMA during the lockout, having fulfilled the role as auditor for a number of years. He was a Primitive Methodist preacher who was "known in the Forest as a clear, earnest and intelligent local preacher".[20]

Charles Luker (1885–1970) was born in Chepstow. His father, Henry, worked as a fish dealer. By 1901, the family had moved to Whitecroft and his father was often seen around the area selling fish from the back of his cart. As a boy, Luker started work as a trammer in the mines and by 1911 he had started working as a hewer at the Crown Colliery. He married Esther Phipps in 1912 and had two children. In 1919, he was elected as Secretary of the FDMA. The following year, the post of Secretary and Treasurer were combined to form the role of Financial Secretary and Thomas Etheridge took over the role, but Luker continued to represent Crown colliery on the FDMA Executive.

David Organ (1876–1954) was born in Oldcroft in West Dean, the son of a farm labourer. He started work in one of the Parkend collieries at

---

19 Thanks to Sheila Bowker, the granddaughter of Wallace Jones, for providing biographical details.
20 *Dean Forest Guardian* March 1914, quoted in Averil Kear, *Bermuda Dick*, (Lydney: Lightmoor, 2002) 146.

the age of thirteen. Organ married Kate Phipps, the daughter of a local stonemason, in September 1896. Soon after their marriage, they moved to Derby where Organ worked as a railway porter. They then moved to Rotherham where their first two children were born. However, in 1900, the family returned to the Forest and moved into a small cottage in Pillowell and Organ gained work at Norchard Colliery in Lydney as a coal hewer. The family supplemented their income selling confectionary and fish and chips. In 1913, Organ was elected checkweighman[21] at Norchard Colliery. In the December 1913 election of officers for the FDMA Executive, Organ was elected Vice President, a role he held until 1919. In 1917, his family moved to a larger house just down the road from their old one. By this time the family had grown to nine children. He was elected President of the FDMA in 1919.[22]

Martin Perkins (1858–1927) was born in Cinderford, the son of a miner, and started work in the pits at the age of fourteen. He was elected as checkweighman at Lightmoor colliery and represented the pit on the FDMA Executive during the lockout. He was President of the FDMA from 1913 to the end of 1917. He was also President of Cinderford Co-operative Society for over a quarter of a century and President of the FDMA's General Accident and Health Insurance Society. After the war, he became a JP and member of the Forest of Dean Council of School Managers. He regularly attended the Baptist chapel.

Enos Cooper Taylor (1862–1941) was born in Cinderford, the son of a miner. When he started work, he trained to operate the engines at Foxes Bridge colliery and by 1901 had been appointed as checkweighman at the pit. He married Annie Baker in 1897 and had five children. He lived at the Colliers Arms, High Street, Cinderford where his wife worked. He represented Foxes Bridge on the FDMA Executive during the lockout.

William Vedmore (1877–1924) was born in Whitecroft, the son of a miner. He worked at Parkend colliery as a hewer. He married Harriett May Thomas from Bream in 1902 and had six children. He represented the Parkend collieries on the FDMA Executive during the lockout.

---

21 See the discussion of the role of the checkweighman on page 31.
22 These biographical details have been taken from David M Organ, *The Life and Times of David Richard Organ, Leading the Forest Miners' Struggle*, (Cheltenham: Apex, 2011).

Albert Wilding (1882–1941) was born in Pontypool where his father, who was born in the Forest of Dean, worked in the mines. The family moved back to Whitecroft where Albert found work in the mines. He married Flora Phipps in 1907 and went on to have six children. He was elected Vice President of the FDMA in May 1919 and remained in that role throughout the 1921 Lockout.

The Craftsmen

Jack B Allen was an ex-official of the Scottish Miners' Association and also worked in Cumberland. He was appointed the agent for the Forest of Dean Craftsmen Association in March 1921.

Charles Cox (1871–1951) lived in Bream. He married Clara Jenkins in 1895 and had three children. Cox worked as a carpenter at Princess Royal and Norchard collieries. He was President of the West Dean Craftsmen Association and Secretary of Bream Co-operative Society during the lockout.

The Railwaymen and Tinplatemen

James Collins Birt (1886–1935) was born in Lydney, the son of a railwayman. His first job was working at a bakery and then he gained employment as a signalman on the railway. He married Jessie Barron in 1913 and had three children. He became active within the NUR and by 1918 was elected to the role of Secretary. In 1918, he was appointed as agent for the Forest of Dean Labour Party and was instrumental in getting James Wignall elected as a Labour MP in December 1918. At this time, he was also elected as a County Councillor. In October 1922, he emigrated to Canada with his family.

Arthur Holder (1862-1932) was born in Randwick, the son of a gardener. He started work as a woollen clothworker and then got a job as a guard on the railways and moved to Gloucester. He married Alice Young in 1906 and had three children. He was President of the local Triple Alliance Strike Committee and Gloucester NUR during the lockout.

James Leonard Jones (1879-1966) was born in Cinderford in 1879, the son of a miner. In 1895, he obtained work on the railway, working as a porter, first at Pen-y-Craig in the Rhondda and then Newnham. In 1898, he was promoted to the role of goods checker at Cinderford and remained in this role for most of his working life. He married Sarah Barnhard in 1905 and went on to have six children. He was a conductor for Cinderford Town Prize Brass Band which often played at trade union rallies. The Cinderford Branch of the NUR was formed in May 1914 with its headquarters at the Railway Hotel and Jones was elected as President. He was elected as councillor for East Dean Parish Council in 1917.

George Powell (1867-1955) was born in Lydney. He started work as a teenager at Lydney tin works as a labourer and worked his way up to a skilled job as a roller man. He married Edith Everett in 1889 and had twelve children. He soon became active within his trade union, the Dock, Wharf, Riverside and General Labourers' Union (DWRGLU), often known as the Dockers' Union, which was to become affiliated to the National Transport Workers' Federation (NTWF). He was a leading member of the DWRGLU during the 1903 tinplate workers' lockout and went on to become Chairman of the Lydney branch. He was a committee member of Lydney Cooperative Society. He was elected President of the Lydney District Trades and Labour Association in 1907 and was elected to Lydney Parish Council in 1910. He was appointed as a magistrate in 1911.

Edwin Rennolds (1879–1954) was born in Bedminster, Bristol, the son of a beer retailer. After leaving school he started work as a cleaner and then as a fireman on the Great Western Railway. He married Edith Kear in 1905 and they went on to have three children. He moved to Lydney in 1907 when he was promoted to engine driver and became active within the Lydney branch of the railway union. In 1911 he was elected as treasurer of Lydney Trades and Labour Association. He was appointed as a magistrate in April 1921.

Miners' Federation of Great Britain

Frank Hodges (1887–1947) was born in Woolaston near Lydney, the son of a farm labourer. As a teenager, he moved to Abertillery with his father and brothers to gain better-paid work in the mines. In 1901, at the age of 14, he started work at the Powell Tillery and soon became an active member of the local miners' union and a member of the ILP. Like many others, Hodges was politicised by the industrial unrest of this period and as a result, involved himself in self-education and workers' discussion groups. In 1909, he obtained a two-year union-sponsored scholarship to Ruskin College where he became involved in the Plebs' League and the establishment of the breakaway Central Labour College. In 1910, Hodges spent ten months studying at the Foyer de l'Ouvrier, Paris, where he became friends with Eleanor Marx.[23]

In May 1912, at the age of twenty-four, Hodges was appointed as the Garw district agent for the SWMF (South Wales Miners' Federation). Hodges immediately started to reform the organisation of the district.[24] One of his first tasks was to build support for the successful 1912 national miners' strike in support of a demand for a national minimum wage. He soon gained a position on the Executive of the SWMF where he argued for workers' control rather than nationalisation by the state. At a special conference of the MFGB on the 21 April 1915, Hodges spoke in favour of an SWMF resolution arguing for strike action to force the employers to grant a 20 per cent war bonus to counteract the rise in the cost of living. The owners refused to negotiate, resulting in 200,000 men walking out on strike in defiance of the Munitions Act and within five days the miners' demands were met in full with a new agreement and 20 per cent increase on their wages.

In November 1918, after the retirement of its part-time Secretary Tom Ashton, the MFGB decided to appoint a permanent official in that role. Hodges, helped by his reputation as a militant, received the nomination of the SWMF and then went on to defeat seven other nominations in the MFGB ballot. At the age of thirty-one, the labourer's son from Wollaston had now become one of the most respected and powerful leaders in the British coalfields. Hodges was a shrewd tactician, confident, intelligent, articulate, and ambitious.

Robert Smillie (1857–1940) was born in Belfast. At the age of fifteen, he moved to Glasgow and began working in the mines of Larkhall. He started to educate himself in the evenings and, as a result, he worked his way up to the post of colliery checkweighman. In 1888, he helped to found the Scottish Workers' Representation Committee, which merged into the Labour Party in 1909. He also helped to found the ILP in 1893. Smillie was a close friend of Keir Hardie, leader of the ILP, until his death in 1915. Smillie became the President of the Scottish Miners' Federation in 1894, a

23 Frank Hodges, *My Adventures as a Labour Leader* (London: George Newness, 1925).
24 Ibid.

Robert Smillie, from an oil painting
by A Mendoza in 1920.

Herbert Smith

post he held to 1918. He played a central role in moving miners' support from the Liberal Party to the Labour Party and in 1908 he successfully campaigned for the MFGB to affiliate to the Labour Party. In 1912, he was elected President of the MFGB and remained in position until 1921.

During the war, he fought to keep the miners outside the provisions of the Munitions Act. He vigorously condemned conscription and became President of the National Council Against Conscription when it was formed in 1915. He was highly respected among his members and had a firm commitment to socialism as an ideal and militancy as a tactic. However, by the end of the war, he had become exhausted after years of struggle and nervous of any action that could put the finances and existence of the MFGB at risk.[25]

Herbert Smith (1862–1938) was born near Kippax in Yorkshire and was orphaned shortly after his birth. He spent his early years in the workhouse but was later adopted. He started working in the mines at the age of 10 and from 1879 held various union branch positions. In 1906, he became

25 Christopher Wrigley, *Robert Smillie*, Oxford Dictionary of National Biography (Oxford: Oxford University Press, 2004).

President of the Yorkshire Miners' Association (YMA) and Vice-President of the MFGB in 1919. He was a stubborn, loyal and class-conscious trade union militant but a political moderate. His characteristic response to requests for concessions during negotiations was 'Nowt doin'.[26]

Triple Alliance

Ernest Bevin (1881–1951) was born in Winsford, Somerset and was an orphan by the age of six. His first job was as a farm labourer. At eighteen, he moved to Bristol where he found work as a van driver and then as a docker. Bevin joined the DWRGLU and by the age of 30 was one of its paid officials. When Ben Tillett and Harry Gosling formed the NTWF in 1910, Bevin was elected to its Executive. Bevin was unsuccessful in his attempt to become the Labour MP for Bristol Central in the 1918 general election. He was considered to be a moderate by most trade unionists.[27] Please note Ernest Bevin should not be confused with Aneurin Bevan, both of whom were members of the 1945 -1951 Labour government.

Charlie Cramp (1876–1933) was born in Kent where he first worked as a gardener, before gaining employment with the Midland Railway. He worked as a porter based in Shipley and then Rotherham, where he was promoted to become a guard, and joined the ASRS. Soon after, he moved to Sheffield where he was elected to the Executive of the ASRS, prior to the first national railway strike of 1911. When the ASRS became part of the NUR, Cramp maintained his position on its Executive and was elected as President in 1917. He was also appointed as Industrial General Secretary of the union, a full-time position, in which he was seen as a deputy to General Secretary Jimmy Thomas.

Jimmy Thomas (1874–1949) was born in Newport, the son of a young unmarried mother. He was raised by his grandmother. He began work at twelve years of age and soon started a career as a railway worker. He became an official of the Amalgamated Society of Railway Servants (ASRS) and, in 1913, helped to organise its merger with two smaller trade unions on the railways to form the National Union of Railwaymen (NUR). His political career started as a Labour Party local councillor for Swindon. He was then elected to parliament in 1910 as the MP for Derby, a post he held until

26 J. J. Lawson, *The Man in the Cap: The Life of Herbert Smith* (London: Methuen, 1941)
27 Christopher Wrigley, *Ernest Bevin*, Oxford Dictionary of National Biography (Oxford: Oxford University Press, 2004).

1936. He was elected NUR General Secretary in 1916, a post he held until 1931. Thomas was on the right-wing of the labour movement and was an intelligent and ambitious opportunist.[28]

Robert Williams (1881–1936) was born in Swansea and began his working life as a coal trimmer at the docks. He became active in the National Amalgamated Labourers' Union and was elected its President. He also served as a Labour Party councillor in Swansea from 1910 to 1912. Williams was elected as the first General Secretary of the NTWF in 1912 when the National Amalgamated Labourers' Union was among the many small unions who affiliated to the Federation. He opposed World War One and was a supporter of the Russian Revolution. He joined the Communist Party in 1920 and in that year was part of a deputation of British trade unionists who travelled to Moscow for talks on the founding of the Red International of Labour Unions. In 1920, he was elected President of the International Transport Workers' Federation and served five years in that position. He was the most left wing of all the senior trade union officials.[29]

Robert Williams.

Labour Party

Ellen Hicks (1864–1948) was born in Bristol and married Arthur Hicks, a Coleford boot maker in 1893. She worked as an assistant boot maker in their shop in Market Square, Coleford. She had two children one of whom died as a child. She joined the ILP before the war and was elected President of the Women's Labour League. She was appointed as a magistrate in August 1920.

Thomas Liddington (born 1875) was born in Aylburton and his father worked on the railways. In 1901 he was working as an engineman at a colliery and in 1911 he was working for an insurance company. He married

---

28 Philip Williamson, *James Henry Thomas*, Oxford Dictionary of National Biography (Oxford: Oxford University Press, 2004).
29 G. A. Philips, *Robert Williams*, Oxford Dictionary of National Biography (Oxford: Oxford University Press, 2004).

Mary Morgan in 1898 and adopted a son called Albert. He was elected as a West Dean District councillor from 1913 to 1915, as Secretary of the Forest of Dean Commoners Association in 1918 and in 1919 was elected onto Coleford Urban Council. Also, in 1919, along with Ellen Hicks and Emily Taylor, he was elected to represent Coleford on the Monmouth Board of Guardians.

James Wignall (1856–1925) was born in Swansea and on leaving school he obtained work on the docks. He became a lay preacher and was known as 'Jimmy the Evangelical'. In 1892, he was employed by the Baptist denomination in Swansea as a parson. In 1900, he was appointed as the first national organiser of the Dock, Wharf, Riverside and General Workers' Union and was elected Vice-Chairman of the Swansea School Board and then appointed as a magistrate.[30] He was elected as the first Labour MP for the Forest of Dean in December 1918.

Francis Henry Yeatman (1884–1962) was born in Lydney, the son of a tailor who had a shop on High Street, Lydney. He worked with his father as an assistant tailor and helped run the shop. He married Victoria Lewis in May 1911 and had two children, Stuart and Barbara. He joined the Norfolk regiment as a volunteer in December 1915. However, he was discharged in May 1917 due to ill health. As a result of the effects of the war, he was unable to carry out manual or physical work. In 1921, he was chairman of Lydney Parish Council and treasurer of the Forest of Dean Labour Party.

Main Characters On The Side Of Capital

Forest of Dean Colliery Owners

Charles Bathurst (1867–1958) was born into an aristocratic family and lived at the family's large mansion house on his Lydney Park Estate. In 1910, he was elected as a Conservative MP for South Wiltshire and remained in parliament until 1928 where he held a series of government offices. In 1911, he formed Park Colliery Limited which bought Norchard Colliery. In October 1918, he was raised to the position of a peer as Baron Bledisloe of Lydney.

---

30 *South Wales Daily Post* 11 July 1925.

Arthur Morgan (1865–1936) was born in Cinderford, the son of George Morgan, an accountant and major shareholder of Henry Crawshay & Co. Ltd., the largest coal mining concern in the Forest of Dean. Arthur Morgan started work for the company as a clerk in about 1880. In 1893, he married Maud Atten and moved to South Wales where he ran a business as a railway contractor. His son, Arthur Cecil Morgan was born in 1900. The family then moved to London for a short period but returned to the Forest and gradually took on more responsible roles within Henry Crawshay & Co. Ltd. In December 1919, after the death of his brother Edwin Morgan, Arthur Morgan was elected as Managing Director and soon became the driving force behind the company. He then moved into the mansion built by the Crawshays on their estate at Abbotswood. Morgan was intelligent, ruthless and ambitious. He was a master of creative accounting and as a result was able to guarantee substantial returns to the company's shareholders, some of whom were members of his extended family.

Details of other Forest of Dean coal owners are provided in the appendix.

The Government

Winston Churchill (1874–1965) was a key figure in the coalition government. Churchill, then a Liberal, became Secretary of State for War and Secretary of State for Air in January 1919. In the period before the war, Churchill sent troops against striking miners during the South Wales Cambrian Combine strike in 1910 and against striking railwaymen in 1911. In both cases, workers were killed by the military.

Robert Horne (1871–1940) was born in Stirlingshire, the son of a church minister. He was elected as a Unionist MP for Glasgow Hillhead in 1918. Horne served under Lloyd George as Minister of Labour between January 1919 and March 1920. He then served as President of the Board of Trade between 1920 and 1921 and as Chancellor of the Exchequer between 1921 and 1922.

Andrew Bonar Law (1858-1923) was a Canadian born Glasgow ironmaster and an arch-Tory. He was elected leader of the Conservative Party in 1911. Law served as Chancellor of the Exchequer in Lloyd George's wartime Coalition which reflected the mutual trust between both leaders and made for a well-coordinated political partnership. He was appointed Leader of the House from December 1916 to March 1921 when he retired due to ill health.

David Lloyd George (1863-1945) was born in Manchester, the son of a Welsh teacher, and brought up on a small farm in Pembrokeshire. He was elected as the Liberal MP for Caernarvon in 1890 and was Chancellor of the Exchequer between 1908 and 1915 when he was a key figure in the introduction of many reforms which laid the foundations of the modern welfare state. He was appointed Prime Minister in December 1916 when he formed a coalition government to replace the earlier wartime coalition under Herbert Asquith. He led the country during the rest of the war and remained Prime Minister until October 1922. Lloyd George was a brilliant political tactician, but unpredictable and sometimes unprincipled.

David Lloyd George.

Chapter One

Miners and Colliery Owners

You had to lie on your side, you dragged on your side in a way or on your belly, to get the coal out. I've seen men, "Mollie" Morris he was a great big man, he used to work in thirteen inches, he used to squeeze his stomach right in. He worked on his side and it was wet, water coming down all the time in that seam, and you dragged yourself in and you dragged yourself out and men worked in that. They lay on their sides to work, hauling the coal out. There was hardly any room to use your pick ... And that's how that was done. That's what I said, we were animals. We were classed as animals and treated as such. They were bad old bosses in those days. They were the boss and you had to beg for bread.[1]

Jesse Hodges (Jnr), Forest of Dean Miner.

The Forest of Dean Miners' Association

In the early twentieth-century coal mining was labour intensive with 75 per cent of production costs being paid in wages, and nationally the industry employed over a million miners, about one in ten of all of the employed male population in Britain. At this time mining was the dominant industry in the Forest of Dean with about 6,000 men employed in the pits. Other smaller industries included transport, quarrying, tin plate making, forestry and agriculture. The mines were privately owned and the conditions and pay for the workers were very poor, resulting in miners living in poverty with a low life expectancy. Children as young as fourteen were employed in appalling conditions. Poverty was widespread. Deaths and serious injuries were common as were deadly diseases such as silicosis and pneumoconiosis.

In response to these conditions, the majority of Forest of Dean miners were members of the Forest of Dean Miners' Association which was affiliated to the Miners' Federation of Great Britain (MFGB). Each district of the MFGB had a full-time miners' agent whose responsibility was the day to day running of the association, recruitment and negotiations with the employers. In addition, each mining association possessed its own district rules, scales of contributions and benefits, forms of administration and

1 Jesse Hodges (Jnr), Gage library.

local customs and traditions. The structure of the MFGB meant that individual districts had a degree of autonomy.

The aims of the MFGB were to campaign nationally to reduce the hours of work, increase wages, improve working conditions and safety in the mines, negotiate compensation for injuries and death and elect MPs to represent the union in Parliament. After World War One, the principal aims of the MFGB were to secure the nationalisation of the coal industry and a permanent national agreement with a guaranteed minimum wage.

FDMA membership disc.

Free Miners

From the mid-nineteenth century onwards, most miners in the Forest of Dean worked in the large, deep pits for the large mining companies—these men made up the membership of the FDMA—but a small number of independent free miners worked small pits, usually drift mines, operated by just a few men.[2] Free mining rights had been claimed from 'time immemorial' by any son of a free miner born in the Forest of Dean who had worked a year and a day in a Forest pit. This right allowed any free miner to open a pit anywhere in the statutory Forest of Dean, provided he paid royalties to the Crown, the owner of the land.[3] By the 1920s, the output of the free mines was small compared to the deep pits, although in terms of culture and Forest identity they were very important. There were about 670 men working about forty small pits in 1918, many of them owned by free miners.[4]

The free miners had an ambiguous relationship with trade unionism. Some worked their own small mines with one or two men, but many registered free miners worked for the large colliery companies as well where it was likely they were members of the FDMA. However, a few were substantial employers in their own right, employing up to a dozen men. The interests of the free miners were represented by the Forest of

2 Drift mining is a process of accessing coal or ore by cutting into the side of a hill or bank, rather than tunnelling directly downwards.
3 At this time, Forest of Dean mining companies paid approximately 6d a ton to the Crown in royalties.
4 See Appendix for details of these pits.

Dean Free Miners' Association but their employees were represented by the FDMA. In 1919, Martin Perkins was elected as the President of the Free Miners' Association. Perkins worked at Lightmoor colliery and was also a longstanding official the FDMA, representing Lightmoor colliery on the FDMA Executive.

Lodges

The FDMA was made up of lodges or branches organised around individual pits or villages. In addition, pit committees were elected at each of the pit lodges to deal with day to day disputes and relations with the management. Each lodge sent a delegate to the FDMA Council to whom the agent was accountable and met on average about four times a year. Every year a ballot of the whole FDMA membership was held for the FDMA Executive Committee, to include a President, Vice President, Secretary, Treasurer, Political Committee, Finance Committee and Auditors. An election could also be held if there was a challenger for the post of agent and the Council agreed. The FDMA held regular meetings attended by the Executive Committee and delegates from the main collieries.

The MFGB held regular national delegate conferences with about 200 delegates and a larger national conference once a year. If votes were taken at a conference the card system would be used and the number of votes per delegate was dependent on the number of members they represented. The agent would usually represent the FDMA at MFGB delegate conferences with a mandate from the membership. The delegate conference could decide that a national ballot of all its members be taken on issues of importance.

Methods of Payment

In any attempt to understand the events leading up to the 1921 Lockout it is helpful to understand the complex way miners were paid (although the reader may wish to ignore the sections dealing with complex wage calculations). Wages varied from district to district, pit to pit and seam to seam and depended on what task the miner was carrying out, his age, experience and skill. Some miners were paid day rates based on a statutory minimum wage but others were paid piece rates.

In the Forest of Dean, the butty system operated in most of the deep mines from the mid-nineteenth century onwards. The buttyman was a

A nineteenth century buttyman with his men and boys.

self-employed contractor who worked a stall hewing coal from the face and employed a small team of daymen and boys. The buttyman was paid a fee for each ton of coal sent to the surface. The rate would be negotiated with the coal mine owner locally by the buttymen, with the support of the FDMA. It was dependent on the conditions at the face, the width and quality of the seam and other factors such as faulting, the condition of the roof or floor, water, type of working system used, etc. The rate paid to the buttyman for an average seam in the Forest of Dean in 1919 was approximately 2 shillings a ton, but this varied considerably depending on the condition of the seam.[5]

The contract system was widespread throughout British coalfields during the 1920s and most hewing teams, timber men and those involved with opening up roadways were normally paid piece rates.[6] The differences between districts on how the earnings were shared out within the teams working on the contract depended on local custom and practice. There were a variety of systems, some more egalitarian than others.[7] In some

5 There were 20 shillings (s) in one pound and 12 pennies (d) in one shilling.
6 A hewer is a man who cuts coal and removes it from the coal face. This was one of the most dangerous jobs in coal mines. The normal procedure for hewers was to cut a slot in the base of the coal seam so that coal would drop, or be coerced into dropping, down under gravity. The roof immediately above the coal was also liable to fall. Hewers, being in the vicinity of this activity, were often killed by accidental falls of coal or stone.
7 See Dave Douglass for a description of systems used in Durham and Yorkshire. Dave Douglass, The Durham Pitman, Raphael Samuel (Editor) Miners, *Quarrymen and Saltworkers*, History Workshop Series (London: Routledge and Kegan Paul 1977) 207-295.

districts, such as Nottingham, a single contractor might employ a large number of daymen and boys working a whole seam.[8] In other districts, the earnings were shared out equally between all the men in the team whilst in another area a pair of buttymen might employ just one boy.

In the Forest of Dean, by the 1920s, most teams consisted of a buttyman or a pair of buttymen with one or two daymen and a boy, although some teams were larger. At Eastern United, the teams varied from about four men up to about nine. Alan Marfell, who worked at Trafalgar Colliery in the early 1920s, remembers:

> Will Reed and Frank Arkell were the two buttymen and had several other men working for them, who were paid a daily wage. Any money earned over and above that was shared by the two buttymen. This system was used in all the house-coal collieries at the time.[9]

The butty system allowed experienced colliers to work unsupervised as small working masters, employing local labourers as required. It allowed the buttymen to define the social relations of work and exert high levels of control over the labour process, backed up by a strong commitment to custom and practice.[10]

Since the buttymen were paid on piece rates and acted as supervisors, there was no need for micro-management of the teams working deep in the mine on the coal face. In addition, the butties employed their daymen, so the colliery owners had no employment obligations such as supervision, the hiring and firing of labourers and health and safety.

So, while the buttymen had a high degree of workers' control, the daymen were reduced to casual day wage workers, subject to the whims of the market, the colliery owners and the buttymen themselves. The actual difference between the earnings of a skilled day rate hewer and a buttyman depended on the size of the hewing team and the system used for extraction of coal.

8 Barry Johnson, *Who Dips in the Tin? The Butty System in the Nottinghamshire Coalfield* (Chesterfield: Nottinghamshire and Derbyshire Labour History Society 2015).
9 Alan Marfell, *Forest Miner, A Forest of Dean Collier remembers life underground during the 1920s*, (Coleford: Douglas McLean Publishing, 2010) 24.
10 Chris Fisher, *Custom, Work and Market Capitalism, The Forest of Dean Colliers, 1788-1888* (London: Breviary, 2016), Chapters 4 and 5.

Systems of Work

The pillar and stall system was used on the thicker steam-coal seams found at a deeper depth such as the Coleford High Delf vein which was up to 2m thick with stalls about 3-5m wide.[11] In this system, the buttymen often worked in a partnership of two or three men (butties) to cover two or three shifts in the same stall and with just one day man on each shift and possibly a boy working as a trammer and labourer.[12] Forest miner Len Biddington described the system:

> There'd be three butty men, one for mornings, one for evenings and another for nights, for each stall and two men at a stall. The butty man would have a man he'd pay day wages, the butty men were paid on the coal and the yardage and all the overplus would be shared out between the dree (sic) butty men.[13]

The longwall system of working was used in the house-coal collieries on the upper, thinner house-coal seams. The width of the stalls was up to 40m, usually 15-20m each side of the stall road. The system generally used more daymen including at least two hewers, hodders and possibly a trammer on each shift. The thinness of the seams meant that hodders were employed to drag the coal out from the face to the roadways under a roof which sometimes was only about 45cm high.[14]

It was quite usual for young boys to start their mining career working for their fathers and often hewing teams were made up of fathers, brothers and sons. Molly Curtis, born in 1912, remembers that her father, who was a buttyman, earned more than the daymen but complained about responsibilities.

> They used to have 'places' and then they had to share out the money and dad used to say "Oh, I hate it on a Friday when I can't give those men as much as I feel they earned" … Dad was the keeper of the place, you know it was his 'place'. He had a lot of responsibilities, you know, and sometimes he used to say if he

11 Tony Oldham, *The Mines of the Forest of Dean*, Self-Published.
12 A trammer is a person who moves the full or empty carts of coal underground.
13 Humphrey Phelps, *Forest Voices*, (Stroud: Chalford, 1996), 49.
14 J. S. Joynes, Description of seams and methods of working in the Forest of Dean, *British Society of Mining Students*, Journal X1 1889. Copy in the Gage Library at the Dean Heritage Centre and Rowe, *Wages in the Coal Industry*, 150-152.

couldn't get enough coal out, then he used to have to go back grovelling to the manager and they didn't like grovelling.[15]

In fact, less than half of the total workforce were employed hewing coal. Other tasks such as road ripping and timbering were carried out by men working for a buttyman or directly for the company. In the majority of pits, an agreement between the FDMA and colliery owners included a local price list which listed the tonnage rates for coal produced and a piecework rate for other jobs such as road ripping (paid by the yard), installing and repairing timberwork and associated work such as clearing dirt, which was not directly productive.[16] Harry Roberts made the point that the price lists were regularly reviewed by the colliery management and adjusted so that the rates earned from piece work were only marginally above the minimum day rates.[17] This was often a source of conflict between management and the FDMA pit committees.

Most other tasks in the pits were carried out by men or boys employed directly by the owners on day rates. These included those involved with the haulage of coal, maintenance of haulage roads and attending to ventilation. The craftsmen and surface workers were also paid day rates.[18]

Minimum Wage

The majority of the miners, including those employed by the buttymen or directly by the company, were paid day rates down to a guaranteed statutory minimum which was agreed by the District Minimum Wage Board, chaired by an independent chairman under the 1912 Minimum Wage Act. The Chairman of the Board in the Forest of Dean was a local aristocrat, Sir Russell Kerr. The buttymen were also paid a statutory minimum day rate if their earnings fell below this level, often the case if the team were working in places where it was difficult to get the coal, which was not unusual in the Forest of Dean coalfield.

15 Molly Curtis interviewed by Elsie Olivey on 20 April 1983, Gage Library.
16 Road ripping is the process of removing two or three feet of the roof as the coal face advances so carts can be brought closer to the coal face to be filled with coal.
17 Harry Roberts, *Memoirs*, Gage Library. Henry (Harry) Roberts was born in Cinderford in 1914. His father was killed in the First World War and Harry started work at New Fancy Colliery in 1928 at the age of 14. In 1930 his mother decided to return to London with the family, so he ceased work at New Fancy and started a new life in London. He returned to the Forest of Dean some 45 years later and provided this graphic account of life at the New Fancy coal face to researchers at Dean Heritage centre in 1983. He died in 2005.
18 The duty of the haulier is to drive the horse and tram carrying coal from the face, where the colliers are hewing the coal, to the mouth of the level or the bottom of the shaft.

In the early twentieth century, in the Forest of Dean, the minimum rate for a hewer was based on the 1888 standard rate of 4s a shift. In most other districts, wages were based on different standards which were usually higher. A percentage was added or subtracted from the standard 1888 rate depending on the local selling price of coal. The minimum rate for a hewer agreed by the Forest of Dean Minimum Wage Board in July 1912 added 30% to the standard 4s, giving 5s 3d a shift. In a similar way, percentages were added or deducted from the 1888 standard for other grades of workers, including piecework rates agreed in the price list.[19]

The average day wage for all underground adult workers, including those on piece work, in the Forest of Dean in 1914 was 5s 10d. The national average wage for all adult underground workers at the time was 7s 7d per shift and the highest was 8s 9d in South Yorkshire. In 1914, the average wage for a hewer, including those on piece work, in the Forest of Dean was about 7s a shift and for an unskilled miner, the figure was 4s 6d. In contrast, the figures for South Yorkshire were about 10s and 6s 4d.[20] It is important to bear in mind that there was a hierarchy of earnings, with the buttymen and hewers receiving the most and some surface workers and boys receiving half of that.

The minimum wage varied from district to district because, up to 1917, most negotiations between miners and the colliery owners took place locally. The Forest of Dean wages lagged behind areas like Nottingham and Yorkshire as a result of lower productivity, due to the poor condition of the pits, thin seams, problems with water and lack of investment.

To put these wages in context, in January 1914, the minimum wage of an agricultural labourer was approximately 16s per week and the average wage of all those employed in the railways was approximately 26s per week. In 1918, the average wage for an agricultural labourer was still only approximately 26s per week.[21] Therefore, it is no surprise that many workers left the land to work in the mines or on the railways, where trade union organisation was well established and there was potential for higher earnings.

19 *Gloucester Journal* 18 May 1912. For instance, if two buttymen, working in July 1912 and employing one boy, agreed to a price of 2 shillings a ton and mined six ton of coal in one day they would be paid 12 shillings, giving each man 5s and the boy 2s. As this was below the statutory minimum, the colliery owner would be required to make the rate up to the statutory minimum rate of 5s 3d for each man and to the minimum rate for the boy.
20 These figures are based on information taken from A. L. Bowley, *Prices and Wages in the UK 1914–1920* (London: Clarendon Press,1921) Chapter 10, J. W. F. Rowe, *Wages in the Coal Industry*, (London: King and Son, 1923), *Dean Forest Mercury* and FDMA Minutes.
21 Nigel Scotland, *Agricultural Trade Unionism in Gloucestershire, 1872–1950* (Cheltenham and Gloucester College of Higher Education, 1991) 91.

Government Control

During World War One, the government took strategic and financial control of large sections of the economy, including the railways and the mines. In 1914, about one hundred railway companies became subject to instructions issued by government departments to guarantee the movement of troops and supplies. The individual railway companies retained ownership and the management of their lines and a system of payment was established which guaranteed their profits based on their earnings in 1913. As a result of on-going negotiations with the NUR and ASLEF, the workers were guaranteed government-financed war bonuses on top of their wages in line with the increasing cost of living.[22]

In 1917, after an increase in profiteering by the coal mine owners and a series of strikes in 1915 and 1916, the nation's mines were taken under financial control by the Mines Department to guarantee the supply of coal for the war effort, while day to day management was to be left to the owners. There was a complex financial arrangement put into place in which the colliery owners were guaranteed a standard profit from a special fund or pool. The agreement was confirmed by the Coal Mines Control Agreement (Confirmation) Act which was passed in February 1918. The Act defined a standard profit for each colliery concern based on its profits for any two out of three pre-war years or any four out of six pre-war years.

This arrangement suited the colliery owners, owing to the exceptional prosperity of the coal trade before the war. The agreement also allowed the colliery owners an additional 5 per cent of excess profits if earned. Eighty per cent of the excess profits went to the treasury and the remaining fifteen per cent was paid into a special fund or pool to be paid out to those colliery concerns which failed to reach their standard profits. But in fact, the government agreed to add 4s a ton to the selling price of coal which covered the employers' contribution to the pool and so the system did not cost the employers a penny and gave them a guaranteed profit.[23] In addition, the colliery owners were still allowed to gain profits from any ancillary undertakings.[24] [25] The colliery companies had to negotiate with the government to determine their standard profits, the selling price of coal, dividend payments and bonuses.

22 Philip Bagwell, Philip, *The History of the National Union of Railwaymen* (London: George Allen and Unwin, 1963) Chapter14.
23 John Thomas, *The Miners' Conflict with the Mineowners* (London: Forgotten Books) 32.
24 G. D. H. Cole, *Labour in the Coal Mining Industry* (Clarendon Press: Oxford, 1923) 54.
25 John Thomas, *The Miners' Conflict with the Mineowners, 32.*

Table 1: Minimum day wage for a hewer in the Forest of Dean 1912 – 1918.*

Date	Pay Award	Calculation	Wage
July 1912	30% above 1888 rate	4s plus 30%	5s 3d
June 1914	5%	4s plus 35 %	5s 5d
February 1915	25%	4s plus 60%	6s 5d
July 1916	20%	4s plus 80%	7s 2d
September 1917	War Bonus 1s 6d	4s plus 80% plus 1s 6d	8s 8d
July 1918	War Bonus 1s 6d	4s plus 80% plus 3s	10s 2d

*These figures are based on information taken from A. L. Bowley, *Prices and Wages in the UK 1914–1920* (London: Clarendon Press,1921) Chapter 10, J. W. F. Rowe, *Wages in the Coal Industry*, (London: King and Son, 1923), the *Dean Forest Mercury* and FDMA Minutes.

At the same time, the MFGB gained a number of national wage settlements based on flat rate increases above the existing district rates, referred to as the war wage and financed by the eighty per cent of excess profits received by the Treasury. Since the nineteenth century, wages had been linked to the price of coal, and up to 1917, a sliding scale had been used in the Forest of Dean to increase or decrease wages in percentage terms as the price of coal went up or down. However, the sliding scale ensured that the standard of living of the miners was at the mercy of the vagaries of the market and the levels of production. The war wage was based on the cost of living and so introduced a completely new principle into wage determination.

Furthermore, the war wage was a flat rate award which benefited the less productive districts like the Forest of Dean and the lower-paid workers within each district. Not surprisingly, the Forest miners were determined to defend the system of flat-rate increases negotiated by the MFGB in the form of national settlements, while at the same time campaigning to remove the district variations on the base rates. During 1917 and 1918 all miners received two flat-rate increases of 1s 6d as a war bonus to cover the increase in the cost of living.

The wage rates in the table above are derived from the Forest of Dean 1888 standard minimum rate of 4s a shift. The figures provided in the text are fairly accurate for the day rate workers and, for the sake of simplicity, the discussion on wages in this text will refer to minimum day rates for hewers. It must be borne in mind that the day rates for other categories of miners were less. However, the exact piece-rate earnings, in particular those of the buttymen are difficult to determine precisely. During the period from July 1914 to December 1918, wages increased by 85% but the cost of living increased by 120%.[26]

Checkweighman

Coal hewed by the buttyman and his team was sent to the pit head in marked trams and then weighed by the employers' weighmen and verified by the FDMA checkweighman, who therefore had to be someone whom the men trusted. The checkweighmen were usually older men who often held responsible positions within the FDMA and the wider community. For instance, Martin Perkins and Ambrose Adams were both checkweighmen and FDMA Executive members as well as local magistrates, which demonstrated they were highly respected members of the broader community.

The buttymen were influential within the FDMA either as FDMA representatives themselves or indirectly through the checkweighmen. A checkweighman was elected by the buttymen and often became the FDMA representative at the pit. One of the problems for the FDMA was that the checkweighmen were also accountable to the buttymen, which could lead to divided loyalties in cases of disputes between the buttymen and their daymen. This was a source of weakness within the FDMA which in the past had been exploited by the colliery owners. As far back as the mid-nineteenth century, there was discontent in the Forest of Dean with a system which encouraged exploitation and division to the advantage of the colliery owners.[27] In the years following the lockout the butty system gradually disappeared from the Forest of Dean coalfield.

---

26 Figures are taken from 1919 Sankey Commission; quoted in R. Page Arnot, *The Miners: A History of the Miners' Federation of Great Britain, from 1910 onwards.* (London: Allen and Unwin, 1953) 196 with an adjustment for Forest of Dean wages.

27 See Chris Fisher, *Custom, Work and Market Capitalism*, Chris Fisher, The Little Buttymen in the Forest of Dean, *International Review of Social History*, 25 (1980) and Royden Harrison, (Editor) *The Independent Collier* (Sussex: Harvester Press, 1978).

Living Conditions

It is a common misconception that living conditions in rural areas were better than those in the cities.[28] This was not necessarily the case, and it certainly did not apply to many miners' homes in the Forest of Dean in the 1920s. Although home ownership was higher than in most areas, few had the resources to upgrade or extend their properties. Some miners were lucky enough to own more than one property, while others took in lodgers. Some miners' homes were owned by wealthy landlords or colliery owners who were not concerned with the state of their properties. Many miners had to rent, and tenants who got behind with their payments could be evicted.

The disparity in wealth between mine owners and miners was large. However, there was also a hierarchy of wealth among the miners themselves, exacerbated by the differentials in earnings at work. As a result, there were significant differences in housing conditions and levels of poverty within the broader community. Some miners owned more than one house and maybe a pub or a shop and some land, while many others were tenants with no other means of support. Winifred Foley in her account of a 1920s childhood in the Forest of Dean recalls:

> The women from the better-off end of the village and a sprinkling of the husbands were regular chapel-goers. Not so the other end. All too often the poorer women 'hadn't a rag to their backs good enough for chapel.'[29]

In January 1920, the *Dean Forest Mercury* reported on the case of James Morgan, a collier living in Whitecroft and employed at Princess Royal Colliery where he had worked for the past 14 years. His family, consisting of an elder son and daughter plus seven younger children, were evicted from their house in November 1919. As a result, they were all forced to live in a room 12 foot x 10 foot, provided by a kindly neighbour.[30]

28 During the war, very few houses were built and more were needed to replace unsafe slums and dilapidated buildings. Christopher Addison, Minister for Health, estimated that 800,000 new council houses were needed. The Addison Act was passed early in 1919 to begin the building but was abandoned in 1922 due to government restrictions on public expenditure and only 213,800 were built across the country. In the years between 1923 and 1931 pressure from Labour councillors in Forest of Dean resulted in local authorities implementing limited schemes of council house building including those at High Nash and Albert and Victoria Roads, Coleford, Berry Hill, Edge End, Brierley, Worral Hill, Parkend and Breams Eaves.
29 Winifred Foley, *Full Hearts and Empty Bellies* (London: Abacus, 1974) 46.
30 *Dean Forest Mercury* 30 January 1920.

In September 1920, Mr L. G. Lyne, the Sanitary Inspector to East Dean Council, gave a talk on the subject of housing conditions to a meeting in Cinderford. The *Gloucester Journal* reported on his talk:[31]

He said they were constantly hearing of natural beauties of the Forest, but no one had the courage to chant the praises of the type of habitation the poor collier and his family occupied … He remarked that there were 3,841 houses on the eastern side of the Forest, and an estimate was that 1,500 fell much below the standard of habitation at which this country was aiming. Today there were four families of six persons each all occupying one bedroom, and 13 families of five persons each in one bedroom. Houses with only two bedrooms each were inhabited by 83 families, each with eight persons. Forty-three families counted nine persons each, 24 had 10, four possessed 11, and three counted 12 each, and in one case, would they believe it, there was a family of 15 all in one house of only two bedrooms … He mentioned three ancient tenements each possessing two bedrooms, and in these 31 persons were cuddled together.

Diseases like tuberculosis and scarlet fever were common and the living conditions meant recovery from illness was difficult. Harry Roberts remembered that after the war finished there had been:

the terrible virus of influenza which killed thousands of people throughout the country. I have heard since that 100,000 were killed by this virus, and lots of people died around here, and "flu" was a word that got in the children's vocabulary because of that, and then there was a series of things that happened after the Great War was finished and children began to grow up. I grew up and the next calamity was the 1921 coal strike.

31 *Gloucester Journal* 25 September 1920.

Gender

The history of working-class women in the Forest of Dean in the nineteenth and early part of the twentieth century remains largely hidden and their voices are rarely heard.[32] However, in the Forest of Dean during this period, Skimmington style protests were sometimes used by women against anyone who offended the morals of the community or engaged in unacceptable behaviour such as male violence.[33] A Skimmington was a rowdy parade in which effigies of victims, or people dressed up to represent them, were used to make a public demonstration of moral disapproval of the individuals responsible. The general intent was the public humiliation of those concerned and it was typically a noisy affair, with rough music made by the clattering of pots and pans. In the Forest of Dean, there are records of women ducking men accused of domestic violence in ponds, burning effigies of men who had deserted their families and using rough music in demonstrations against blacklegs during strikes.[34] Despite being hidden from history, this shows that working class women were very much a part of the social and political life of their communities.

In the years before World War One, there is evidence that local women supported equality and more formal political action, as this report from the *Gloucester Journal* in 1912 illustrates:

Encouraged by the reception afforded them on the occasion of their first visit, some representatives of the National Union of Women's Suffrage Societies, who claim to be non-militant and also devoid of party bias, held a meeting in the Cinderford Town Hall on Sunday afternoon last, for women only. This was

---

32 There is a fair amount of research on women from the South Wales coalfield including Sue Bruley, *The Women and Men of 1926* (Cardiff: University of Wales Press, 2011), Carole White and Sian Rhiannon Williams (Editors), *Struggle or Starve, Women's Lives in the South Wales Valleys between the two World Wars* (Powys: Honno, 2002) and Angela V. John (Editor) *Our Mothers' Land: Chapters in Welsh Women's History, 1830-1939* (Cardiff: University of Wales Press, 2011). As far as I know there has been little research done on working class women from the Forest of Dean coalfield. However, there is now a large amount of oral history on a wide range of subjects, including miners' wives, available at Gage Library for the period between the wars.

33 Buchanan Sharpe, *In Contempt of All Authority——Rural Artisans and Riot in the West of England, 1586 -1660*, (London: Breviary Stuff Publications, 2010).

34 Forest miner Alan Drew remembers such protests during the 1926 Lockout when "if they thought you were going back, they would come outside your home and batter pans and tins and make a hell of a row". See 'Lively Scenes at Whitecroft Level' *Lydney Observer* 25 June 1926. For examples of the treatment of wife beaters and burning effigies of men see 'Wife Beater Lynched at Coleford' in *Illustrated Police News* 31 August 1878 and the interview with Archie Freeman by Bess Anstis on 25 March 2003, Gage Library.

followed up by a public meeting in the same building on Monday evening, and there were large attendances on both days.

In 1911, some socialist women organised a branch of the Women's Labour League in the Forest of Dean. The League had been founded In 1906 to promote the political representation of women in parliament and on local bodies and was affiliated to the Labour Party. The main organisers of the Forest of Dean branch were Ellen Hicks who was the wife of Arthur Hicks, a bootmaker, and Mary Liddington who was the wife of Tom Liddington, an insurance worker and an ex-collier. One of their members, Annie Pope, stood for election for Coleford Parish Council in April 1913 but failed to get elected.[35] Pope was a trained nurse and helped run the Waverley Hotel in Coleford with her husband. In 1919, Ellen Hicks was elected to represent Coleford on the Monmouth Board of Guardians and in 1920 she was appointed as a magistrate.

At least one woman went further and used direct action to argue her case for equality. On 11 July 1914, the Miners' Association held its demonstration meeting at Speech House and provided an opportunity to protest:

> At this point, there was considerable interruption among the crowd, chiefly caused by a supposed suffragette, who by her repeated ejaculations interfered with the speakers. There were cries of "Duck her" and "Throw her out" and after something like order had been restored, and responding to repeated invitations to get upon the platform, she did so, much to the amusement of those present. Even after she had mounted the platform, the lady interrupted upon several occasions with "Votes for Women", "Home Rule for Ireland" and other interpolations.[36]

This incident demonstrates that for most miners a woman's place was at home carrying out domestic duties and providing care for her family. However, one consequence of this was that the bonds between women were strong and mutual support was an essential component of everyday life. Poverty meant that families were linked into an interdependent network of neighbours and kin and developed a strong sense of community and class consciousness.

35 *Gloucester Journal* 12 April 1913.
36 *Gloucester Journal* 18 July 1914.

The life of the miner's wife was hard and she had no choice but to struggle to fulfil her role as the backbone of the family. The men would rarely carry out domestic work and would expect a meal on the table before and after their shift in the pit. The women had to manage their receipts from the weekly wage packet, making sure there was money left over for rent and bills. They had to provide food, care and shelter for their children, the elderly, the sick and disabled, often by going without themselves. Some men kept back more than their share of the wages to spend on alcohol or tobacco and magistrates' court records reveal some women had to deal with drunkenness and domestic violence by taking their husbands to court.

The poor condition of the housing stock, overcrowding, infestation, ill-health and disease added to the burden, which was exacerbated by the lack of good health care. As a result, the death rates among babies and children were high and life expectancy low. Some women died in childbirth or while having back street abortions. It was not unusual for miners' wives in the Forest of Dean at this time to have at least twelve children. Forest of Dean miner, Fred Warren, who was born in 1899 lost eight of his siblings as a child.

> Mother had a dozen or more but her only managed to rear four of us. We was the good ones.[37]

Similarly, for Amy Adams' family, only four children survived.

> My mother had twelve but of course, some died in infancy. The last 4 of us lived, the youngest of them was 16, and the oldest was 72 as died.[38]

Domestic Schedules

The day often started at 4 am with lighting the fire and cooking breakfast for the men, boys or lodgers on the early shift. Then meals and baths had to be prepared for those returning from their shift. The three-shift system, including night-shift, meant that women could be working a seventeen-hour day. Childcare, cooking, cleaning, walking to the shops and back, baking, making and mending clothes and many other tasks would take up the whole day and evening. Monday was washing day but for large

37 Fred Warren interviewed by Elsie Olivey on 16 March 1983, Gage Library.
38 Amy Adams, interviewed by Elsie Olivey on 1 October 1983, Gage Library.

families the task could take several days. Washing involved hand cleaning dirty sheets and clothes thick with dirt, coal dust and sweat. It was back-breaking work, filling a heavy cast iron boiler with water over the fire and then carrying boiling water to the zinc bath, washboard, rinsing tub, starch bowl, mangle and clothesline in the back yard.

The busy domestic schedule often had to be carried out during pregnancy or while carrying a newborn baby. In addition, many women became carers for men who were disabled early in their lives from injury or suffered from lung disease as a result of their work in the pits. Some war widows and mothers struggled to cope with the devastating loss of loved ones and others had to help men disabled by the war to recover and build a new life.

As a result, some women became the main breadwinner, dependent on low paid work as cleaners for the wealthy, taking in washing and sewing and housing lodgers. Harry Toomer was born in 1902 and started work on horse lighting at Trafalgar colliery when he was fourteen and then, after about a year, moved to Waterloo colliery to work on the coal face.[39]

> My home life was very very hard times, my mother was left a widow when my father died. I was two years old then. She was left with seven children. There was no dole, no income whatever. She brought us up practically, they call "on the washtub", doing work for other people. It was very hard times.[40]

During World War One, some local women worked in munitions-related work at Lydbook cable works and at Speech House wood distillation and refinery plant which produced acetone. The majority of teenage girls went into service in nearby cities where they soon learnt how to stand up for themselves. They usually sent a significant part of their earnings home. This is Molly Curtis talking about her sister Nancy.

> She was working in one place and the lady said to her "If I had known you were one of these beastly collier's daughters, I would not have employed you." Of course, my sister was naturally very cross and she said "If it was not for the beastly colliers you would

---

39 Horse lighting involves running in front of the horse, which was pulling the drams of coal, with a light.
40 Harry Toomer interviewed by Elsie Olivey and Helen Nash on 9 February 1984, Gage Library. Harry Toomer's father started work as a farm boy in Dorset where he was born before moving to Ross and then to the Forest of Dean to work in the pits.

be without a fire in your drawing room", and she was told she was very rude, but she gave her notice in because of it.[41]

After the war, gender stereotypes were challenged by the extension of the franchise to women of property. In reality, this did not include women in mining communities, where the opportunities outside the domestic sphere continued to be limited and where miners' wives were underrepresented on the committees of formal political organisations.[42] However, in 1919, most women were determined to provide decent homes for returning soldiers and shared the desire for peace and prosperity with their men. As a result, some women attended meetings and joined demonstrations and picket lines during the 1921 Lockout and played a significant role in maintaining solidarity.

Working Conditions

The working conditions in the Forest pits were among the worst in the country as a result of lack of investment, water, damp, thin seams and frequent roof falls. Deaths and serious injuries were common as were deadly diseases such as silicosis and pneumoconiosis, leading to a low life expectancy. Miners earned more than agricultural workers but often their work led to ill-health and early death. Forest miner Albert Meek recalled how his father suffered from silicosis:

which was then called 'colliers' asthma', never got anything for it. I often think about it, my father was rasping for years before he died and he died before he was fifty.[43]

Nationally, in the decade before 1921, there were between 160,000 and 176,000 notified pit casualties every year and between 1,500 and 1,700 deaths.[44] In the Forest pits during the war years, eighteen men or boys died, and there were numerous severe injuries.[45] A survey in 1912

41 Molly Curtis, The Gage Library.
42 The collection of the oral histories of miners' wives in the Forest of Dean in the interwar period, as held at the Gage library, reflects that their role remained mainly confined to the domestic and community sphere. However, gradually more working-class women became active in formal political organisations and were elected to positions on their committees. As an example, Minne Allen was elected as Vice President of the Forest of Dean Labour Party in 1928.
43 Albert Meek interviewed by Elsie Olivey on 6 April 1983, Gage Library.
44 Cole, *Labour in the Coal Mining Industry*, 82.
45 Dave Tuffley, *Mining and Quarry Fatalities in the Forest of De*an, CD (Forest of Dean: Forest of Dean History Society, 2006).

showed that there were approximately twenty accidents a week requiring medical attention in Forest pits.[46]

It was common for injuries to lead to permanent disability which could mean a whole family living on the meagre compensation available under the Compensation Act. There was no compensation available to the many men who suffered severe disability followed by an early and agonising death from lung disease at this time. Children as young as fourteen were employed in appalling conditions. Albert Meek, who was born in 1898 and started work at Crump Meadow in 1911, remembers:

> We left school at thirteen—the times were poor, very poor, and the girls used to go into domestic service at thirteen to try and get a bob for mum, and the boys to the pit.[47]

Hodding

FDMA President, David Organ, started work as a hodder at the age of 13. This job involved transporting coal from the coal face to the dram loaders in a hod, which was a large wooden box on skids. Hodders were mainly employed by the buttymen working the house coal pits where the seams were thin and boys were employed to drag the coal out to the roadways. Hodders had to drag the hod along by hands and knees using a chain attached to a leather harness that ran between their legs and over their shoulders. Some of the seams were only about 12 to 18 inches high, so the work often resulted in injuries to their back, knees and genitals.[48] Hodders were employed in some Forest pits as late as the 1940s.

House coal, or block coal for domestic use, was mined from the upper thinner seams. Steam coal, which is a clean and free burning coal used for forge and steam purposes, was mined from the deeper Coleford High Delf seam which reached up to seven feet in thickness in places. The steam coal pits had very different production methods and improved productivity compared to the house coal pits, where the miners often worked narrow seams on all fours. Forest miner Eric (Ky) Warren described the difference thus:

---

46 *Gloucester Journal* 30 November 1912.
47 Albert Meek, Gage Library.
48 The No-Coal-Seam in the house coal pits was only 12 inches high in places, and the Brazilly Seam was only 18 inches in places.

Bill James of Cinderford demonstrating hodding at Lightmoor

You could always tell a house coal collier from a steam coal collier. The house coal collier was thicker in the shoulder. He had to lie on his back to work. He did everything from that position. There wasn't a tougher man in Britain than the house coal collier, he worked hard, played hard and drank hard.[49]

Fred Warren, Eric's father, started work as a hodder at Foxes Bridge Colliery in 1913 and described his first day at work in Forest dialect as follows:

Oh, I d'aim I was 14 or more, just about 14, because we had to go up to the pit in the morning, stand by the cabins and see all the men go down and if there were two butties on there and they hadn't got nurn a boy, they would come out and look around at you. You were like cattle in a market. They would look at you and if your backside did stick out a bit, they did say "he might be able to do a bit of hodding".[50]

Similarly, for Albert Meek whose experiences of working in the pit, followed by blacklisting, led him to leave the mining industry.

49 Phelps, *Forest Voices*, 86.
50 Fred Warren, Gage Library.

The Hod Boy, by John Wakefield, is situated between Soudley and Ruspidge. The statue was inspired by Erik Warren who was the last hod boy at Lightmoor Colliery and who started work at the age of 13.

You'd cry all day and you would cry all night. You would get sore shoulders; you would get sore knees. And you would say to your parents "what would you do for my sore knees?" "Put them in the jerry!" [51]

Some boys were keen to work as hodders as they could earn twice the money as working on the ventilation doors, the screens or other menial jobs. Having served their apprenticeship as hodders most young boys progressed to work as fillers and trammers and then to work on the coal face as a hewer. Some continued working as daymen, while others aspired to be buttymen. Alan Marfell described the conditions at Trafalgar in the 1920s.

Sometimes the seam was only eighteen inches high (or even less) to work under. You had to learn how to work under that height, how to lie out to use a pick, how to use a sledge for driving a wedge to bring the coal down after undercutting, and how to use a shovel to put your undercutting in the 'gob' behind you.[52]

51 Albert Meek, Gage Library.
52 Marfell, *Forest Miner*, 14. The gob is the void from which all the coal in a seam has been extracted and where the roof is allowed to collapse in a controlled manner.

One of the consequences of working in these conditions was the development of a strong sense of comradeship, solidarity and class consciousness, which was unique to the mining industry. When asked what they would do if they had their time again, Fred Warren, his son Erik and his son-in-law, Alan Drew all said, without hesitation:

> Go down the pit, there was far better comradeship there than in any factory. We was all butties there.[53]

However, when Albert Meek was asked if he enjoyed his time in the pit, he replied:

> I didn't. I had some damned hard work in the pit—for nothing! Mind you, comradeship yes! You met a lot of mates there, they were all comrades, and you don't see it today somehow, I don't know why.[54]

53 Fred Warren, Erik Warren and Alan Drew interviewed by Elsie Olivey on 16 March 1983, Gage Library.
54 Albert Meek, Gage Library.

Chapter Two

Labour and Capital

I want this Alliance of ours to be strong when we shall require the strength. I want it to face the great industrial problems we shall have to face after the War. And should the time ever come— we all hope that time will not arrive—when the strength of this organisation is tested, then this Alliance must either win or go under.[1]

Robert Smillie

The period 1919–1921 was characterised by momentous battles between the forces of capital and labour. In the Forest of Dean, capital was symbolised by the directors of Henry Crawshay & Company Ltd, the largest mining company in the Forest, who ruthlessly pursued the interests of their shareholders at the expense of their own workers.

The forces of labour were represented either by the advocates of industrial action within the FDMA and MFGB or by the advocates of constitutional reform in the Labour Party and the national trade union leadership.[2] The period was characterised by tension between these two approaches as they sought to represent the interests of the Forest of Dean mining community in its battles with capital.

In an attempt to explain the background to this tension, this chapter will focus on the influence of syndicalism on the development of the political philosophy of Herbert Booth before he took up his post as the FDMA agent in 1918. It will describe how he found allies in the FDMA, including David Organ, Reuben James and William Hoare, in his attempt to apply this approach to industrial relations in the Forest of Dean coalfield. It will then reflect on the electoral success of the Labour Party in the Forest and the formation of the Triple Alliance of the three main British trade unions. Thirdly it will provide some background information on the main Forest of Dean colliery companies. Finally, it will flag up the key personalities from the government who intervened on the side of capital when the final battle took place.

1 Jeroen Sprenger, *The Triple Alliance, London School of Economics and Political Science (1975-1976)*. See http://www.jeroensprenger.nl/Triple%20Alliance/the-1919-railway-strike.html (Last accessed on 18 November 2019).
2 In this context, constitutional reform refers to an emphasis on the methods of electoralism and parliamentarism to achieve social change.

George Rowlinson

From 1886 to 1918, the agent of the FDMA was George Rowlinson who was a member of the Liberal Party and closely tied to the political establishment in the Forest. In the period before the war, Rowlinson had opposed attempts by the FDMA to affiliate to the Labour Party. He was rooted in a non-conformist religious and cultural tradition which included Liberal politics and a conviction that cooperation between miners and employers should be fostered whenever possible. As a result, he advocated moderation, arbitration and an emphasis on parliamentary activity, which sometimes stifled rather than realised the aspirations of the rank and file miners. Rowlinson worked closely with the buttymen and the checkweighmen who dominated the FDMA Executive Committee during his period of office.[3]

Although the MFGB had affiliated to the Labour Party in 1908, the election of the Liberal candidate, Sir Henry Webb, as MP for the Forest of Dean in 1911 and 1912 appeared to show that Liberal values still retained a purchase on the community as a whole.[4] Webb held considerable financial interests in the coal industry, including a directorship of the Ocean Coal Company Ltd in South Wales, and was a shareholder of the Norchard Colliery in Lydney.[5]

However, at this time, the dominance of the Liberal Party and its values came under attack from rank and file trade unionists and members of the ILP. On a number of occasions, Rowlinson had been accused by FDMA members of being in the pocket of the colliery owners and he was reluctant to support any independent action by his members. In 1912, Reuben James from Bream who worked at Princess Royal colliery accused Rowlinson of:

> not being an agent of the Forest of Dean Miners but had been for a long while the agent of the Forest of Dean coal owners.[6]

It appears that Rowlinson had a cosy relationship with the Crawshays. An inspection of the Crawshay accounts for 1919 reveal that he received payments directly from the company, although it is unclear what these

---

3 Ian Wright, *Coal on One Hand, Men on the Other, The Forest of Dean Miners and the First World War 1910–1922* (Bristol: Bristol Radical History Group, 2nd Edition, 2017) 18-22.
4 There were no elections during the war and so Webb remained the MP for the Forest of Dean until December 1918.
5 Wright, *Coal on One Hand*, 31-32.
6 *Gloucester Journal* 19 October 1912.

were for.[7] World War One veteran and miner Harry Barton who worked for his father, a buttyman at Lightmoor colliery in the years before the war said:

> Well, the Union at the time I was in Lightmoor was very poor. G.H. Rowlinson was the agent for the district when I was in there, I didn't think much of him, we'd come out and have a meeting up by the pit head and he'd say, "Men, as far as I am concerned, we must put our shoulder to the wheel." Him, "put his shoulder to the wheel", he didn't do damn all. I used to laugh my head off, I used to tell my father, "I have heard some things in my life, I can't see him putting his shoulder to any wheel."[8]

In 1917 and 1918, conflict within the FDMA over attitudes to the Labour Party, industrial action and the conscription of miners resulted in a new generation of men gaining positions on the FDMA Executive. They sought to make the union more democratic and were willing to advocate industrial action to pressurise government and employers to concede to union demands. One of these men was Reuben James who was elected President of the FDMA in January 1918 and another was David Organ, who was elected President of the FDMA in January 1919, a post he held until 1939.

Organ believed that working-class people should have representatives in parliament and, as a result, was a strong supporter of the Labour Party which brought him into direct conflict with Rowlinson, who continued to support the Liberals. In 1913, Organ was elected checkweighman at Norchard Colliery, which soon gained a reputation as being a militant pit. During the war, Organ helped build the FDMA into a more democratic organisation with a nearly

George Rowlinson.

7 Board Minute Book of Henry Crawshay & Co. Ltd. (O) 1919-1921, October 1919 Accounts (Gloucestershire Archives, D8729/1/1/15). The 1919 accounts list two payments to Rowlinson, £23 8s 9d and £7 15s., equivalent to about 60 days' work on the coalface.
8 Harry Barton interviewed by Elsie Olivey on 7 June 1984, Gage Library.

The Organ family in 1917.

full membership. In particular, he was instrumental in uniting miners from the steam coal pits in West Dean with miners from the house coal pits in East Dean.[9] In March 1916 he spoke out against military conscription and was among the miners who came into conflict with Rowlinson over the issue of the conscription of miners in 1917.[10]

Herbert Booth

In May 1918, Rowlinson was voted out of office in a ballot of the FDMA membership over his support for the conscription of miners and his policies of moderation and conciliation. Herbert Booth was appointed in his place.[11] Along with Organ, Booth was a key figure in the FDMA at the time of the 1921 Lockout and so it is important to consider how his background and political philosophy impacted on the course of events.

As a young man working in the Nottingham coalfield, Booth would have participated in the greatest explosion of industrial discontent that Britain had ever experienced. In 1910, strikes and violent confrontations between the community and the police and the army spread through the

9 Wright, *Coal on One Hand,* 39-46.
10 *Labour Leader* 23 March 1916.
11 Wright, *Coal on One Hand,* 114-115.

mining areas, in particular the South Wales valleys. This was followed by the first national miners' strike in 1912, lasting six weeks, which successfully led to a minimum wage for all mine workers.[12] This would have been Booth's first experience of a significant industrial dispute and he played a leading role, travelling the county to address mass meetings.[13]

Syndicalism

The unrest made a considerable impact on a new generation of leaders committed to greater militancy and opposed to the way that the old leaders were conciliatory to the colliery owners. Booth was among the young miners who came under the influence of a spectrum of new ideas generated at this time. In 1912, Welsh syndicalists produced a pamphlet entitled *The Miners' Next Step* which demanded rank-and-file control of a centralized and industrial union, called for antagonistic relations with employers and rejected the demand for nationalisation of the mines in favour of workers' control. In addition, the pamphlet argued that socialists needed to organise from below to gain control of the leadership of the union and, with this aim in mind, organised Unofficial Reform Committees (URCs) to apply pressure from below.[14]

However, the labour historian John Lovell has suggested it was the mood of syndicalism, not the doctrine, that made headway, as it emphasised the primary importance of direct action over parliamentary pressure as a means of settling grievances.[15] In practice, for many miners syndicalism simply meant using an aggressive industrial policy to achieve better working conditions and was part of a diverse political tradition that included anything from militant trade unionism to revolutionary politics.[16]

Also influential was the growth of industrial unionism which advocated that all workers in the same industry should be organised into one union, thus giving workers more leverage in bargaining. Industrial unionism contrasted with craft unionism, which organised workers along

12 Alan. R. Griffin, *The History of the Nottingham Miners 1881- 1914* (Nottingham: Nottingham Printers Limited) 165.

13 *Dean Forest Mercury* 29 March 1918.

14 Some syndicalists went further and argued for an aggressive industrial policy to force the colliery owners out of the industry leaving the mines in control of the workers. In theory, industrial unions covering all industries of the country would then become the basis of a completely new social structure. One of the strongest advocates of this idea was a young miner from the Rhondda called Noah Ablett.

15 John Lovell, *Stevedores and Dockers* (London, 1969), 156.

16 Ralph Darlington, *Syndicalism and strikes, leadership and influence: Britain, Ireland, France, Italy, Spain and the United States* (University of Salford, http://usir.salford.ac.uk/id/eprint/31003/, 2017) 23.

lines of their specific trades, sometimes leading to multiple unions with different contracts, pay and working conditions in the same workplace.

The most notable success of the advocates of industrial unionism was the formation of the National Transport Workers' Federation (NTWF) in 1911, and of the National Union of Railwaymen (NUR) in 1913. The MFGB had almost always been an industrial union and, although there were some small unions that recruited the craftsmen and white-collar workers, the MFGB organised the great majority of the miners in their industry. One of the reasons Booth opposed the butty system was that it maintained the existence of differentials and contradicted the principles of industrial unionism.

Migration

Some of these radical ideas impacted on the growing militancy across the British coalfields as miners migrated from district to district seeking work. The 1911 census shows that in the Rhondda alone there were 2,875 men and boys from Gloucestershire working in its pits, about half the number of those working in Forest pits.[17] Some travelled more widely. Twenty-two-year-old collier Frank Baynham left the Forest of Dean in 1907 and travelled to work in the mines in New Zealand. He returned in 1911 and, in 1914, registered as a free miner. In 1917 he bought the free mine New Speedwell, near Berry Hill, with Henry Brown and they ended up employing about ten men in the 1920s.[18]

Graham Morgan, the Labour county councillor for Cinderford, described how various members of his family had to migrate to other coalfields to find work. His great grandfather, George Morgan, born in Mosley Green in 1856, went to Yorkshire in the 1870s and joined his brother, William, working at a pit near Normanton. William died of typhoid in 1875 and George then moved to the Fryston colliery near Castleford, living on Smith Street next to the colliery.[19] Graham reported that at the time there was a strong community of Forest of Dean miners working at Fryston colliery, with five Cinderford families living on Smith Street. George returned to Cinderford in the 1880s and worked on the railway.

17 Hywel Francis and David Smith, *The Fed*, (London: Lawrence and Wishart, 1980) 45.
18 Information supplied by Dave Morris, Frank Baynham's grandson.
19 The census forms for the Castleford area reveal there were dozens of families migrating from the Forest of Dean to the Pontefract and Castleford area from the 1870s onwards. The author's grandfather-in-law also went from pit to pit in the Castleford area seeking work in the 1920s and 1930s

Men at a pit near Mile End (probably Speedwell Colliery).

Graham's grandfather, Sam Morgan, born in 1890, left home at sixteen and moved briefly to Yorkshire. During his life, he worked at thirty-nine different collieries, first near Castleford and then back and forth to South Wales. He was working in Wales during the 1921 Lockout at Cefn Fforest, where Graham's father, Merlin, was born the following year. The family returned to Cinderford in 1925 after Merlin's mother died. When Merlin was older, he joined his father working at Eastern United. Graham said:

> Grandfather Sam was born at the Works Cinderford on the 23 March 1890. He started work at 12 as a coal miner leaving home at 16 following his father's footsteps to find work in Yorkshire, then ending up in South Wales and back to the Forest working in some 40 different collieries. He used to tell me with pride he was a coal hewer and was paid to get coal by the ton.[20]

In a similar way, members of Jesse Hodges' family went to work in the pits of Yorkshire and South Wales to earn higher wages. Migration was not unusual for Forest mining families and it would be expected they would have come under the influence of some of the radical political

20 Interview with Graham Moran by the author, November 1917.

ideas spreading around the coalfields. This challenges the often-repeated misconception that the Forest community was somewhat isolated and cut off from the outside world.

It is likely that some Forest men, returning home after working in South Wales and Yorkshire, would have been influenced by the growth of syndicalism and would have brought news of the industrial unrest which spread through the coalfields from 1910 to 1921.

Central Labour College

Syndicalism started to influence a number of young miners in the Nottinghamshire coalfield. Among these was Herbert Booth who, in September 1912, was the first to win a Nottinghamshire Miners' Association scholarship to attend the (CLC) which had been established in August 1909 by a group of working class students and former students of Ruskin College, Oxford. Most of these were members of the Plebs' League which was formed in 1908 and was active until 1926. The Plebs' League aimed to provide independent working-class education based on the idea that working people should produce their own thinkers and organisers.

South Wales miner, Noah Ablett, was central to the formation of the League and was at the core of a group of students at Ruskin who challenged the lecturers' opposition to Marxism. Ruskin College specialised in providing educational opportunities for adults with few or no qualifications but insisted on a formal and orthodox curriculum. In the 1907–1908 academic year, Ablett and some other students began organising unofficial classes in Marxist political economy. Ablett returned to South Wales in 1908, where he began organising Marxist education classes with the Plebs' League.[21]

Encouraged by Ablett, the students continued to oppose Ruskin College's teaching methods and campaigned for a curriculum based on their life experiences, including working class history and philosophy. In 1909, the students went on strike, refusing to attend classes after the Principal, Dennis Hird, was dismissed for supporting their campaign.

As a result, Hird and the students set up the CLC, with the aim of providing independent working class education outside of the control of the University of Oxford. The CLC was supported financially by the Amalgamated Society of Railway Servants (later the NUR) and the South

21 Robert Turnbull, *Climbing Mount Sinai: Noah Ablett 1883-1935* (Socialist History Occasional Publication 40, 2017)

Wales Miners' Federation (SWMF). In 1911, the college moved to Earl's Court, London and existed until 1929.

This intellectual climate had a huge impact on Booth when he arrived at the CLC in 1912. During the next two years, he came under the influence of a mixture of radical ideas ranging from parliamentary socialism, which advocated the common ownership of the means of production to be achieved by reform through constitutional means, and syndicalism which advocated industrial action and an aggressive industrial policy leading to workers' control of industry. It was the latter which was the dominant doctrine at the CLC and in some respects the college became a training ground for syndicalism and industrial unionism.

One of the other students at the CLC with Booth was Arthur Cook, who went on to be elected the General Secretary of the MFGB and led the miners during the 1926 Lockout. Booth and Cook became lifelong friends and would later become allies in the struggles in the Nottingham coalfield. Booth's time at the CLC had a deep effect on the development of his political philosophy and he was keen to put theory into practice.[22]

Nottinghamshire

Booth returned to Nottinghamshire in August 1914 and joined the ILP which campaigned for a Labour government. However, branded as an agitator, he initially found it difficult to get work in the local mines and moved to Nuneaton to obtain work. After two months, he disguised his appearance and changed his identity and returned to the Nottingham coalfield where he managed to get work as a miner. The manager soon discovered who he was, but fearing trouble if he sacked him allowed him to remain. As a result, Booth was able to concentrate his energy on trade union work and was part of a group of young militants who started to challenge the NMA leadership.[23]

---

22 Alan R. Griffin, *The Miners of Nottinghamshire*, 239–240. Arthur James Cook (1883–1931) was born in Wookey, Somerset. At the age of twelve, he began work as a labourer on the farm, but in 1901, he joined the exodus of agricultural workers from the West Country attracted by higher wages in the South Wales coalfield. Moving to the Rhondda, Cook began work in the Trefor colliery in Trehafod and soon began to take an interest in trade union and political matters. He publicly opposed the war. In April 1918, he was charged with sedition under the Defence of the Realm Act and was sentenced to three months' imprisonment, of which he served two. In November 1919, Cook was elected as miners' agent for the Rhondda no. 1 district, a full-time post through which he automatically became a member of the SWMF Executive. He was elected onto the Executive of the MFGB in 1921 and as General Secretary of the MFGB in 1924.
23 *Dean Forest Mercury* 29 March 1918.

Inspired by the Plebs' League, Booth began teaching classes on politics and economics to other miners. He soon built up a network of keen socialists among the miners who had attended his classes. The group campaigned on a range of issues such as pit head ballots for the election of branch officials, elections every three years for full-time officials and the abolition of screens for removing small coal which impacted on colliers' earnings.[24]

At this time, the NMA Executive, led by George Spencer, its president from 1912 to 1918, operated a policy of moderation and conciliation. Since the conditions in the pits in Nottinghamshire were favourable to good productivity, Spencer argued he could achieve better terms for the men by continuing to undertake wage negotiations locally rather than through national agreements with the MFGB.

Booth and his fellow socialists supported MFGB national policy which sought to bring the mines under public ownership and to negotiate wages nationally to reduce or eliminate district differentials. They argued for a combative industrial policy to force concessions from the colliery owners. Soon after his return from the CLC, Booth found himself at odds with Spencer and the NMA leadership.

Spencer was closely associated with the Liberal MP John Hancock and had fallen out with the MFGB over his support for the Liberal Party. In addition, Spencer was a strong patriot and disliked the anti-war sentiments of the MFGB President, Robert Smillie, and the close links between the MFGB and the anti-war majority within the ILP. As a result, Spencer proposed to withdraw the NMA from contributing to the MFGB political fund which was used to finance the Labour Party.[25]

Booth responded by organising a campaign against this proposal and addressed meetings up and down the county, issuing 30,000 leaflets, partly funded from his own pocket. He forced the NMA leadership to run a ballot and won a majority in favour of keeping the NMA contribution to the MFGB political fund. This was to be the first battle in a long-running war between the MFGB and those who wanted a 'non-political' union in the Nottinghamshire coalfield led by Spencer.[26] In 1917, Booth held a public debate with Spencer at the Eastwood Empire cinema over what direction the NMA should take. Booth put forward a powerful argument for a left-wing programme in front of an audience of 1,700; following the debate, he won the vote almost unanimously with Spencer only receiving eleven votes.[27]

24 Griffin, *The Miners of Nottinghamshire*, 1914–1944, 39-40.
25 Ibid. 22.
26 Ibid. 39-40.
27 Ibid. 40.

Election of Booth

In March 1918, Booth applied for the post of agent for the FDMA and was selected by a ballot of the whole membership from a shortlist of six.[28] The main issues during the election campaign were the approach to industrial relations, the conscription of miners and the butty system. He won the ballot with a clear majority over all the other candidates, receiving 3,420 votes, with his nearest competitor only receiving 677 votes.[29] Booth had been involved in organising the daymen in Nottingham and his belief in industrial unionism did not sit well with the widespread use of the butty system in the Forest coalfield. He made this clear during the election campaign and, as a result, won the ballot with the support of the daymen. His first task was to set about building up the FDMA at pit and lodge level and to make sure the daymen had representation. In spite of this, Booth was careful not to alienate the buttymen, most of whom were good union men, and he was willing to work with the existing Executive of the FDMA.

It wasn't long before he made an impact when, in October 1918, he was involved in a controversial dispute at Norchard colliery over the reinstatement of a single victimised and sacked worker, William 'Bingy' Hoare. The dispute, which soon turned into a threat of an all-out strike in the whole Forest coalfield, in defiance of the Munitions Act, had its roots in an event which took place a year earlier.[30]

William Hoare

At the end of November 1917, a case was brought against William Hoare before the local magistrates by James Hooper, the manager of Norchard colliery. Hoare was accused by the management of contravening the Mines Regulations Act of 1911 by travelling over a haulage road while the haulage was in motion. He was found guilty and fined £3. However, this practice was common in Forest mines at the time and his fellow workmen at Norchard believed the case was a clear example of the victimisation of a union activist, subsequently confirmed when Hoare was dismissed by Hooper.[31]

As a result, on Tuesday 4 December 1917, 350 miners walked out in an unofficial strike and demanded his reinstatement. After a meeting

28 *Dean Forest Mercury* 29 March 1918.
29 *Western Mail* 19 March 1918.
30 During World War One the government introduced the Munitions Act which made strikes illegal and the restriction of output a criminal offence.
31 *Gloucester Journal* 1 December 1917.

with Rowlinson, the men returned to work on Thursday 6 December but resolved that unless Hoare was reinstated, they would take the necessary steps to issue notices of an official strike.[32]

Negotiations continued over the next year between the Forest of Dean Coal Owners' Association and the FDMA. As a result, Hoare was offered work at collieries on the other side of the Forest, some of which were over ten miles away. This was unlikely to be acceptable because miners had to walk to and from work and then up to a mile underground to reach the coal face. After Booth was appointed, he continued to insist on Hoare getting his job back at Norchard, near where he lived.

Consequently, in October 1918, in defiance of the Munitions Act, the dispute at Norchard Colliery over the sacking of Hoare turned into a threat of an all-out strike by over 5,000 Forest miners. The miners at Norchard had the full backing of Booth and the new FDMA Executive, who threatened to close down the whole Forest coalfield. On 18 October, Booth sent letters to all the collieries in the Forest giving two weeks' notice of strike action unless Hoare was reinstated. The situation was deemed so serious that Sir Guy Calthrop, the Coal Controller, asked the MFGB to intervene. He then travelled to the Forest and, on Saturday 2 November, addressed the men's delegates at Cinderford. He appealed to them "to brush aside their local trouble till the victorious end of the war, which might soon come.[33]

There was a mass meeting of miners at Speech House the following Sunday morning chaired by Reuben James. During his speech, Booth made it clear that they would continue to insist Hoare get his job back at Norchard and the meeting resolved to abandon the strike subject to further negotiations and to return to work on Monday morning.[34] In the end, Booth obtained an agreement which allowed Hoare to return to work at Norchard. The dispute marked a significant watershed in terms of the development of a new combative leadership within the FDMA, one which refused to be intimidated by the government or employers.

Booth also set about promoting independent working-class education. He persuaded the FDMA Executive to sponsor a student to attend a two-year residential course at the CLC and encouraged miners to apply. The successful candidate was William Hoare who, according to his daughter in law, Madeline, attended the college in 1919 and 1920, the first miner to attend the college from the Forest of Dean.[35]

32 *Gloucester Journal* 8 December 1917.
33 *Gloucester Journal* 2 November 1918.
34 *Gloucester Journal* 8 November 1918.
35 Thanks to William Hoare's grandson, Andrew Davies-Hoare, for passing on this information.

William Hoare on the Bream Miners Welfare Hall Committee in 1926.
Back Row: Tom Nash, Charlie Brice, Tom Carter. Middle Row: Oliver
Hoare, Freddie Watkins, Jim Price, Jesse Miles, Jack Kent. Front Row:
Arthur Saunders, Fred Wicks, Albert Brookes, Tom Kear, William Hoare,
George Hall.

Aneurin Bevan

The college had been closed during the war and was formally reopened in
October 1919 by Noah Ablett, the chairman of the Board of Governors,
before a large gathering. Hoare travelled up to London and joined a
select group of students which included the twenty-one-year-old Aneurin
Bevan, a South Wales miner who went on to become Minister of Health
in the Labour government between 1945 and 1951. It must have been
a daunting experience considering sixteen CLC students would become
Labour members of Parliament during 1944-55.[36] The principal from
1919 to 1924 was William Craik, a railway guard who was expelled from
Ruskin College during the student protests in 1909. In his 1964 book he
remembers October 1919:

36 W.W.Craik, *Central Labour College, A Chapter in the History of Adult Working-class Education*
(London: Lawrence and Wishart, 1964) 125.

Twenty-nine students were now in residence. The majority of them were miners, most of them from the South Wales Miners' Federation, but, in addition, also students from the Northumberland and Forest of Dean Miners, and one from the Dyers' and Bleachers' Federation, as well as six railwaymen.[37]

Among the tutors in 1920 was William Mainwaring, a South Wales miner who was a prominent member of the syndicalist Unofficial Reform Committee and who collaborated with the authorship of the *Miners' Next Step*.[38] At this time, the Russian Revolution had a deep impact on this new generation of post-war students and, as a result, about one third joined the newly formed Communist Party (CPGB).[39] Others, including Bevan at this stage of his career, kept their faith with syndicalism and continued to oppose the idea of social and economic transformation by means of a political party. During his two years at the CLC Hoare undoubtedly would have got to know Bevan well and probably joined him:

> debating with other students, when he could, into the small hours of the morning, the merits of direct action and the demerits of parliamentary action.[40]

James Wignall

Bevan would later change his mind and throw his weight behind the parliamentary Labour Party. Throughout the war years, the ILP and the Labour Party had grown in strength as working class people sought political representation in parliament. By the end of the war, most of the leading figures within the FDMA and MFGB were members of the Labour Party, including people like Martin Perkins who had changed their allegiance from the Liberals to Labour.

At first, the support for working class political representation complemented rather than conflicted with syndicalist sentiments. In

37 Ibid. 114.
38 William Henry Mainwaring (1884–1971) was born in Swansea . At the age of thirteen, he started work at the Cambrian Colliery, Clydach Vale. He played a prominent part in the 1910 miners' strike and was strongly influenced by syndicalism. He was subsequently secretary to the Unofficial Reform Committee and was a joint author of *The Miners' Next Step*. He was sponsored by the SWMF to attend the CLC where he studied economics. After two years, he returned to the coal face. During World War One, he was a conscientious objector. After the war, he returned to the CLC where, from 1919- 1924, he lectured in economics and served as vice-principal.
39 Craik, *Central Labour College*, 125.
40 Ibid. 123-124.

the short term, most trade unionists recognised that measures like the Workmen's Compensation Acts and the nationalisation of the mines demanded the presence in Parliament of men who directly represented, and were amenable to, the wishes and instructions of the workmen.

However, there were differences and this was reflected in the debates at the CLC. The majority of those who had joined the ILP continued to prioritise the election of a Labour government as a means to social and economic change. In contrast, others in the trade union movement prioritised industrial action as a means of forcing the employers and the government

James Wignall

to improve their conditions and were keen to use their newly-acquired industrial muscle.

One thing that characterised the FDMA from 1918 onwards was that the agents, Booth, and from 1922 John Williams, came from a background firmly rooted in the tradition of syndicalism and this approach to industrial relations was fully supported by Organ and a number of others on the FDMA Executive. This was in marked contrast to most other districts where militancy was driven by the rank and file and the agents had a more moderating influence. As a result, there was no need for organisations like the United Reform Committee (URC) which existed outside the formal union structure as was the case in South Wales, Scotland and Nottinghamshire.[41]

The consensus on which the pre-war prosperity and liberal ascendancy rested was torn asunder by the industrial and class conflict of the early 1920s. After the war, the more strident and confrontational response from the FDMA, represented by the new generation of miners' leaders such as David Organ, Reuben James, William Hoare and Herbert Booth, was reflected in a change in the nature of political representation in the Forest of Dean.

41 Martyn Ives, *Reform, Revolution and Direct Action amongst British Miners*, (Chicago: Haymarket, 2017) Chapters 3, 4 and 5.

At the end of May 1918, James Wignall was adopted as the first Forest of Dean Labour candidate at a meeting attended by over 70 delegates and presided over by David Organ.[42] In the December 1918 election, Wignall beat the sitting Liberal MP, Harry Webb, who stood with the support of the Conservative Party. Wignall received 9731 votes and Webb 5765 votes. Nationally Labour won more seats than ever before with 22 per cent of the vote and was able to field over 350 candidates compared to 56 in 1910. The Labour vote was boosted by the extension of the franchise to women over the age of thirty who met the property qualification and to all men over the age of twenty-one (men in the armed forces could vote from the age of nineteen). The Labour Party also made sweeping gains in the Municipal Elections in 1919. However, Lloyd George's wartime coalition held a large majority on the back of his promise to deliver homes fit for heroes.

Wignall was a political and trade union moderate and a popular MP, going on to be re-elected in 1922, 1923 and 1924 and holding his seat until his death in 1925.[43] The 1918 election manifesto contained the famous Clause 4, committing the Labour Party to the common ownership of the means of production, which included the nationalisation of the mines.[44] Although ineffectual in parliament, the election of men like Wignall reflected the growing power of the Labour Party in working class areas like the Forest of Dean. However, James Hinton argues:

> during 1919 the fate of war collectivism was decided, and the commitment of the Labour leadership to the maintenance and extension of state control over the economy was put to the test. The Labour Party, deprived of its expected representation in the House of Commons by the "hang the Kaiser" election of 1918, could do little to resist the rapid dismantling of the war economy … Faced with the impotence of the parliamentary Labour Party many trade union leaders began to talk the language of Direct Action, of the political general strike. The phenomenal growth of the unions during the post-war boom and their militancy lent plausibility to this threat.[45]

42 *Gloucester Journal* 25 May 1918.
43 *Dean Forest Mercury* 20 December 1918.
44 Ralph Milliband, *Parliamentary Socialism* (Merlin Press, 2009) 60-61.
45 James Hinton, *Labour and Socialism: A History of the British Labour Movement 1867-1974* (Massachusetts, University of Massachusetts Press, 1983) 108. Lloyd George made the trial of the Kaiser part of his election campaign, using the slogan 'hang the Kaiser'.

Triple Alliance

The development of the three major industries of mining, transport and docks in the pre-war years meant that industrial action in one sector would automatically impact upon other sectors. As a result, at an MFGB national conference in October 1913, the South Wales and Garw Valley miners' agent, Frank Hodges, moved a resolution in support of an alliance of mining, transport and railway unions in which he proposed they agree to co-ordinate industrial disputes and support each other through solidarity action. The proposed triple alliance included the MFGB, the National Transport Workers' Federation (NTWF) and the National Union of Railwaymen (NUR). As a result, the Triple Alliance was formed in 1914 with an informal agreement to support each other during industrial disputes.

The senior partner in the alliance, the MFGB, had a membership of 870,000 in 1913. The NTWF, with a membership of 163,000, had been created in 1910 as an amalgamation of the trade unions representing dockers, seamen, tramway men and others and included the Dock, Wharf, Riverside and General Labourers' Union, the National Union of Dock Labourers and the National Sailors' and Firemen's Union. The NUR, with a membership of 268,000, was created in 1912 as a merger of a large number of local and sectional organisations representing rail workers.

Although the NUR represented the vast majority of railwaymen, they did not represent all the engine drivers and firemen or white-collar workers. As an industrial union, the NUR set out to appeal to all railway workers, however some drivers and firemen chose to remain members of the Associated Society of Locomotive Engineers and Firemen (ASLEF) and some white-collar workers chose to remain with the Railway Clerks' Association (RCA). In 1919, the Secretary of the Lydney branch of the NUR was James Birt and the Secretary of the Lydney branch of ASLEF was William Wintle.

At the end of July 1914, a meeting was organised in Lydney with the purpose of bringing together local representatives of the miners, railwaymen and transport workers to form a local branch of the Triple Alliance. The meeting was presided over by Edwin Rennolds from Lydney NUR and George Powell, a tin plate worker from Lydney and a member of the Dock, Wharf, Riverside and General Labourers' Union which was a constituent of the NFTW.

A march was held through Lydney followed by speeches from local trade unionists including William Smith, from the FDMA and ILP, who had challenged Rowlinson for the role of agent in 1912 but was defeated in a ballot of FDMA members.[46] The atmosphere was full of optimism as it was believed that improvements in living and working conditions for the working class could be achieved through international solidarity and industrial action.[47] All hopes of this being realised were shattered as international solidarity broke down and large sections of the European working class responded to the call to arms.

One of the consequences of the war was that trade unions, in particular the MFGB, extended their autonomy and power. In December 1915, a joint conference of the three unions making up the Triple Alliance met and ratified its constitution and pledged to support each other in industrial disputes.[48] The NUR was now led by Jimmy Thomas as General Secretary, and the NFTW by Robert Williams as General Secretary with Ernest Bevin an influential member of its Executive. These men were now committed to a formal alliance with leaders of the MFGB which included Robert Smillie, President, Frank Hodges, Secretary and Herbert Smith, Vice-President. The war saw a dramatic growth in trade union membership across Britain, rising from just over 3 million in 1912 to 8.25 million in 1920.[49] As a result, Smillie, Hodges, Smith, Thomas, Williams and Bevin were now very powerful men.

The unions affiliated to the Triple Alliance all believed in the advantages of industrial unionism over craft or occupational unionism. The leaders were dissatisfied with a system of society in which labour power was treated as a mere commodity and they demanded that trade unionists become real partners in industry, jointly sharing in the determination of working conditions and management of the workplaces. In spite of this, there were fundamental weaknesses inherent in the Alliance as a result of the constituent bodies and their leaders having conflicting ideas about how to bring about social change. Consequently, virtually no attempt was made to bring more coherence in organisation and ideology. However, in general, all the main leaders were opposed to syndicalism because they did not believe trade unions should challenge the power of the State.

46 Wright, *Coal on One Hand,* Chapter 2.
47 *Western Daily Press* 27 July 1914.
48 R. Page Arnot, *The Miners,* (London: Allen and Unwin, 1953) 181.
49 H. A. Clegg, *A History of British Trade Unions since 1889. Volume Two. 1911-1933*, (Oxford: Oxford University Press, 1987) 302.

In addition, the strength of the Alliance was impaired by the unequal measures of power possessed by its three constituent bodies, and the fact they had different constitutions hindered the decision-making process. The power invested in the Executive Committees of the NUR and the MFGB by their respective organisations was far greater than that of the Executive Committee of the NTWF. The NUR was tightly controlled from above by Jimmy Thomas and Charlie Cramp. The MFGB was more democratic because, when it determined important national policy, the Executive consulted with its membership through delegate conferences or by a ballot of the whole membership. In contrast, the power within the transport Federation lay in the hands of a loose alliance of 26 constituent unions, some of which were controlled by right-wing leaders.

The constitution of the MFGB required that a ballot of all its members must achieve at least a two-thirds majority before calling a strike. The NUR had the power to declare strike action through its respective Executive or delegate conference and so, in theory, could call a sympathetic strike to assist the miners if required without going through the long process of a ballot of all their members. In June 1919, the NTWF introduced a rule that required each affiliated union to conduct a ballot before the Executive could call a strike. In addition, the leaders of the Alliance made no concerted attempt to set up local Triple Alliance Committees and the organisation was run from the top, partly because the leaders were fearful of losing control of local action within the various districts, and this hindered the involvement of rank and file workers.

The Craftsmen

One of the weaknesses for trade unionism in the mining industry was that large numbers of the craftsmen remained members of smaller craft unions. There were about 700 craftsmen, including enginemen, stokers, pumpmen, masons, carpenters, blacksmiths, banksmen, onsetters and ostlers working in the Forest of Dean coalfield at this time. Up to 1918, they had been members of the FDMA with separate lodges in East Dean and West Dean. However, in May 1918, most of the craftsmen left the FDMA and affiliated to the South Wales Colliery Enginemen, Stockers and Craftsmen Association.[50] This organisation was affiliated to the National Association of Colliery Enginemen and Mechanics. The craftsmen on the west side of the Forest were represented by C. R. Jones and on the east side by Frank

50 *Gloucester Journal* 18 May 1918.

Princess Royal colliery blacksmiths.

Ferley. The decision of the craftsmen to leave the FDMA caused bad feeling to develop between the craftsmen and the miners. This was exacerbated by the implication that the craftsmen were more skilled than colliers. Despite this, a handful of craftsmen remained loyal members of the FDMA and committed to industrial unionism.

In October 1920, the South Wales Colliery Enginemen Stokers and Craftsmen Association voted to amalgamate with the SWMF.[51] The Forest of Dean craftsmen were not included in this arrangement and so set about forming their own organisation. At the same time, they approached the FDMA seeking to affiliate with both the FDMA and MFGB. The FDMA Executive agreed to accept their membership provided they became full members on the same basis as before 1918. However, the craftsmen still wanted to maintain a separate organisation and constitution while at the same time seeking to affiliate to the MFGB. In December 1920, FDMA Executive agreed to meet with them to agree on a working arrangement.[52] In March 1921, the craftsmen appointed Jack Allen, an ex-official of the Scottish Miners' Association, as a full-time agent.[53] Allen immediately met with FDMA officials with the view to working together but as independent organisations.

51 *Daily Herald* 11 October 1920.
52 FDMA Minutes 7 December 1920, Richard Burton Archives.
53 *Daily Herald* 28 April 1921.

Other mining unions representing workers in the Forest coalfield were the National Union of Clerks (NUC) and the Colliery Examiners and Overseers Association.

The Colliery Owners

In opposition to the growing confidence of labour were the forces of capital in the form of the Mining Association of Great Britain (MAGB) and the Forest of Dean Coal Owners Association (FDCOA). The MAGB was established in 1854 to represent the interests of the employers in the mining industry. Initially, its main purpose was to lobby the government on any proposed legislation that could affect the profits of its members. After the formation of the MFGB in 1888, the MAGB participated in negotiations over miners' wages, hours and employment conditions. In 1919, Evan Williams, Chairman of the Monmouthshire and South Wales Coal Owners' Association and a formidable South Wales colliery owner, was elected President of the MAGB.

The FDCOA was formed in the 1870s in response to the formation of the FDMA. Its Chairman for many years, up to his death in 1935, was Thomas Deakin, Managing Director of Parkend Deep Navigation Collieries Ltd. Its Secretary was Sir Francis Brain who owned the Trafalgar colliery up to December 1919. After Brain's retirement from the role of Secretary in 1913, his place was taken by Walter Champness, the manager of Foxes Bridge colliery. Harold Fisher took over as Secretary after the death of Champness in January 1918. The FDCOA had an ambiguous relationship with the largest coal mine company in the Forest of Dean, Henry Crawshay & Co. Ltd., which generally preferred to negotiate agreements directly with its own workforce rather than through the FDCOA and its Managing Director, Arthur Morgan, had a huge influence over the course of events in East Dean during the 1920s and 1930s.

The Government

David Lloyd George was appointed Prime Minister in December 1916 when he formed a coalition government to replace the earlier wartime coalition under Herbert Asquith. The Tory leader, Andrew Bonar Law, was given senior positions in Lloyd George's war cabinet which reflected the mutual trust between the leaders and made for a well-coordinated political partnership.

Table 2: Forest of Dean Mining Companies employing over 100 men in 1921.

Mine	Company	Managing Director	Location	Coal	Men	Operated
Princess Royal	Princess Royal Colliery Ltd	Percy Moore	Bream	Steam	700	1840-1962
Lightmoor	Henry Crawshay & Co. Ltd.	Arthur Morgan (from December 1919)	Cinderford	House	900	1840-1940
Crump Meadow and Duckpit	Lydney and Crump Meadow Collieries Ltd	Joseph Hale	Cinderford	House	625	1824-1929
Foxes Bridge	Foxes Bridge Colliery Co. Ltd	Arthur Morgan (from December 1919)	Cinderford	House	730	1830-1931
Eastern United	Henry Crawshay & Co. Ltd.	Arthur Morgan (from December 1919)	Ruspidge	Steam	210	1909-1959
New Fancy, Parkend Royal & Crown	Parkend Deep Navigation Collieries Ltd	Thomas Deakin	Parkend	House	630	1827-1944
Norchard	Park Colliery Ltd	Lord Bledisloe	Lydney	Steam	320	1842-1957
Cannop	The Cannop Coal Company Ltd	Montague Maclean	Cannop	House & Steam	630	1906-1960
Arthur and Edward (Waterloo)	Lydney and Crump Meadow Collieries Ltd	Joseph Hale	Lydbrook	House	550	1841-1959
Howbeach	Jointly Owned	Lord Bledisloe	Parkend	Steam	140	1831-1921
Trafalgar	Henry Crawshay & Co. Ltd.	Arthur Morgan (from December 1919)	Drybrook	House	460	1860-1925

Lightmoor colliery.

The general election held in December 1918, just after the armistice, resulted in a landslide victory for Lloyd George and his Coalition government, giving him 522 seats made up of Conservative Party (382), Coalition Liberal (127), National Labour Coalition (4) and Coalition National Democrats (9). The Labour Party, with 22 per cent of the vote, won only 57 seats and the Liberal Party 36 seats. However, after the 1918 election, Lloyd George was increasingly reliant on the Tories for support and soon Bonar Law became the real power behind the Coalition.

Across Europe, massive numbers of demobilised men searching to find a role in civilian life produced widespread social and political destabilisation. Economic crisis, unemployment and inflation compounded the problems of peace. In Britain, many returning servicemen expected the world to be a better place, where their life could return to normality in a secure and safe environment with jobs and decent housing for all. This expectation was raised by Lloyd George's speech the day after the armistice where, amongst other promises, he said there would be "habitations fit for the heroes who have won the war ".

In addition, low levels of taxation and big spending on the war effort left Britain £7.4 billion in debt, including £1.6 billion to America.[54] Gold

54 The war loans were finally paid off in 2015.

and foreign currency reserves had been severely depleted and the pound, which had gone off the gold standard, was worth less than half its 1914 value by the end of 1919.[55] Consequently, returning servicemen soon found the government unable or unwilling to respond to their demands and needs. The traditional class system, underpinned by deference, had been transformed and soon the government began to see the working class as its enemy.

The appointment of Winston Churchill as Minister for War in January 1919 strengthened the hand of those in the government committed to the maintenance of a large army and to curbing the power of the trade unions. Churchill was a staunch advocate of foreign intervention and a strong supporter of British involvement in the Russian Civil War. He argued that Bolshevism must be "strangled in its cradle" both at home and abroad and was fearful of the influence of communism in the labour movement. The miners, on the other hand, bolstered by the war-time government intervention in the economy, were demanding nationalisation, higher wages and shorter hours. Churchill argued for an aggressive policy towards the trade unions and was often in dispute with Lloyd George who believed the government strategy should be more tactical.

The ruling elites and big business had done very well out of the war, particularly if their industries were tied into the war economy. In early 1919, the price of coal, in particular steam coal for export, was still rising. Speculation was rife and vast profits could be made selling shares at inflated values. The colliery owners wanted to end the war-time government control of their industry and believed that even larger profits could be made in an unfettered free market. They had powerful friends in government and men like Bonar Law and Robert Horne, the Minister of Labour, were fundamentally hostile to government intervention in the economy.

However, in 1919, Lloyd George was happy to pocket any excess profits from the coal industry for the exchequer under the war-time agreement. At the same time, he argued with his government colleagues that the growing militancy in the labour movement could be deflected by keeping the trade union leaders on side by maintaining government control of the coal industry.

As Minister of Labour from 1919 to 1920, Robert Horne dealt with the wave of industrial unrest which spread through Britain during those years. On becoming president of the Board of Trade in March 1920, he

55 John Foster, Prologue: What Kind of Crisis? What Kind of Ruling Class? in John McIlroy, Alan Campbell and John Gildart Keith (Editors) *Industrial Politics and the 1926 Mining Lockout: The Struggle for Dignity* (Cardiff: University of Wales, 2009) 16.

negotiated a trade agreement with Soviet Russia. However, he continued to resist pressure from the MFGB to nationalise the mines despite handling renewed disputes over wages in the coal industry. On his appointment as Chancellor of the Exchequer in April 1921, Horne introduced severe cuts in public expenditure and reduced income tax.

David Low on the David Lloyd George coalition (1918).

Chapter Three

Direct Action or Constitutional Reform?

Everything was in trim for the most smashing blow that had ever been delivered at the system which had governed the coal industry since its inception.

Frank Hodges, My Adventures as a Labour Leader, 1925.

At the end of the war, returning miners joined those who had remained in the pits during the war and demanded a land fit for heroes. As a result, the early 1920s marked the ascendancy of a more militant leadership within the miners' union, both nationally and in the Forest of Dean. Although in 1919 the majority of the Executive of the MFGB were still men of moderate view, militants were being elected to influential positions within the local associations and were beginning to have an influence at the delegate conferences. As a result, the MFGB demanded a living wage and an industry where safety came before profit, where men did not continue to die due to lack of investment and where there was a concern for the wellbeing of the workforce. The MFGB believed these demands could only be achieved if the mining industry was brought into public ownership and run jointly by the workers and the state.

However, there was considerable debate within the MFGB over how this could be realised. Some on the left-wing of the movement argued that the coalition government could only be forced to make concessions on work conditions, wages and public ownership by industrial action. Others of more moderate opinion argued that industrial action should be a weapon of last resort and that concessions could be best achieved by constitutional means, including education, campaigning, arbitration and reform through parliament.

After the end of the war, the government was reluctant to demobilise the troops because of industrial unrest and the threat of revolution in Europe.[1] The Ministry of Labour was very concerned that many strikes "have not been taken with the sanction of the trade unions".[2] Coal was in such short supply that the government was concerned that:

---

1 Brock Millman, *Managing Dissent in First World War Britain* (London: Frank Cass, 2000).
2 Quoted in Chanie Rosenberg, *1919, Britain on the Brink of Revolution* (London: Bookmarks,1987) 39.

unless the supplies of coal in this country were increased, it was not impossible that there might be a revolution. Even now the spirit of lawlessness was apparent, and no one could say what might happen if, for instance, there was no coal in the East End in December.[3]

There remained a shortage of men working in the Forest pits, with only 4,407 men and 709 boys employed in November 1918.[4] As a result, by mid-December 1918, the war cabinet released 100,000 miners from the armed forces to reduce the immediate threat of scarcity of coal.[5] Most healthy and fit miners returning to the Forest had no problem getting their old jobs back, although it would take a while before those who were unwell or injured were re-deployed into suitable work. It is possible that some men and boys, who had only recently been employed, were asked to make way for returning soldiers. In other districts there were problems. For instance, in December 1918, 3,000 miners at the Glamorgan colliery in the Rhondda Valley went on strike in protest against the non-employment of demobilised miners.[6]

The MFGB was determined that demobilised miners would return to an industry with decent pay and work conditions. However, the MFGB was fearful that the coalition government, under Lloyd George, would return the mines to the owners. If this happened, it was expected that the owners would undermine the wages and work conditions that had been established during the war and that wages would again be dependent on the price of coal and local conditions. The MFGB tried to exert pressure on the government to nationalise the mining industry, with Hodges, Smillie and Smith at the forefront of this campaign. At an MFGB conference in January 1919, a resolution was moved by SWMF Vice President, James Winstone, seconded by Hodges, which included a statement that argued for a degree of workers' control:[7]

3 Cabinet minutes quoted in Supple, *The History of the British Coal Industry*, 118.
4 Cyril Hart, *The Industrial History of Dean* (Newton Abbott: David and Charles, 1971, 289.
5 Cabinet minutes quoted in Supple, *The History of the British Coal Industry*, 118.
6 *Pall Mall Gazette* 1 January 1919
7 James Winstone (1863-1921) was born in Risca, in Monmouthshire. Winstone worked from the age of eight, first at a local brickwork, then at Risca United Colliery. He was elected checkweighman and became a prominent founder member of the SWMF. Winstone was also active in the ILP and was a Baptist lay preacher. In 1912, he was elected as Vice President of the SWMF, the first socialist to such a position.

It is clearly in the national interest to transfer the entire industry from private ownership and control to State ownership, with joint control and administration by the workmen and State.[8]

The resolution was passed and included a request to the Labour Party to co-operate in ensuring a nationalisation bill would become law. In addition, the MFGB demanded the reinstatement of demobilised miners on full pay and for any displaced miners to be paid an out-of-work allowance equivalent to full pay. They also demanded that miners injured in the war should be provided with rehabilitation and be retrained in a suitable occupation on full pay. In addition, the MFGB demanded a 30 per cent increase in wages, and hours to be reduced from an eight to a six-hour day. The demand for a six-hour day was important because it would reduce unemployment among miners returning from the war.[9] All the more remarkable was that these demands fell short of what some districts were calling for. In fact, the Forest of Dean, Lancashire, Cheshire and South Wales districts argued that the increase in wages should be 50 per cent.[10]

On 31 January 1919, representatives of the MFGB met with the Minister of Labour, Sir Robert Horne, who agreed to refer their demands to the Cabinet. On 5 February, Horne informed the MFGB that the government was prepared to offer an increase of one shilling a day but could not accept their demobilisation plans and proposed referring the remaining demands to a Committee of Inquiry. On 12 February, the MFGB Executive submitted the government's reply to a special conference of the MFGB which rejected the offer and decided to refer the question to a ballot of the whole membership, recommending members vote for strike action.[11] However, Smillie warned the delegates:

We would not be acting as honest citizens of the state if we took advantage of our power to enforce claims on our fellow citizens that were unjust.[12]

8 Cole, *Labour in the Coal Mining Industry*, 70.
9 Ibid. 71–72.
10 *Gloucestershire Echo* 17 January 1919.
11 Cole, *Labour in the Coal Mining Industry*, 72-73.
12 Quoted in M. G. Woodhouse, Mines for the Nation or Mines for the Miners? Alternative Perspectives on Industrial Democracy, 1919-1921, *Llafur*, (Volume 2, Number 3, 1978) 95.

On 22 January 1919, Henry Wallace James Smith of Cinderford, aged 27 and an experienced collier, was killed after a roof fall covered him with several tons of rocks at Waterloo Colliery in Lydbrook. Smith had recently returned from France and had only been employed at the colliery for ten days. He had been in the army for two and a half years and served as a gunner in the Royal Artillery.

Government Crisis

To attempt to understand how the ruling class responded to the demand for substantial reform from mining communities, some background information is necessary on how events elsewhere impacted on government policy.

It is difficult to overestimate the crisis facing the government in early 1919. There was violence in India and the Middle East and warfare in Ireland. Churchill was prosecuting bloody wars in Iraq and Afghanistan and had sent conscripts to Russia to fight against the Red Army. In early 1919, the shortage of necessities combined with the unmet expectation by millions of troops that there would be immediate demobilisation created an explosive situation. As a result, increasing insubordination resulted in mutinies and strikes at home and abroad which directly challenged ruling-class authority. In a memorandum to the Versailles Conference of 1919, Lloyd George wrote:

> Europe is filled with revolutionary ideas. A feeling not of depression, but of passion and revolt reigns in the breasts of the working class against the conditions of life that prevailed before the war. The whole of the existing system, political, social and economic, is regarded with distrust by the whole population of Europe. In some countries, like Germany and Russia, this unrest is leading to open revolt and in others, like France, England and Italy, it is expressed in strikes and in a certain aversion to work. All signs go to show that the striving is as much for social and political changes as for increases in wages.[13]

13 Quoted in Jack T. Murphy, *Preparing for Power* (London, 1972) 172.

Mutiny

Immediately after the armistice, protests erupted in the army and navy over the issues of demobilisation, military discipline and drafting to Russia. Two days after the armistice, 7,000 soldiers marched from their base at Shoreham to Brighton and demanded to be released from the army.[14] There were strikes and demonstrations by discontented servicemen at Biggin Hill, Aldershot, Winchester, Lymington, Bristol, Milford Haven, Plymouth, Falmouth, Felixstowe, Bedford, Kettering, Leeds, Manchester, Blackpool, Edinburgh, the Isle of Wight, Lewes, Southwick, Osterley Park, Bromley, Park Royal and Kempton Park.[15]

The protests continued into early 1919 and in some cases developed into outright mutiny as soldiers disobeyed orders, took over bases and even arranged their own demobilisation. On 3 January, the *Daily Herald* reported that in Folkestone:

> Ten thousand soldiers marched through the town, held a mass meeting at which they formed a soldiers' union, elected 140 men to act as clerks, took over the demobilisation department, and in one day issued all the necessary pass papers, ration books and railway warrants for the whole camp. By the Sunday the camp was clear.[16]

At the end of January, the trouble spread to Calais where up to 20,000 men were involved in demobilisation protests and linked up with striking French railway workers closing the ports to prevent the movement of troops.[17] In mid-January, sailors on several ships mutinied and refused to be sent to fight against the Red Army in the Russian civil war.[18] In most cases, the scale of the protests meant that the authorities had no choice but to concede to the men's demands. On 8 February, the loyalty of professional soldiers in the Grenadier Guards and the Household Cavalry was tested when they were ordered to fix bayonets and confront over one thousand armed soldiers who were marching towards parliament, having refused to board trains to France. Churchill wrote later: "I remained in my room, a prey to anxiety".[19]

14 *Daily Herald* 11 January 1919.
15 G. Dallas and D. Gill, *The Unknown Army, Mutinies in the British Army in World War One* (London: Verso, 1985) and Simon Webb, *1919, Britain's Year of Revolution* (Barnsley: Pen and Sword, 2016) 43.
16 *Daily Herald* 11 January 1919.
17 Webb, *1919*, 40-41.
18 Ibid. 24-25.
19 Ibid. 43.

During January and February, some estimates have up to 100,000 men directly or indirectly involved in these disturbances and so it is likely the events would have impacted on men from the Forest of Dean.[20] The government was concerned that it could no longer rely unconditionally upon the loyalty of its soldiers and sailors, particularly if conscripts were ordered to act against their communities. The government's greatest fear was that the diminishing deference towards the ruling class could mean Bolshevism would spread to Britain. On 14 January 1919, Churchill circulated a secret memorandum to all commanders of British forces asking whether their forces would serve overseas and particularly in Russia, whether they would serve as strike-breakers, and for details of the soldiers' attitudes to trade unions.

Strikes

During January and February 1919, serious industrial unrest spread across Britain. On 11 January, there was a strike at New Fancy colliery near Parkend in a dispute over the minimum wage.[21] On the 18 January, 150,000 South Yorkshire miners struck in support of the right of surface workers to take a break for food. As a result, within twenty-four hours the demands of the Yorkshire miners were met by the owners under the instruction of the Coal Controller.[22] During the rest of 1919 and early 1920, the demand for coal remained high and, as a result, it was not unusual for the Coal Controller to rule in favour of the trade unions in disputes with the owners, so as to avoid strikes and disruption.

In Belfast, on 25 January, shipyard workers, electricians and engineers walked out in defiance of their national leaders, in an unofficial strike demanding a 44-hour week. The demand for a reduction of hours was directly linked to the issue of unemployment facing demobilised soldiers and sailors on their return. Just like the mutinies, the strike appeared to be a spontaneous mass action and this was very menacing to the established order. Within days the city was in the grip of a general strike.[23]

Similarly, in Glasgow, on 27 January, an unofficial general strike led by engineering and shipbuilding shop stewards demanded a reduction in their hours from 57 to 40 a week. This was in opposition to a deal just

20 Ibid. 44.
21 *Gloucester Journal* 18 January 1919.
22 Ives, *Reform, Revolution and Direct Action*, 279-280.
23 David Mitchell, Ghost of Chance: British Revolutionaries in *1919, History Today*, (November 1970) 758.

negotiated by the official trade union leaders of a 47-hour week. Many of the men involved in picketing were identified as ex-servicemen by their army coats.[24]

At the same time, the whole of the nearby coalfields of Fife and Lanarkshire were closed down in an unofficial strike over issues relating to surface men's shift patterns. The miners quickly linked up with the general strike in Glasgow and escalated their demands to a six-hour day and a minimum wage of five pounds a week. The strike was led by the syndicalist Fife and Lanarkshire URC without the backing of the official leadership. At one point the offices of the Scottish Miners' Association were occupied by armed strikers who raised the red flag. However, by the 5 February the strike had collapsed after the official leadership called for a return to work.[25]

In Glasgow, the general strike continued, and the raising of the red flag on a municipal flagpole, followed by rioting, raised concerns about the spread of Bolshevism. At least 10,000 loyal troops were brought in from other districts and backed up by machine guns, armoured cars, field artillery and tanks. The strike came to an end on 11 February when some of the strikers were arrested and imprisoned. The government was happy for the official trade union leadership to step in and the compromise deal of a 47-hour week was agreed. The Belfast men returned to work a few days later on 19 February under similar circumstances.

In the meantime, the strikes had spread to the docks on the Thames, and with the threat of more strikes in the capital's generating stations, together with the strong likelihood of disruption on the railways, the government felt it was losing control. Many of the strikes were unofficial, a fact which contributed to the atmosphere of insurgency and caused the government serious problems in devising a strategy to deal with the unrest. Tom Jones, Deputy Secretary to the cabinet, wrote to Lloyd George warning that:

> Much of the present difficulty springs from the mutiny of the rank and file against the old established leaders [who] no longer represent the more active and agitating minds in the labour movement.[26]

24 Webb, *1919*, 60
25 Ives, *Reform, Revolution and Direct Action*, Chapter 3 and *Sunday Post* 2 February 1919.
26 Ibid. 39.

In South Wales, where many Forest of Dean miners worked, the URC had grown in strength and as a result, an upsurge in unrest erupted, leading to 242 strikes in the South Wales valleys during 1919, most of these between January and August and many of them unofficial.[27] In early January, James Winstone, a moderate by the standards of the day, announced at a post-election rally after a disappointing parliamentary election result that:

> There is a force rising up in this country that all the forces of darkness will never stem. This crowd, this coalition crowd of capitalists and landlords and their henchmen will be snuffed out as a bit of snowflake before the sun.[28]

How this would be achieved was open to debate, particularly when the Labour Party was still struggling to win seats in working class areas. However, the opinion of Siegfried Owen Davies was much more in tune with the mood in the coalfields:

> the trade union weapon was the only weapon to contend with the new government.[29]

Men like Davies, Ablett and Cook joined forces with other members of the South Wales URC like John Williams, the Secretary of the Garw Valley district of the SWMF and young communists like Arthur Horner who was checkweighman at Maerdy Colliery in the Rhondda.[30] These men had a significant presence at the SWMF delegate conferences and

27 Ibid. 157.
28 *Merthyr Pioneer*, 4 January 1919.
29 *Merthyr Pioneer*, 4 January 1919. Siegfried Owen Davies (1886-1972) was born in Aberdare and at the age twelve began work in the Cwmpennar mine and attended adult education classes. In 1913, he obtained a BA in social sciences from University College, Cardiff. In December 1913, he was elected miners' sub-agent for the Anthracite district of the SWMF. He opposed World War One, advocated workers control of industry and supported the Russian revolution. In 1918, he became an agent of the SWMF for Dowlais.
30 Arthur Horner was born in Merthyr Tydfil and gained work in Merthyr railway goods station. In 1915, he went to work in the Rhondda coalfield where he became a protégé of Noah Ablett. Horner opposed the First World War from the standpoint of class solidarity and fled to Dublin in 1917 to avoid arrest for ignoring his call-up papers. On his return to Britain, he was arrested by the authorities for avoiding conscription and sentenced to six months hard labour at Wormwood Scrubs. After he had served his sentence, he was refused the amnesty made available after the war to most conscientious objectors. He was rearrested and sent to Carmarthen jail. The SWMF campaigned for his release and to this end secured his election in absentia as checkweighman at Maerdy Colliery. The campaign led to his release in May 1919. Horner joined the CPGB and was elected President of the SWMF from 1936 to 1959 and General Secretary of the National Union of Miners from 1946 to 1959.

increased their influence on events in the South Wales coalfield through the support they received from newspapers like the *Daily Herald*, the *Workers Dreadnought* and the *Merthyr Pioneer*. During this period the Executive of the FDMA had developed a close relationship with the socialist newspaper the *Daily Herald* which nationally had a circulation of about 250,000.[31] Jesse Hodges (Jnr) remembered:

> My father was the man who brought the *Daily Herald* into the Forest, gave his life's blood for the worker.[32]

In the early months of 1919, the paper championed the idea that the industrial power of the working class expressed through a general strike was the key to the transformation of society and for a short period, the paper appeared to abandon the idea of the parliamentary road to socialism. In early February, George Lansbury, the editor of the *Daily Herald* wrote:

> Do none of these Parliamentarians, these preachers of constitutional methods, these finger-shaking pundits, realise that the old world is breaking up under their feet, that a new spirit is moving on the face of the waters, that a new spring is in the air? It is not too much to say that the constitutional method is on its last trial and the sands are running out.[33]

The situation was compounded by severe unrest in the police force when the National Union of Police and Prison Officers threatened to strike for recognition.[34] The rail unions were pressing the government for an eight-hour day, higher wages, a national agreement to standardise wages and nationalisation of the railways. Meanwhile, unrest continued in the army camps.[35] The government was beginning to panic and could not countenance a nationwide strike in the rail industry or coal industry. The

Jesse Hodges (Snr).

31 FDMA Minutes, 22 March 1919.
32 Jesse Hodges (Jnr), Gage Library.
33 *Daily Herald* 8 February 1919.
34 Ives, *Reform, Revolution and Direct Action*, 40.
35 Webb, *1919*, Chapter 6.

demobilisation protests and strikes created a fear among the ruling class of shadowy and disorderly forces operating within working class communities which they had expected to show deference.[36] Despite having little understanding of the hopes and aspirations of ordinary miners and their families, this fear had a profound impact on government policy towards the mining communities.

In fact, unlike in Scotland and South Wales, there is little evidence that rank and file miners in the Forest of Dean had come under the influence of Bolshevism. Nonetheless, the influence of syndicalism was present in their determination to fight for substantial reforms. Forest miners were keen to defend their status as skilled workers with a strong belief in custom and practice, with the right to a living wage and a degree of control over the production process. Many had volunteered to fight in World War One and they now demanded to be treated with respect.

Royal Commission

The unrest in other parts of the country indirectly impacted on the Forest of Dean because the mutinies and strikes meant that the government could not afford to take any risks and was determined to prevent a national miners' strike in such an unpredictable environment. As a result, in a very shrewd move, Lloyd George proposed a Royal Commission to look into the running of the industry and promised that the Commission would be required to present an interim report by 20 March, provided the MFGB called off its threat of a strike.

In December 1918, nine days before the election, Churchill declared that he supported a plan to nationalise the railways.[37] In January 1919, the government set in motion the Ministry of Ways and Communication Bill to re-organise the transport industry.[38] The Bill included a clause enabling the government to nationalise the whole transport industry, including the railways, docks and roads.[39] However, it soon became clear that Churchill was just electioneering and the majority of MPs believed that the wartime control of all industries should be removed with all possible speed and wages reduced by removing the wartime bonus. A confrontation between the railway workers and the government and the railway companies appeared to be inevitable.

36 Bonar Law stated he was in fear of being strung up on one of London's lamp-posts.
37 Bagwell, *The Railwaymen*, 405.
38 The name of the Bill was changed to the Ministry of Transport Bill in August 1919.
39 Bagwell, *The Railwaymen*, 405-406.

On 25 February 1919, the results of the miners' strike ballot were announced and revealed that nationally six to one were in favour of strike action, with 615,164 in favour and 105,082 against.[40] In the Forest of Dean, where the FDMA Executive argued for a strike, the figures were twenty-six to one in favour of a strike with 4,020 for and 154 against.[41] This is in marked contrast to South Wales where it was only three to one in favour of a strike, mainly as a result of the two elder statesmen of the SWMF Executive, Tom Richards and William Brace, arguing against strike action.[42] The next day, on 26 February, miners' delegates met for a conference to hear a report on the Commission proposal from the MFGB Executive and to discuss the options.

Among the delegates were members of the new generation of young syndicalists such as Booth, Cook and Ablett, who had started to influence events locally. However, most members of the MFGB Executive were moderates accustomed to the language of conciliation and arbitration. For instance, Thomas Cann (Durham), William Buckley (Derbyshire), Charles Bunfield (Nottingham), William Straker (Northumberland) and William Brace (South Wales) had their roots in nineteenth-century liberalism. Thomas Cape (Cumberland), John Sutton (Lancashire), Frank Hall (Derbyshire), Samuel Finney (Midlands), Samuel Roebuck (Yorkshire) and John Hoskin (Yorkshire) were all in their fifties and sixties. These men were fully aware of recent events in Belfast and Glasgow and nervous of the consequences of a national strike. William Brace warned:

Starting a war is easy; stopping it once it has started is another matter.[43]

In addition, Smillie and Hodges had recently come under the influence of Sidney and Beatrice Webb from the Fabian Society, who were

40 Cole, *Labour in the Coal Mining Industry*, 73.
41 *Gloucester Journal* 22 February 1919 and *Dean Forest Mercury* 21 February 1919.
42 Ives, *Reform, Revolution and Direct Action*, 176.
Tom Richards (1859–1931) was Secretary of the SWMF from 1898 to 1931 and MP for West Monmouthshire until 1918. He was then elected MP for Ebbw Vale from 1918 until he retired in 1920. He became a member of the Privy Council in 1918.
William Brace (1865–1947) was elected as President of the SWMF from 1912 to 1915. At the 1906 general election, he was elected as a Lib-Lab member of parliament for South Glamorganshire, holding the seat at the next two general elections. During the First World War, he held the post of Under-Secretary of State for the Home Department in the Lloyd George Coalition Government. When the South Glamorganshire seat was abolished at the 1918 general election, he was elected unopposed to represent the new Abertillery seat as a Labour Party MP.
43 *Rhondda Leader* 22 March 1919.

On 31 March 1919, Henry John Evans was crushed to death by a roof fall while working at Lightmoor colliery. Evans was born in Littledean in April 1870, the son of a coal miner. He followed his father into the mines. In 1894, he married Emily Church and had eight children, one of whom died at the age of two. His last child, Reginald, was born ten months before his father was killed.

instrumental in persuading them to accept the offer of a commission.[44] The Fabian Society believed that socialism should be achieved gradually by reform in parliament by the Labour Party and was hostile to syndicalism.[45] As a result, Hodges had now started to move away from the syndicalism of his Welsh colleagues and had become attracted to a form of guild socialism which argued that social transformation could be achieved by constitutional means alone, by gradually democratising the state and introducing joint workers' control by parliamentary reform. Consequently, he believed he could achieve his aims through negotiation, influence and persuasion in his dealings with the government.

Smillie, at 62 years old, was exhausted and reluctant to commit the MFGB to a major confrontation with the government which could threaten the finances of the MFGB. He was also fearful of the use of state violence against striking miners. He knew that in the past Churchill had sanctioned the use of troops against workers, resulting in deaths. In addition, on 20 March, Bonar Law warned that the government would "use all the resources of the state without the smallest hesitation" to defeat the miners.[46] Hodges later recalled that he and Smillie:

> threw in the whole weight of our argument and our influence to get the men and delegates to accept the Royal Commission.[47]

As a result, the Executive persuaded the conference to suspend strike notices, providing the MFGB would be given adequate representation on the Commission.[48] This suited the government and the MFGB leadership,

44 Margaret Cole (ed), *Beatrice Webb's Diaries, 1912-1924* (London: Longmans, 1952) 150-151.
45 For a detailed discussion of the Webbs' critique of syndicalism see J. M. Winter, *Socialism and the Challenge of War* (London: Routledge, 1974) 29-66.
46 Ives, *Reform, Revolution and Direct Action*, 193.
47 Hodges, *My Adventures*, 80.
48 Cole, *Labour in the Coal Mining Industry*, 73-74.

who were both concerned that they could lose control during a nationwide miners' strike.

Lord Sankey

The government soon set about establishing a Commission of Inquiry and appointed Sir John Sankey as Chairman.[49] The Commission's brief was to enquire into many aspects of the coal industry, including health, safety, costs, profits, hours of work and conditions of employment. It was tasked to consider alternative methods for the future conduct of the industry in terms of ownership and control.

Hodges, Smillie and Smith were appointed as the miners' representatives on the Commission. Sidney Webb, who had helped persuade the MFGB Executive to accept the Commission proposal, also sat on the Commission.[50] The essence of the miners' case was essentially ethical. Smillie, Hodges and Smith set out to convince the Commission, the public and the government that industrial cooperation was a higher ideal than the greed and clash of interests associated with private enterprise. They argued that the dictates of justice and the right to a living wage and shorter hours were more important than the dictates of the market. William Straker, speaking on behalf of the MFGB, claimed: "that which is morally wrong cannot be economically right".[51] The miners argued this was directly linked to the issue of public ownership and joint control which they believed would provide the basis of a humane, efficient and prosperous coal industry.

The miners' representatives concentrated on five main points: (1) a wage advance which would provide a living wage to counter the rise in the cost of living; (2) a reduction of hours on human and social grounds and to reduce unemployment; (3) improvement in housing and social amenities; (4) a limit on the enormous profits made by the colliery owners as was the case during the war; (5) a strategy to deal with the inefficiency of the existing system of production and distribution.[52]

49 John Sankey, 1st Viscount Sankey (1866-1948) was a British lawyer, judge, Labour politician and Lord Chancellor of Great Britain.
50 The Coal Industry Commission held its first meeting on March 3rd. It was composed of the following men: Hon Justice Sankey (Chairman); Robert Smillie, Herbert Smith, Frank Hodges and Sir Leo Chiozza Money (nominated by the MFGB); R. H. Tawney and Sidney Webb (Government nominees agreed to by the MFGB); Arthur Balfour, Sir Arthur Duckham and Sir Thomas Royden (Government nominees); Evan Williams, R. W. Coope; and J. T. Forgie (representing Coal Owners).
51 Woodhouse, *Mines for the Nation or Mines for the Miners?* 95.
52 Cole, *Labour in the Coal Mining Industry*, 79.

Hodges, Smillie and Smith contrasted the privilege and wealth of the colliery owners and landed gentry, who gained a huge amount of their wealth from profits and royalties, with the poverty faced by mining communities. Smillie cross-examined peers of the realm and other landowners, questioning how they could justify the huge earnings they made from their royalty payments. In particular, the issue of profiteering by the colliery owners during the war created a sense of revulsion among the general public, the majority of whom were now convinced by the miners' case. Beatrice Webb later commented that during the enquiry the colliery owners were completely outclassed by the miners' leaders and added that the colliery owners had not the remotest inkling of the wider political and social issues. On Hodges' negotiating skills and eloquence Webb reported:

> his extraordinary command of facts and the dexterity with which he marshalled them, his clever cross-examination of hostile witnesses, commanded universal admiration.[53]

During the enquiry, Sir Francis Brain, representing the Forest colliery owners, claimed that increasing miners' pay and reducing hours would make the Forest pits unviable.[54] In fact, the Commission revealed that:

> The private ownership and distribution of coal had not merely meant swollen profits wrung out of the low wages paid to the miner and high prices paid by the public, but also had severely hampered the national effort during the war by its inefficiency and wastefulness.[55]

The Commission failed to produce a unanimous report. However, on 20 March 1919, it published three separate interim reports: one by Sankey and three business representatives, one by the miners and their allies and one by the colliery owners. Sankey's report, which was the one officially adopted, proposed an increase of two shillings per shift for adults and one shilling for boys and a reduction of the maximum hours from eight to seven, with the aim of reducing the hours to six by 1920.

The report also recommended a levy of one penny a ton on all coal mined to finance educational, welfare and recreational facilities for miners and their communities. In addition, it recommended the colliery owners

53 Beatrice Webb, *Diaries Vol.* 1, 161.
54 *Western Daily Press* 14 March 1919.
55 Arnot, *The Miners*, 189.

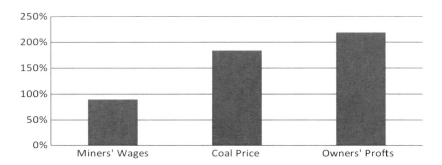

Percentage Increase in Forest of Dean Miners' Wages, Coal Price and Owners' Profits (1913 to 1918).

Figures from the Sankey Commission quoted in Arnot, *The Miners*, p190 and Forest of Dean newspapers.

should receive a maximum profit of one shilling and two pence a ton to make sure the excessive profits made during the war years were not repeated. Sankey also recommended that state control of the mines be continued, pending a full decision on the future of the industry.[56] Sankey's report added that the present system of ownership was fragmented, inefficient and created recrimination between the colliery owners and the men:

> Even upon the evidence already given, the present system of ownership working in the coal industry stands condemned, and some other system must be substituted for it, either nationalisation or a method of unification by national purchase and/or joint control.

> It is in the interests of the country that the colliery worker shall in the future have an effective voice in the direction of the mine. For a generation, the colliery worker has been educated socially and technically. The result is a great national asset. Why not use it? [57]

The miners' representatives on the Commission stuck to their original demands and recommended joint state and workers' control. The owners, of course, rejected nationalisation and recommended no change to the system of private ownership.

56 Cole, *Labour in the Coal Mining Industry*, 85–87.
57 Ibid. 87.

The Railwaymen

Meanwhile, the rail unions, the government and the railway companies were negotiating with each other over wages, conditions and the introduction of an eight-hour day. The companies were fearful that the government would agree a deal leaving them with an intolerable wage bill and rigid conditions of work, if and when the railways were returned to private control. The companies accepted the principle of an eight-hour day from 1 February but insisted this would not include meal times and breaks. In some areas, including on London's tube trains, railway workers went on strike over the eight-hour issue and unofficial actions spread, resulting in most of the railway companies backing down.[58]

Jimmy Thomas warned that unless the other main points of the NUR's demands were agreed upon by 20 March, he would have no alternative but to withdraw from the negotiations. He pointed out that on 20 March the Sankey report was to be published and his partners in the Triple Alliance were due to meet the following day to discuss the miners' response. The NUR Executive then voted to ask the Triple Alliance to intervene if necessary. Horne was aware of the danger and advised the war cabinet on 19 March:

> It is worthwhile to pay the extra cost of the railwaymen's demands in order to secure their support at the present time. If the miners came out on strike the railwaymen might come out too, but with this difference, that if the above concessions were now granted, they would be striking without a grievance.[59]

The government and the rail companies quickly responded with a revised offer on wages which included a guarantee of the war bonus to 31 December 1919 and the principle of the standardisation of wages. In addition, the negotiations achieved a guaranteed day and week, a week's holiday after a year's service and extra money for night work, Sunday duty and overtime. As a result, on 24 March 1919, both the NUR and ASLEF accepted the revised offer which was scheduled to come into effect on 7 April 1919. The issue of the standardisation of wages based on a nationally negotiated agreement was left to further negotiation.[60]

---

58 Bagwell, *The Railwaymen*, 377-378.
59 War Cabinet Minutes, CAB 23/9/34, The National Archives, Kew.
60 Bagwell, *The Railwaymen*, 379.

Meanwhile, the powerful railway companies and their representatives in parliament had made it clear to government ministers that they would never accept nationalisation. In the same way as the government used the Sankey Commission to defer the issue of nationalisation of the coal industry, it exploited the introduction of the Ministry of Ways and Communication Bill to sidestep the issue of nationalisation of the railways. In May 1919, under pressure from the private transport companies, the government deleted the nationalisation clause from the Bill, leaving the NUR with the weaker option of campaigning for some participation in the management of the railways by its workers.[61]

Bonar Law

On the evening of the day on which the Sankey Commission's reports were issued, Bonar Law, the Tory leader of the House and the real power behind the coalition government, stated in the House of Commons the government's readiness to accept the proposals contained in the Sankey Report. He made conciliatory gestures to the MFGB, suggesting the issue of nationalisation would remain under review during the second stage of the Commission.

He also intimated that if a miners' strike took place, the whole resources of the state would be used without hesitation to deal with the emergency.[62] When the MFGB national conference assembled on 21 March, some delegates expressed resentment at Bonar Law's threat.[63] After considerable discussion and questioning, especially from South Wales, Hodges read the following letter addressed to the Secretary of the MFGB from 11 Downing Street, Whitehall, S.W.1., and dated 21st March 1919 :

> Dear Sir, Speaking in the House of Commons last night I made a statement with regard to the Government's policy in connection with the Report of the Coal Industry Commission. I have pleasure in confirming, as I understand you wish me to do, my statement that the Government are prepared to carry out in the spirit and in the letter the recommendations of Mr Justice Sankey's Report.

> Yours faithfully, A. Bonar Law.[64]

61 Ibid. 408.
62 Ibid.
63 Cole, *Labour in the Coal Mining Industry*, 87-88.
64 R. Page Arnot, *South Wales Miners, 1914-1926*, (Cardiff: Cymric Federation Press, 1975), 169.

However, at the same time, in private meetings, Bonar Law was assuring the Cabinet he would not be prepared to pass the necessary legislation needed for the nationalisation of the mines.[65] The MFGB conference was convinced by Bonar Law's assurances and agreed to suspend the strike notices. When it met again on 26 March, it agreed to organise a ballot on the government's offer of two shillings per shift for adults and one shilling for boys and a reduction of the maximum hours from eight to seven.[66]

Smillie, Hodges and others on the MFGB Executive argued that the Commission had highlighted that radical social change could be brought about by constitutional means alone and recommended acceptance. This decision was backed by the influential South Wales members on the MFGB Executive, Vernon Hartshorne and William Brace.[67] However, some South Wales miners disagreed, and by the end of March, nearly 80,000 South Wales miners were on strike in an unofficial and short-lived protest against the decision to recommend acceptance.[68] In addition, on 29 and 31 March, in opposition to its leadership, an SWMF delegate conference voted to recommend a rejection of the offer in the ballot.[69] At the end of March, there was also an unofficial stoppage involving 30,000 miners in Nottingham and unofficial strikes in South Yorkshire, the Black Country, Chesterfield, Staffordshire and Warwickshire against acceptance of the Sankey offer.[70]

The national ballot result was announced on 15 April and showed that nationally 693,684 were for and 76,992 against the government's offer.[71] In the Forest of Dean, the FDMA Executive recommended acceptance with the result that the Forest miners voted 14 to 1 to accept the government's proposal with 5431 in favour and 393 against.[72] In the end, even South Wales voted for acceptance.

---

65 Patrick Renshaw, *The General Strike*, (London: Eyre Methuen, 1975) 59.

66 Cole, *Labour in the Coal Mining Industry*, 88–90.

67 Vernon Hartshorne (1872–1931) was born in Pont-y-waun and started work as a miner as a boy. For a time, he was a clerk at Cardiff in one of the docks offices; but he returned to the coalfield, finding work at Risca where he was appointed as checkweighman. Hartshorne was one of the pioneers of the ILP in Wales. In 1905, he was appointed the agent for the SWMF in the Maesteg district. In 1911, he was elected to the National Executive Council of the MFGB, one of a number of young militants who displaced more established figures, following the Cambrian Combine Strike of 1910–11. He took a leading part in the minimum wage strike of 1912 and was prominent in local government. However, in recent years he had moderated his views and now was often in conflict with syndicalist and left-wing miners within the SWMF.

68 *Western Mail* 24-31 March 1919.

69 Ives, *Reform, Revolution and Direct Action*, 178-182.

70 *Sheffield Evening Telegraph* 28 March 1919.

71 Cole, *Labour in the Coal Mining Industry*, 89.

72 *Dean Forest Mercury* 18 April 1919.

The majority of the miners and the whole trade union movement believed that the government had pledged itself to the ending of the private ownership of the coal mines. Consequently, the threat of a national strike was dissipated, to the relief of the government and the majority of the MFGB Executive.

Local Government

At this time, the government started cutting back on its programme of investment in the economy, which impacted on local government's plan to invest in public services. The government was keen to restore pre-war British predominance in international trade, which it believed would require a return to the gold standard and the stabilising of the value of sterling around the pre-war dollar exchange rate. The government believed this required equilibrium in the balance of payments and the reduction of money in circulation. As a result, Austen Chamberlain, the Chancellor of the Exchequer, introduced a budget which cut back government spending and reduced the supply of money, followed by an increase in the bank rate to 6 per cent later in the year.[73]

Meanwhile, the Labour Party had been making gains in local elections. The Labour Party was traditionally strongest in West Dean where it had a significant number of members in the ILP, whilst East Dean had traditionally been the base for Rowlinson and the Liberal Party. Rowlinson was chairman of East Dean District Council, but after the local elections in April 1919, the Labour Party had gained a majority of councillors in the Cinderford ward, including Frank Ashmead and Jim Jones from the NUR, and a significant minority of councillors on East Dean District Council.[74] However, the cuts in government expenditure curtailed the ability of the newly elected Labour councillors to implement municipal projects such as housing, water and sewage schemes.

Minimum Wage Dispute

On the ground, miners were continuing to use localised industrial action to push for more reform. Between January and March 1919, the Board of Trade lists fifty-four serious disputes nationwide in the coalfields, involving almost half a million miners and making an aggregate of over two million

73 John Foster, *Industrial Politics and the 1926 Mining Lockout*, 27.
74 East Dean District Council was made up of five wards which included Cinderford (six seats), Abbenhall (one seat), Littledean (one seat), Joys Green (one seat) and Drybrook (three seats).

days lost through strikes.[75] This does not even take into account the instances when just the threat of industrial action forced a concession from the colliery owners.

In May 1919, a dispute erupted in the Forest coalfield over the minimum wage agreement. Under pressure from the FDMA, a new standard minimum rate had been introduced by Russell Kerr, chairman of the local minimum wage board, an increase from 4s per shift to 4s 7d. However, the employers insisted the increase was just for hewers and did not apply to other workers and those on a lower standard rate. As a result, on 10 May, after consultation with the workforce, strike notices were issued by the FDMA Executive. Booth released a statement to the *Dean Forest Mercury* which included:

> However, apart from this matter, the real cause of the tendering of notices was the failure of the owners to meet the workmen at many of the collieries on little matters, and these little matters have accumulated to such an extent that only a spark was necessary to produce an explosion.[76]

Consequently, on 15 May, the FDMA Executive agreed to arbitration by the Coal Controller and eventually a compromise was reached, giving the men about half of what was in the original application. As a result, face workers would still get the 4s 7d, but other workers on the 4s standard would now get 4s 4d and men on a 3s standard would now get 3s 3d, etc.[77] A mass meeting was held at Speech House on 25 May where, despite some dissent, the majority of the miners agreed to accept the results of arbitration.[78] During the dispute the *South Wales News* reported Booth's views on the dispute:

> He did not personally look for the emancipation of the workers from sending Labour men to Parliament, but rather from the combined and united efforts of the workers through their trade union organisations, by which means they could compel Parliament to legislate in accordance with their wishes.[79]

75 Board of Trade, *The Labour Gazette*, January to April 1919.
76 *Dean Forest Mercury* 16 May 1919.
77 Minutes of FDMA Executive 14 May *1919*, and *Dean Forest Mercury* 30 May 1919.
78 *Dean Forest Mercury* 31 May 1919.
79 *South Wales News* 6 May 1919.

As a result of this dispute, the minimum wage for a day rate hewer in the Forest of Dean was now 13s 2d which included the additional percentage, the war wage and the Sankey award (4s 7d plus 80%, plus 3s, plus 2s, giving 13s 2d). This was a pay rise of one shilling which was a significant amount. The Craftsmen Association met with the Forest of Dean colliery owners under the chairmanship of the Deputy Coal Controller and agreed on an increase of 4d a day on their standard wages.[80]

Joint Control

On 24 April 1919, the second stage of the enquiry began and concentrated in more detail on broader issues of policy, in particular, the question of ownership and control. On 20 June, the Commission published four reports but with no clear majority position. Sankey and the miners recommended nationalisation with differing views on the degree of workers' control. The miners proposed that management of the mining industry should pass from shareholders and directors to public ownership and be placed, both nationally and locally, as far as possible in the hands of the workers as opposed to a state bureaucracy. The owner's representatives were for continuing private ownership.[81]

The fourth report produced by Sir Arthur Duckham was a compromise between nationalisation and private ownership and recommended that the collieries should be acquired by district coal boards owned by individual companies and operated with a limit on profits. All four reports proposed abolishing royalties and placing coal distribution in the hands of public bodies.[82]

Meanwhile, the MAGB had re-organised itself with substantial funding from the mine-owners, set up an office with paid officials and re-elected Evan Williams as the President in a permanent full-time role. The MAGB immediately went on a propaganda offensive against nationalisation. The MAGB was influentially represented in the House of Commons, and a large proportion of the members of the coalition parties had pledged themselves to resist any attempt to introduce nationalisation. The ruling classes did not want to set a precedent which would undermine private enterprise. The government now stated it was not obliged to act on any of the reports.

80 *Western Mail* 28 May 1919.
81 Cole, *Labour in the Coal Mining Industry*, 90-100.
82 Ibid.

On 8 July, under pressure from the MAGB, the government decided to postpone introducing a bill to limit colliery owners' profits.[83] On 9 July, despite receiving massive profits from the export trade, the government increased the retail price of domestic coal by six shillings a ton, blaming the recent wage increase to the miners in an attempt to turn public opinion against them.[84]

No More War

Every year in July, the Forest of Dean miners held a demonstration at Speech House which combined politics with music by the colliery bands and the fun of the fair. Caroline Nicholls, who was born in 1908, remembers:

All the people as was in the unions, and the MP, they had the lot there in the morning. And believe me, men did go to hear what they'd got to say, and I'll tell you another thing, the men was allowed to have their say. And some of them did, without any arguments … There was never an argument, you know what I mean, it was just a clean straightforward talk. Anybody could ask questions and they'd listen to the questions and they'd give them an answer.[85]

At the demonstration on 12 July 1919, the miners were full of confidence, but the atmosphere was politically charged with many war veterans present. It was clear that the Forest community had had enough of war and did not want to be drawn into another conflict, particularly with their old ally. As a result, a resolution was passed demanding the withdrawal of British troops from Russia and the end to conscription. Another resolution was passed, calling for a reduction in the cost of living, progress with housing schemes and proper provision for the care and maintenance of the soldiers and sailors disabled by the war, with ample pensions secured to the widows and children of those killed. In addition, a resolution was passed calling for the nationalisation of the mines without further delay.[86]

However, many members of the establishment found these demands unacceptable and argued the miners should put nation before class. The

---

83 May, *A Question of Control*, 224.
84 Cole, *Labour in the Coal Mining Industry*, 101–103.
85 Caroline Nicholls, interviewed by Elsie Olivey on 1 March 1984, Gage Library.
86 *Western Daily Press* 14 July 1919.

day after the demonstration, Bishop Frodham, a canon at Gloucester Cathedral, spoke in Bream at an open-air memorial to the dead of the Forest of Dean Battalion and the Gloucestershire Regiments where he attempted to invoke the memory of the fallen to persuade the miners to drop their demands for better living and working conditions. The *Gloucestershire Chronicle* reported:

> In the name of the brave dead, he appealed to the true patriotism of the living miners to put England first of all.[87]

Keswick Conference

On 15 July, Bonar Law offered to withdraw the increase in the price of coal if the MFGB agreed to a no-strike deal for three months and to sign a productivity agreement. However, when the MFGB annual conference at Keswick started on 16 July, the delegates made it clear they would have nothing to do with Bonar Law's offer, despite some attempts by members of the Executive, in particular, Hartshorne and Brace, to persuade them to accept it.[88]

In the end, the majority at the conference decided on a compromise of accepting the proposals made by Sankey, as opposed to the MFGB scheme, and to campaign for their implementation. However, there was much debate over how the award would be implemented, with concerns expressed on how hours reduction would impact on piece rates, and the failure to include surface workers in the award. In fact, surface workers were already on an unofficial strike over the issue in South Wales, where many pits were at a standstill. Hartshorne and other members of the Executive appealed to them to return to work and accept the Sankey report.

Moderates like Hartshorne, Brace and Richards were able to limit the influence of the URC within the SWMF, but this only resulted in widespread unofficial activity, which was not the case in the Forest of Dean where militants like Booth and Organ held key positions in the much smaller FDMA. In Yorkshire, Herbert Smith expressed concern over how the Sankey award would affect the piece work rates of his members. In the end, a resolution was passed at the conference in favour of standardisation of wages and conditions across all the nation's coalfields.[89]

87 *Gloucestershire Chronicle* 19 July 1919.
88 Ives, *Reform, Revolution and Direct Action*, 234.
89 *Western Mail* 19 July 1919.

On 24 July 1919, 77 year-old Henry Winston Smith died after falling over at Princess Royal Colliery.

A new MFGB Executive was appointed at the conference, the majority of members of which were still of moderate views and in their fifties and sixties. Most of these men were anxious to avoid any conflict and were fearful of a government that in the words of Smillie was prepared "to shoot down our people".[90] Booth, who at thirty-three years old was elected as a representative of the small regions, was frustrated by the failure of the MFGB Executive to use direct action.[91]

However, the Executive made it clear that whatever its internal differences over the use of the strike as a weapon of last resort, it remained committed to constitutional means to achieve the implementation of Sankey's proposals.[92] As far as the rank and file miners were concerned, the opportunity to consolidate their power by using their industrial muscle appeared to be slipping away. Hodges told the *Daily Herald* on 31 July 1919:

the marvel is that the whole of the miners of this country were not on strike on Monday of this week. Only a few men realised how near we were to a general stoppage.[93]

On Wednesday 23 July, Wignall asked Horne in the House of Commons if he was aware that three large places of employment had been closed down in Mitcheldean since the signing of the armistice. This included the cement works which formerly employed 200 persons, the brickworks which employed 150 persons, and the Wigpool iron mine, which employed about 100 persons. Wignall asked if Horne would consider the possibility of the government taking over the brick and cement works and also continuing the development of the iron ore mine, thus providing employment for the returned soldiers who were then in receipt of unemployment benefit. Wignall also raised the issue of £320 still

90 Triple Alliance Conference held on 23 July quoted in Ives, *Reform, Revolution and Direct Action*, 194.
91 *Daily Herald* 19 July 1919.
92 Ives, *Reform, Revolution and Direct Action*, 305.
93 *Daily Herald* 31 July 1919.

owed to the iron ore miners as a result of the Sankey award. Horne replied that the Sankey award only applied to coal miners and that his department would get back to him on the closures.[94] However, the government was now committed to reducing its expenditure and there was little chance of them subsidising these industries.

Land Fit for Heroes

The government was still concerned that it had failed to contain the threat from organised labour and the atmosphere of insurgency continued throughout the summer. Following the signing of the Versailles Peace Treaty on 28 June 1919, Lord Downham announced that the British Government had decided that Saturday 19 July would be the day for a national celebration of victory and peace. However, in some parts of the country riots erupted during the Peace Day Demonstrations, in particular in Luton, Greenwich, Swindon, Coventry, Edinburgh, Hull, Wolverhampton, Salisbury and Liverpool.[95] One of the causes was the exclusion of ex-servicemen from lavish banquets enjoyed by the great and the good, many of whom had made fortunes from profiteering during the war.[96]

In the Forest of Dean, the Peace Day demonstrations were hampered by heavy rain. As a result, most of the outdoor processions were cancelled and took place the following weekend. The Forest was primarily a working-class community and there were no attempts to exclude ex-servicemen from indoor events.

In fact, in the vast majority of cases, the Peace Day Celebrations across the country went ahead without incidents. However, the government was still concerned about the threat and knew its ability to send troops into mining areas would be undermined if it could not rely on the military. The fact that ex-servicemen anywhere were involved in unrest only confirmed the government's fears that dangerous forces were at work.

94 *Gloucester Journal* 26 July 1919.
95 *The Times*, 21, 22, 23 July 1919 and *Daily Herald* 1, 7, 21, 23 July 1919.
96 This was the case in Luton where the town hall was attacked and the building ransacked and burnt down after ex-servicemen were excluded from a banquet. Tension had been building up all week after the council refused the ex-servicemen the use of a park to hold an alternative memorial service for their fallen comrades. Neil Gordon Orr, Keep the Home Fires Burning: Peace Day in Luton, *Family & Community History* (2:1, 1999) 17-32.

Soudley peace march.

Veteran Organisations

In response to the grievances of ex-servicemen, several veteran organisations were established towards the end of the war and organised campaigns around issues such as profiteering, back pay, pensions and employment. The National Federation of Discharged and Demobilised Sailors and Soldiers (NFDDSS) formed a number of branches in the Forest of Dean with miners as members.[97] The FDMA worked closely with the NFDDSS by sending delegates to the local War Pension Committees and making sure ex-soldiers gained employment in the mines.

Maurice Woodman was President of the Cinderford NFDDSS and Wallace Jones was Secretary.[98] Jones was also one of the founders of the Soldiers and Sailors Club in Cinderford. In October 1919, the NFDDSS joined forces with the Labour Party to contest seats in local elections in Gloucester.[99]

97 On 26 May 1919, the NFDDSS organised a march to Parliament Square in an attempt to get into Parliament. The march was baton charged by mounted police, resulting in a riot by the ex-servicemen. As a result, the Secretary of the newly formed police union apologised to the ex-servicemen for the behaviour of some its members among the metropolitan police and called for an end to militarism in the police, recognition of their union and closer links with organised labour. (*Globe* 27 May 1919).
98 Woodman joined the Gloucestershire Regiment in 1915 but was discharged in August 1916 due to sickness. He worked as a colliery clerk and was a proprietor of the Temperance Hotel in Cinderford.
99 *Gloucester Journal* 4 October 1919.

The NFDDSS was run by ordinary ex-servicemen and independent of the authorities. It had a strong anti-officer bias and membership was only open to the ranks or those officers who had been commissioned from the ranks.[100] In contrast, the Comrades of the Great War was founded by Edward Stanley, 17th Earl of Derby, as a right-wing alternative to the other veteran organisations. Some ex-military officers from the Forest of Dean organised Comrades of the Great War branches in Drybrook, Bream and Blakeney.[101]

The government was keen to quell any unrest due to veteran unemployment, and miners who had served in the military were quickly re-employed in the pits. By September 1919, about 80 per cent of the 15,000 ex-servicemen from Gloucestershire had been re-employed, with the rest mainly made up of the disabled.[102] As a result, the government issued an order demanding all employers take on at least five per cent disabled ex-servicemen. The FDMA was active in ensuring local colliery owners obeyed this order by employing disabled veterans, mainly on the surface. However, the authorities were still concerned about the threat of the independent ex-service organisations and made sure they were closely monitored by the security services.[103]

Government fears were compounded by a national police strike in August 1919 which led to the use of troops to quell serious disorder in Liverpool.[104] This was the third time that the military was used against working class communities on the British mainland since the end of the war. The government could not allow the police strike to continue and in a draconian measure dismissed all the strikers from its ranks. The authorities

100 A more militant organisation called the National Union of Ex-Servicemen (NUX) was founded in London in early 1919. Many of its members were formerly supporters of the Soldiers, Sailors and Airmen's Union (SSAU) which was formed during the demobilisation protests. Within six months, NUX had grown from one branch with fifty members to over one hundred branches. (David Englander, The National Union of Ex-Servicemen and the Labour Movement, 1918-1920, *History*, (1991).)
101 *Gloucester Journal* 17 August 1918, *Gloucester Journal* 22 May 1920 and *Gloucester Journal* 3 July 1920 .
102 *Gloucester Journal* 27 September 1919.
103 Stephen R Ward, Intelligence Surveillance of British Ex-Servicemen, 1918-1920, *The Historical Journal* (1973). Field Marshal Haig feared that "revolutionary ideas" were widespread among ex-servicemen, and argued that "the only solution was to get those men back to their old leaders, the officers." As a result, in 1921, the government encouraged the NFDDSS, NADSS and the Comrades of the Great War to combine to form the British Legion, which was run from the top by members of the British establishment, including Haig. The Cinderford branch of the Royal British Legion was established in July 1921.
104 Renshaw, *The General Strike*, 69-70. Yet again the government feared it was losing control and sent in 2500 armed soldiers to patrol the streets, resulting in one man being shot dead. The troops were backed up by four tanks, a battleship and two destroyers with their guns trained on Liverpool.

believed the purge was necessary because the government could not risk divided loyalties within the police ranks with the threat of major industrial disputes on the horizon.

Summer of Discontent

The government continued to view working class communities like the Forest of Dean as dangerous, particularly if their organisations were independent of the authorities. Meanwhile, some miners had started taking matters into their own hands. In the weeks following the Keswick conference about 400,000 miners in different parts of the country went on strike over issues raised in the debates arising from the Sankey Commission award on pay and hours. The primary demand was that piece workers should receive an increase in their rates to cover the loss of earnings as a result of shorter hours. Another issue was that the surface workers were not covered by Sankey's proposals on hours of work. Districts affected included Yorkshire, Scotland, the North East, Lancashire, Nottinghamshire, Derbyshire, the Midlands, South Wales and Kent. Many of these strikes were unofficial and included nearly half the total membership of the MFGB.

At the centre of the unrest were nearly 200,000 Yorkshire miners who went on strike at the end of July over a demand that the daily rates of pay for those on piece work should be increased. The strike did not receive the support of the MFGB but had the full backing of Herbert Smith and the YMA. The strike started just after the Keswick conference ended and by 21 July the coalfield was at a standstill. The Kent miners came out on strike over similar issues, and unofficial stoppages took place within other districts, including Lancashire where riots spread through the coalfield. Nearly 200,000 miners in South Wales threatened to strike in sympathy.[105] The Special Branch was keeping a close eye on the situation and issued daily reports to the Cabinet, for an example of this see appendix eight.

Significantly, the Yorkshire miners pulled out the safety men including the pumpmen, leading to flooding in some of the pits. This was the first time such drastic action had been taken with the sanction of an official trade union. As a result, the government sent in the navy to operate the pumps and troops to guard the pits, triggering fears of a repeat of the Featherstone massacre of 1893 when troops opened fire and killed striking miners. Eric Geddes, the transport minister, announced that troops had been brought back from the Rhine and:

105 Ives, *Reform, Revolution and Direct Action*, Chapter 9.

the government is determined that all the resources of the State, whether of citizens or armed forces of the Crown shall be used to prevent ruin to the community.[106]

On the tenth day of the strike, the MFGB secured a national agreement to cover a proportion of the loss of earnings for piece-rate hewers. However, the Yorkshire miners, backed by Smith, would not budge from their original demand. The Yorkshire miners were accused of being irresponsible by some members of the MFGB Executive, who argued they were undermining the case for nationalisation. The strike lasted until 12 August when, starved into submission, the Yorkshire miners returned to work defeated, demoralised and blaming the MFGB for not supporting them.[107]

In the Forest of Dean, the FDMA agreed to accept 12 per cent on piecework rates in line with the national settlement.[108] The YMA leadership made little attempt to spread the strike and miners in the Forest of Dean had little knowledge of the action or the significance of this defeat. However, with the Yorkshire miners contained and defeated, many within the ruling class felt they now had the upper hand.

Deception

Despite Bonar Law's seemingly unequivocal statement that the Government accepted the Coal Commission report, including nationalisation, "in the spirit and in the letter", the Cabinet was deeply divided over the nationalisation issue, the majority, including Lloyd George, being against. However, the government played for time, waiting until it was clear that the current unrest among the police had been contained and that among the armed forces had evaporated. The announcement of the rejection of nationalisation was held over until 18 August 1919 when, in a scandalous breach of faith, Lloyd George issued a statement that the government would not commit itself to nationalisation in any form.[109] He announced that they intended to hand the coal industry back into private ownership in August 1921 and said:

106 *Sheffield Daily Telegraph* 24 July 1919.
107 Ives, *Reform, Revolution and Direct Action*, Chapter 9.
108 FDMA Minutes 21 August 1921.
109 However, he did accept the recommendation that the state should purchase the mineral rights, although he did nothing to act on this.

Friends and many outside seem to assume that when a Government appoints a Commission, it is in honour bound to accept all its recommendations and to put them into operation. I never heard of that doctrine in the whole history of the House of Commons.[110]

The MFGB was appalled by this decision and Vernon Hartshorne, an SWMF representative on the MFGB Executive, summed up the views of the miners of the country when he said: "We have been deceived, betrayed, duped".[111] Despite this, Hartshorne, still nervous of the consequences of industrial action in the current politically charged climate, warned that in the event of a Triple Alliance strike:

within a week or ten days, revolutionary conditions will have developed in this country to the extent that nobody will be able to control the situation.[112]

As a result, at its conference on 3 September, the MFGB resolved to avoid industrial action but to immediately seek the help of the broader trade union movement, including the Trades Union Congress (TUC) and the Triple Alliance, to campaign politically for the implementation of the Commission's recommendations. It is possible that most on the MFGB Executive were so overwhelmed by the moral power of their arguments that they still believed that they could win by constitutional means alone and continued to argue against any form of industrial action to force through their demands. The miners presented their case to the TUC conference the following week and gained near-unanimous support for their campaign, but with no commitment to solidarity industrial action.[113] The government continued to make it clear to all concerned that under no circumstances would it consider nationalising the mines.

Consequently, the main result of the Sankey Commission was to defuse the potential for a general strike involving the Triple Alliance, which Lloyd George feared would be a direct challenge to the authority of parliament. The only immediate result was a seven-hour day which was imposed by an Act of Parliament passed on 15 August, while the wage advance was wiped out by the increasing cost of living.

110 *Hansard* 18 August 1919 volume 119 cc2000-1.
111 Cole, *Labour in the Coal Mining Industry*, 114.
112 *Rhondda Leader* 23 August 1919.
113 Cole, *Labour in the Coal Mining Industry*, 116.

Railway Strike[114]

By now, many rank and file miners and workers in other industries had given up relying on politicians. During 1919, there was an extraordinary number of strikes, amounting to 34,969,000 days lost, which averaged out as 100,000 workers on strike every day of the year. More than one in five of these strikes were in the nation's coalfields, and most were unofficial.[115]

The rail unions continued to press for their original demands. In April and June, negotiations between the government and the NUR and ASLEF resulted in some more concessions to the railwaymen but there was no resolution on the main issues. On Saturday 10 August, a parade and demonstration were held in Cinderford in support of the railway workers and £27 was collected in support of their campaign from a population mainly made up of mining families.[116] On 20 August, ASLEF agreed a deal with the government and owners that the footplatemen would receive a standardised wage based on the best rate paid on the railway in July 1914 plus the war bonus. However, the government was reluctant to extend the offer to other grades of railway workers.[117]

On Thursday 25 September 1919, the engagement of the Triple Alliance in an industrial dispute became a real possibility when the NUR issued strike notices. The strike was called by the NUR without consultation with ASLEF but in spite of this, a special conference of the ASLEF executive voted the following day to strike in solidarity.

In reality, the use of the Triple Alliance at this time was problematic, not least because the miners would need to ballot their members before striking and this would take a while to carry out, with an unpredictable result. Also, Thomas was determined to keep the Triple Alliance out of the strike so he could continue to keep

Jimmy Thomas.

114 Thanks to Philip Kuhn who provided me with information and analysis about the 1919 Railway strike.
115 Department of Employment, *British Labour Statistics 1886-1968*, Table 197 (1971) 396.
116 Collection receipts held at the Gage Library, Dean Heritage Centre.
117 Bagwell, *The Railwaymen,* 381.

control of the union and thereby block any attempts by the rank and file at unofficial action or to link up with other workers. However, the veiled threat of the use of the Triple Alliance impacted on the government's response to the strike.

The government was so nervous that 23,000 troops were mobilised and sent to all the industrial centres, where machine gun posts were set up at strategic points. About 1600 fully mounted cavalry troops made their way through Cinderford on their way to Gloucester where the *Dean Forest Mercury* reported:

> Gloucester presents, for the time being at any rate, the appearance of a military centre by reason of a large number of troops, both cavalry and infantry, who have been sent out for duty in various places in case of emergencies arising in connection with the railway strike.[118]

In addition, the government invoked the wartime Defence of the Realm Act and signed up 70,000 'Citizen Guards' from the middle class to aid the police and army. The rest of the available army, navy and air force were put on standby or used to secure ports, power stations, railway stations, etc. In Gloucester, a large body of middle-class citizens, as well as members of the Comrades of the Great War, came forward to swear in as Special Constables or to offer their services as 'Citizen Guards'.[119]

The rail strike began at midnight on 26 September and involved a formidable display of solidarity between the drivers and firemen from ASLEF and other grades from the NUR. A key feeling during the strike was that the government had not acknowledged sacrifices made during the war. In the words of NUR General Secretary, Jimmy Thomas:

> the short issue is that the long-made promise of a better world for railwaymen which was made in the time of the nation's crisis, and accepted by the railwaymen as an offer that would ultimately bear fruit, has not materialised.[120]

The effect of the railway strikes locally brought both the Great Western and Midland railways to a standstill, and several large collieries and

---

118 *Dean Forest Mercury* 3 October 1919.
119 *Gloucester Journal* 11 October 1919.
120 Warwick Digital Collections, http://contentdm.warwick.ac.uk/cdm/ref/collection/tav/id/2357. Last accessed 24 April 2019.

RAILWAY STRIKE

THAT 14 SHILLINGS

The Government says the Country cannot afford to make this part of the War Wages permanent.

It says **54** shillings a week is too much money for a Railwayman.

BUT

GEDDES, who slammed the door, gets **£96** a week, and received **£50,000** when he left the North-Eastern Railway.

BONAR LAW, who refuses standardization upwards to the Railwaymen, wants the salaries of Ministers "standardized upwards" from **£38** to **£96** a week.

NUR poster.

Lydney tin works ceased work.[121] By Thursday 2 October, Lightmoor and Eastern collieries were completely closed due to a shortage of trucks and work was disrupted at most of the other collieries. Mine managers warned they would have to close the pits within days.[122] On Saturday 4 October, a meeting of the FDMA Executive agreed to instruct their members to refuse to work with any blackleg labour employed by the railway companies and informed the local railway authorities that:

> we will not be responsible for the action of men if other coal trucks are put in by blackleg labour.[123]

The strike came to an end after nine days when the government agreed to maintain wages at existing levels for another year and agreed that negotiations on the standardisation of wage rates should be completed before 31 December 1919. Subsequent negotiations resulted in a national agreement with a national wages board and standardisation of wages across the railway companies, and an increase for the worst paid men.

A hitch occurred in the resumption of work at the Midland and the Great Western Stations in Cheltenham. Arthur Chandler, the Midland stationmaster and NUR member, had joined the strikers and took an active part in the dispute. When he arrived to return to work on Monday morning he was turned away by the management, despite the condition in the agreement that there would be no victimisation. Consequently, a demonstration of about 400 local railway workers marched to the Midland station and demanded his reinstatement. In reference to the strike, one of the speakers said:

> Mr Chandler has nobly stood by us and we must now stand firmly by him; if we do, we are bound to win, as we have won in our struggle against the Government.[124]

As a result, the management quickly caved in and he was re-instated. This incident highlighted the conflict between the rail unions and the rail companies over who had the right to manage the railways. The railway companies felt increasingly under threat as the unions started to chip away at their policy that the railways should be run along military lines with the

---

121 *Gloucestershire Chronicle* 4 October 1919.
122 *Dean Forest Mercury* 3 October 1919.
123 FDMA minutes 4 October 1919.
124 *Gloucester Journal* 11 October 1919.

attendant discipline. However, although the strike successfully frustrated the attempt to reduce railwaymen's wages, it did nothing to settle the bigger problem of the future organisation of the transport industry. The views of many in the local labour movement were summed up by the industrial correspondent of the *Dean Forest Mercury*.

> In this district, a surprising solidarity was displayed by the workers involved to the general satisfaction of other organised bodies. The view taken here was that any success which attended the Cabinet to reduce wages of one section of workers would be a signal for a general reduction. In other words, to quote the strikers rallying cry "If the railwaymen lose, it will be your turn next". So far as I have been able to obtain expressions of opinion of representative railwaymen locally, the result of the strike is not so much a complete victory for the men but is a strategic retreat on part of the Government. To those who say the ballot box is the best medium to obtain redress of grievances, may I point out the fact that the last General Election proved the falsity of this argument. Approximately 250,000 Labour votes only returned 46 Labour members, whereas approximately 100,000 more Conservative votes returned over 300 Conservative members. So long as seats are distributed in this manner so long it will be necessary for Labour to use other means to gain their ends.[125]

It was clear to many that the Labour party in 1919 was also unable to produce any meaningful legislative reform to improve the conditions of the working class. Although, as Robert Williams remarked, it did manage to reduce the tax on tea by two pence in the pound.[126] Consequently, more workers were taking industrial action to defend or improve their work conditions.

Other Workers

At the end of October, carpenters employed by the Railway Wagon Repair Company at Lydney came out on strike as a result of a threat by the manager to impose piecework rates on the workforce. After three weeks, on 12 November 1919, the other employees at the Lydney depot walked

---

125 *Dean Forest Mercury* 17 October 1919.
126 Robert Williams quoted in Ives, *Reform, Revolution and Direct Action*, 33.

out on strike in sympathy, bringing the workplace to a standstill. The men were being paid strike pay by their union, the Railway Vehicle Engineering Association.[127] The following week the company caved in and awarded a five per cent increase to some grades and a five-shilling increase to other grades, along with other improvements in work conditions.[128]

On 18 October, in an attempt to consolidate the relationship between the trade union movement and the Labour Party, Booth invited representatives of local trade unions to a meeting at the Globe Hotel to discuss forming a Cinderford branch of the Labour Party. Local delegates from a wide range of trade unions turned up including representatives of FDMA lodges based at the George Inn, Nags Head, Forge Hammer, Royal Union, Royal Oak and Queens Head. Delegates also included representatives from the Craftsmen Association, National Union of Clerks (NUC), Colliery Examiners and Overseers Association, NUR, Bakers Union, Amalgamated Union of Co-operative Employees and Workers Union. The meeting elected officers and a committee of sixteen delegates with the view of advancing the cause of Labour in Cinderford.[129]

In South Wales in June 1919, a successful strike by the NUC over union recognition led to the spectre of industrial unionism when the NUC held talks with the SWMF over joint action and amalgamation. In the Forest of Dean, some of the clerical workers working for local colliery companies had joined the NUC and in an attempt to get the union recognised Ben Griffiths, the national organiser of the NUC, met with Arthur Morgan from Henry Crawshay & Co Ltd. However, when Morgan reported back to the Crawshay board on 20 November 1919 they decided that:

> they might be disposed to recognise a local union but they did not want their staff to be identified with a national union.[130]

In the end, in June 1920, the Crawshay clerks resigned from the NUC in return for a bonus from the company. In this instance, this paternalistic approach to industrial relations bore fruit for the company.[131]

Despite the success of some of these strikes, the majority of MFGB Executive remained reluctant to use industrial action to force the government

---

127 *Dean Forest Mercury* 14 November 1919.
128 *Dean Forest Mercury* 28 November 1919.
129 *Dean Forest Mercury* 24 October 1919.
130 Board Minute Book of Henry Crawshay & Co. Ltd. Ltd (O) 1919-1921.
131 May, *A Question of Control*, 227–229.

Albert Webb was born in 1864 in Brierley. He married Ellen Harris in 1883 and had 14 children. He started work as a coal miner and later became a mine inspector. On 22 November 1919, he was killed at Trafalgar Colliery when the cage broke away and went hurtling down the pit shaft while he was working on the top of it. Liz Hiatt, Albert Webb's granddaughter told how it happened: "Well he used to do fettling (repairing the shaft, the main shaft in the pit). Anyways he was working this one weekend on a Saturday evening at about 10.30 at night. They had finished and the cage man brought them up to the top and the one fellow stepped off, but grandfather was still on there … And of course, grandfather was smashed to smithereens".

to implement Sankey's proposals. In December 1919, the MFGB and TUC launched the Mines for the Nation campaign, which sought to educate the public and bring pressure onto the government to nationalise the mines. Meetings were held throughout the country. However, the campaign was not a great success and, seven months after the Commission published its report, any hope within the labour movement that the government could be pressurised into nationalising the mines was flagging.[132]

Meanwhile, the shareholders, directors and senior managers of the colliery companies were doing very well. Morgan negotiated with the Mines Department to sanction extra dividend payments and bonuses. Morgan's salary was £1,350 plus bonuses, usually about £750, amounting to an income of about £2,000 which is equivalent to £112,000 today. In addition, he gained an income in the form of dividends from his shares in the company. In 1917, 1918 and 1919 Henry Crawshay & Co. Ltd. paid out £56,700 in dividends to its shareholders and bonuses to its senior managers and directors.[133] This would be worth £3,166,230 today.[134]

Therefore, it was no surprise that the Forest colliery owners were keen to keep control of their industry and so fervently resisted nationalisation. They argued their case in a propaganda war with the MFGB in the local and national papers which regularly covered the debate throughout

132 Cole, *Labour in the Coal Mining Industry*, 116–121.
133 Board Minute Book of Henry Crawshay & Co. Ltd. Ltd (O) 1919-1921.
134 This is Money, https://www.thisismoney.co.uk/money/bills/article-1633409/Historic-inflation-calculator-value-money-changed-1900.html (Last accessed on 18 November 2019).

this period. In November 1919, the Gloucester Chamber of Commerce organised a debate at the Assembly rooms at Gloucester.[135] William Brace MP put the case for nationalisation and Sir Francis Brain, Lord Bledisloe and Sir Ashton Lister, Liberal MP for Stroud, put the case against.[136]

In February and March 1920, Ernest Bevin was instrumental in establishing a court of enquiry into dockers' wages, which came up with a minimum rate for dockers' pay, the end to casual employment and the establishment of a Joint Industrial Council.[137] In January 1920, agricultural workers negotiated a minimum wage of 42s for a 50 hour week rising to 54s for a 60 hour week for stockmen and shepherds.[138] Members of the Triple Alliance and other groups of workers were gradually having their grievances settled. However, in the coalfields pay continued to stagnate as a result of inflation and the miners started to focus their attention on issues to do with earnings and conditions of work. Everybody knew a significant confrontation was on the horizon, and that it was just a matter of time.

Victimisation

Another challenge made by miners was about the right of managers to discipline workers as they chose. This led to a number of disputes over accusations by the workers of victimisation. One case involved Richard Kear, a preacher who was influenced by socialist politics. Kear represented New Fancy colliery on the Executive of the FDMA, having fulfilled the role as its auditor for a number of years. His grandson, Alec Kear remembers:

> I remember a room in his cottage which no one was really allowed into. However, when going in there one day, I found the room was full of political and communist-influenced books.[139]

In December 1919, there was a threatened strike at New Fancy colliery over the dismissal of Kear. The issue came up at an Executive meeting on 29 November when Harper, the lodge secretary at New Fancy, was invited to explain the background to the case, which he argued was one of

135 *Gloucester Journal* 29 November 1919.
136 Sir Robert Ashton Lister (1845–1929) was founder of R A Lister and Company in Dursley, in 1867. He was elected Liberal MP for Stroud December 1918.
137 Clegg, *A History of British Trade Unions*, 257-258
138 Scotland, *Agricultural Trade Unionism*, 111.
139 Statement to the author by Richard Kear's grandson, Alec Kear.

victimisation. The meeting agreed on a deputation, consisting of Booth, Organ and Perkins, to be sent to the Managing Director, Deakin, in an attempt to resolve the matter.[140]

The deputation failed to get an agreement, and as a result, a ballot was organised resulting in 214 for strike action in support of Kear with 44 against. On 13 December, a meeting of the Executive resolved to make another attempt to achieve a settlement backed up by the threat of strike action. If a strike occurred, the FDMA agreed to pay Kear a 'locked out' rate of 15s a week plus 1s 6d per child. On 20 January, Booth reported to the Executive that Kear's case had been settled and he had returned to work at New Fancy.[141]

Richard and Martha Kear.

The use of the strike weapon to change government policy was raised at a mass meeting of miners and ex-servicemen at Speech House at the end of December. The issue was about the restriction on the sale of alcohol, which had been imposed during the war to curb consumption, which the government believed was hindering production. This was followed by a public meeting in Coleford two weeks later. The *Gloucestershire Chronicle* reported that ex-sergeant Gregory appealed to the large number of comrades present:

> After fighting in France, he came home on leave and was dumped down at Lydney Junction with his kit and rifle and proceeded to walk some miles to his home. On the way he called at an inn and asked for refreshment in the form of a glass of beer, but was politely told by the barmaid that he could not be served as there were restrictions in the Forest now.[142]

The meeting was chaired by Tom Liddington and members of the FDMA, including Frank Ashmead, spoke against the restrictions. There was talk

140 FDMA Minutes 29 November 1919.
141 FDMA Minutes 13 December 1919 and 20 January 1920.
142 *Gloucestershire Chronicle* 03 January 1920.

of a down tools policy to force the government to act and a resolution was passed protesting vigorously against:

> the restrictions of their right to obtain reasonable refreshment at public-houses on Sundays; also, against the restricted and unsuitable hours for opening and closing on weekdays in that area.[143]

The government still needed coal, particularly as it was making large profits out of the export trade and so could not allow alcohol to hinder production. In the end, the men did not carry through their threat.

In December 1919, a conglomerate of local colliery owners acquired Howbeach colliery. These included Lord Bledisloe from Norchard colliery as Chairman, Arthur Morgan from Henry Crawshay & Co. Ltd. as Vice Chairman, Percy Moore from Princess Royal colliery as Secretary and Richard Thomas, owner of Lydney and Lydbrook tin works. Their first task was to lay off the majority of the men, amounting to 200 miners, with the view to developing the colliery and re-employment at a later date.[144] It was no surprise that miners in the Forest of Dean were beginning to feel vulnerable.

Workers' Control

At the heart of the syndicalist challenge to trade union orthodoxy was the idea of workers' control and industrial democracy, a contributory factor to the rise in unofficial actions during 1919 and 1920. On 2-3 February 1920, there was a two-day unofficial strike at Foxes Bridge, although it is unclear what the dispute was about. The FDMA Executive expressed concern that the men had taken unofficial action without their authority and it was quickly resolved.[145]

In February 1920, another dispute arose which directly challenged the right of the owners to discipline their workers and to manage their pits. This occurred when one of the carpenters at Crump Meadow Colliery, a World War One veteran, was transferred from the mechanical department to a job at a lower grade by the foreman. His workmates tendered seven days' notice to take strike action unless the man was reinstated in his old job. The men were all members of the Monmouthshire, South Wales and

143 Ibid.
144 *Gloucester Journal* Saturday 20 December 1919.
145 FDMA Minutes 7 February 1920.

Crump Meadow colliery.

Forest of Dean Colliery Enginemen, Stokers and Craftsmen Association, which was affiliated to the National Association of Colliery Enginemen and Mechanics and had about 700 members in the Forest of Dean.[146]

The colliery management, backed by the FDCOA, insisted they had the right to dismiss a man for any reason they considered sufficient and to transfer men to other duties as required. They were determined to stick by this principle. In response, the craftsmen insisted that this was a case of victimisation. They made the point that no evidence had been provided that the man was incompetent and they were equally determined to stick by the principle that they had the right to defend their jobs and conditions of work. On Saturday 14 February the FDCOA passed a resolution:

> The principle that the employers have a right to dismiss a man for any reason they consider sufficient, or to re-arrange their duties of any person employed, cannot be departed from in any way or to any extent whatever, but subject to this, the employers are prepared to meet the representatives of the craftsmen to see if the misapprehension which the employers believe exists can be removed with a view to settling the dispute.[147]

The principles at stake were fundamental, and as a result, on Tuesday 17 February, a conference of senior representatives of the employers and employees was held at Speech House.[148] In attendance were both national and local officials of the Craftsmen Association and senior representatives

146 *Dean Forest Mercury* 20 February 1920.
147 *Dean Forest Mercury* 20 February 1920.
148 *Dean Forest Mercury* 20 February 1920.

of the principal colliery owners in the Forest.[149] However, the conference broke up after four hours without a resolution after the colliery owners insisted on an adjournment for a week to consult with the MAGB.

On the same evening, a mass meeting was held in Cinderford with the officials of the Craftsmen Association. Frank Ferley, the President of Crump Meadow and Waterloo Craftsmen Association, was in the chair. The men insisted they would continue with their plan to strike the following week unless they received confirmation of their workmate's reinstatement. D. B. Jones, the Craftsmen Association full-time agent, argued that:[150]

> These men ran risks every day of being injured or fatally injured in the course of their employment. All the risks the employers ran was to lose the capital they had sunk in the pit … They had fought five years on the continent to protect the weak against the strong and they were now honour bound to protect the workman against the employer.[151]

Seven hundred craftsmen from the other collieries in the Forest also threatened to join the strike unless the matter was resolved. This would bring the coalfield to a standstill, throwing 6,000 men out of work. The removal of pumpmen and other safety men could lead to flooding and possible long-term damage to the pits. Consequently, the government intervened and a telegram arrived from the Coal Controller in London to the Craftsmen Association office asking the men to withdraw their notices and to accept arbitration. Jones persuaded the men to agree to this and, after arbitration, the Coal Controller recommended reinstatement of the man involved to his old job and insisted the employers accept his advice.[152] This was because the demand for coal was still high and the government was keen to maintain supplies, particularly as it was making huge profits out of the export market.

This dispute was significant in that it was about principles. The owners argued that they could not allow the men to determine how the workforce

149 This included John Rowe (President), W. Hopkins (General Secretary), D. B. Jones (agent), John Yemm and L. Morgan from the Craftsmen's Association. Senior representatives of the principal colliery owners in the Forest included Winterbotham (solicitor), William Meredith (manager at Lightmoor Colliery), John Joynes (manager at Cannop Colliery), J. Morrison (manager at Foxes Bridge Colliery) and Harold Fisher (Secretary of the FDCOA).
150 D. B. Jones was the General Secretary of Monmouthshire, South Wales and Forest of Dean Colliery Enginemen, Stokers and Craftsmen Association. He was appointed as the agent in 1915 and was the first craftsman to be elected to this position.
151 *Dean Forest Mercury* 20 February 1920.
152 *Dean Forest Mercury* 12 March 1920.

was managed. In response, the men argued that this was not the issue and the dispute was about their rights as workers to protect their livelihoods and prevent victimisation. In reality, there was a grey area between these two positions and the issue of workers' control was highlighted by the dispute.

Price Lists

One of the most important issues impacting on miners in the Forest of Dean was out of date price lists which did not specify the necessary details for different seams, types of rock and timber work at a time when production methods and conditions were constantly changing. The price lists provided a framework for piece rates on a wide range of tasks including timberwork and road ripping as well hewing. Therefore, the precise details in the price lists were important and had to be carefully negotiated and continuously reviewed.

In December 1919, Booth was asked by his Executive to demand a revision of the price lists at all the steam coal collieries.[153] At Princess Royal colliery, Booth, James and Fred Isles set about negotiating detailed costings with the manager Percy Moore.[154] This was soon replicated at other pits across the Forest. Booth was also involved in negotiations over shift allowances and schedules, Saturday hours and pay, etc which were often a source of conflict.

An examination of the minutes of the FDMA during 1919 and 1920 reveals weekly disputes over issues associated with price lists, shift patterns, compensation cases, minimum wage agreements, dismissals, overtime etc, which often directly challenged the managers' right to control the workforce. Most of these issues were quickly resolved with the threat of industrial action or the use of the courts. These disputes reflect the concern of Forest miners to defend custom and practice and control their labour at the point of production.

Mining was highly skilled and based almost exclusively on knowledge gained through extensive experience in a range of geological conditions. The buttymen and the experienced daymen had expertise in all the jobs done in the mine. Albert Meek explained:

153 FDMA Minutes 13 December 1919.
154 They eventually agreed on a price list for the high delf seam at Princess Royal in February 1922 which included detailed prices for the tonnage of coal, pillar work, boring, filling, road ripping, timber work and moving coal.

Men at the coalface, Lightmoor Colliery in the 1930s.

Then you got rock road to drive and one thing and another; timbering—we were complete colliers we used to do the shot firing. They've got shot firing separate these days. We used to do all the timbering and we used to do everything that you could call a collier. You had to be complete colliers at that time.[155]

The buttymen, in particular, were autonomous in the organisation of their work tasks and responsible for all aspects of coal extraction with little external supervision.[156] In most respects, Forest miners were mining coal practically independently of the colliery's management and were in a strong position to claim they could run the pits themselves.

However, at this time, there was little debate within the FDMA Executive about creating a more equitable system of distributing earnings among the contract teams or even demanding a universal day wage for all jobs. Booth continued to encourage the daymen to get involved in the FDMA and was instrumental in arranging sponsorship for William Hoare to attend the CLC. Booth also recruited another young miner, Harold Craddock from Whitecroft, who worked at Princess Royal colliery, and arranged sponsorship for him to attend the CLC from September 1920.

155 Albert Meek, Gage Library.
156 J.W.F. Rowe, *Wages in the Coal Industry*, (London: 1923) 150-152.

However, with the possibility of a major conflict on the horizon, the issue of differentials and inequalities among working miners was put on hold.

Lost Opportunities

Meanwhile, on 2 February 1920, a special conference of government ministers met to discuss how, if necessary, industrial action or unrest could be put down by force of arms. The meeting was attended by Lloyd George, Winston Churchill, Andrew Bonar Law, Robert Horne, Edward Shorn (Home Secretary), Lord Inverforth (Minister for Munitions) and W. H. Long (First Lord of the Admiralty) among others. Agenda items included the ability of the RAF to use machine guns and bombs and the arming of loyal militias.[157]

On 10 March 1920, an MFGB delegate conference voted in favour of seeking support from the Triple Alliance and the TUC for a general strike to force the government to nationalise the mines. The result of the card vote was not conclusive with 524,999 in favour of a general strike and 344,000 against.[158] The Forest of Dean was one of the districts voting in favour.

In the hope that the miners could sway public opinion in their favour and gain support from the TUC, the FDMA arranged a debate on the issue of nationalisation between Booth and H. G. Williams, a London Engineer and a staunch opponent of the Sankey recommendations. The debate took place at Double View School on 13 March. Booth had no trouble convincing the audience of the case for public control, particularly as it became clear Williams had no understanding of the mining industry in the Forest of Dean.

In fact, Booth went further and emphasised the demand for genuine workers' control, arguing that the pit committees could take over the management of each colliery, making the directors redundant and therefore cutting costs.[159] This idea, taken directly from the *Miners Next Step*, argued that the MFGB district executives would become boards of production which would be supervised nationally by the MFGB.

On 18 March, a Special TUC Conference met to consider the MFGB's request for a general strike in support of their demand for implementation of the Sankey recommendations. When it came to a ballot on the issue, a majority of TUC delegates voted against industrial action with 3,732,000

157 Webb, *1919*, 134-135.
158 Cole, *Labour in the Coal Mining Industry*, 120.
159 *Dean Forest Mercury* 19 March 1920.

for continuing with the political campaign and 1,050,000 for a general strike. It was possible the delegates were influenced by the small majority in the MFGB delegate conference ballot.[160] Another factor was that the railway workers and dockers had successfully achieved a satisfactory resolution to their grievances and some may not have wanted to commit themselves to further industrial action. The opportunities presented in 1919 appeared to be lost, and realistically this marked the end of the line for the MFGB to use the strike weapon in support of its nationalisation campaign, at least for now.

Cost of Living

The cost of living index continued to rise and by February 1920 reached 130 per cent above pre-war levels.[161] As a result, miners focused their attention on their living standards. On 12 March, the day after the TUC had rejected their call for industrial action in support of nationalisation, the MFGB put in a claim for an extra three shillings a shift.[162] On Sunday 28 March, a mass meeting was held at Speech House where Booth, Kear and Organ gave a report back from the recent London meetings. Booth pointed out that some estimates revealed that the increase in the cost of living was higher than the official figures.

> The late Food Controller Mr Roberts admitted the cost of living had gone up 170 per cent. How was a man with a wife and family to live decently unless he received a higher wage than at present? The miners would find a solution for the problem if the government failed and their solution would be the stopping of the pits.[163]

Booth continued organising public meetings but now concentrated on putting the case for a wage increase. On Tuesday 28 March he organised a meeting with Sidney Jones, a checkweighman from Blackwood, who argued that:

160 Cole, *Labour in the Coal Mining Industry*, 120.
161 Ibid. 122.
162 Ibid. 122–126.
163 *Dean Forest Mercury* 1 April 1920. George Roberts was elected as Labour MP for Norwich in 1906. He was a minister in the Lloyd George Coalition Government as Parliamentary Secretary to the Board of Trade from 1916 to 1917, Minister of Labour from 1917 to 1919, and Minister of Food Control from 1919 to 1920. He was appointed as a Privy Counsellor in 1917. Roberts stood in 1918 as a Coalition Labour candidate, opposed by the official Labour Party candidate.

the representatives of the landlord and capitalist classes had thrown down the gauntlet to trade unionism, and the challenge was accepted. Labour and Capitalism had always been antagonistic. The class struggle had in fact been the very basis on which Labour's past successes had been achieved and the same struggle would only perfect trade unionism and bring it greater success in the future. An injury to one member of the Labour organisation was an injury to the organisation itself.[164]

On March 29 the government, still nervous, offered two shillings a shift. The same day an MFGB conference decided to call a ballot on industrial action in support of the MFGB claim. The results of the ballot were announced in mid-April resulting in 442,704 for acceptance and 377,569 for strike action.[165] In contrast, the Forest of Dean miners were in favour of strike action with 1,176 voted for acceptance of the offer and 3,508 for strike action.[166]

Within a few weeks of the signing of this agreement, the government raised the price of household coal by 14s 2d a ton and of industrial coal by 4s 2d a ton.[167] The leaders of the MFGB saw this increase as an attempt to turn public opinion against the miners once more and, at the same time, facilitate the return of the industry to profit-making private enterprise.

At the same time, Austen Chamberlain increased interest rates to seven per cent and introduced a budget which further cut back government spending. The government was fully aware that the budget would increase unemployment but hoped that this would undermine the power of the trade unions rather than lead to unrest. However, it failed to foresee that its deflationary policies would be one of the factors leading to a devastating depression in the British economy by the end of the year.[168]

May Day

May Day rallies across the country attracted thousands of men, women and children. In the Forest of Dean, this was the first time such an event had been held. Mines, ironworks, stone works and tin works were all closed and workers joined the rally at Speech House. Organ chaired the

164 *Dean Forest Mercury* 1 April 1920.
165 Cole, *Labour in the Coal Mining Industry*, 128.
166 Arnot, *The Miners,* 235 and *Daily Herald* 15 April 1920.
167 Ibid. 236.
168 John Foster, *Industrial Politics and the 1926 Mining Lockout*, 28.

meeting and was supported by Vice President Albert Wilding, Charles Luker and Booth.

Organ explained that the strategy of the FDMA and MFGB was to achieve a further reduction in hours; an amendment of the Compensation Act so injured workmen would receive the same compensation as they would receive in wages while at work; an increase in the allowance for widows of men killed in the mines; an improvement to the Coal Mines Regulation Act to reduce death and injury; the establishment of pithead baths; and decent accommodation for miners and their families. Organ emphasised that the MFGB would not be satisfied unless it achieved nationalisation, with joint control by the state and workers, with the view to freeing the mines from the control of the capitalists. Finally, Organ claimed the MFGB would resolve:

to do all in its power to secure for the people the control of banking and credit in conjunction with the workers in other countries, so with national ownership and joint control of vital industries, the political and economic revolution, which can alone bring the emancipation of the working classes, can be achieved.[169]

At the same, Thomas MacNamara, the new Minister of Labour, announced to the government that wage rewards in future should not be based on the cost of living but subject to the laws of the market.[170] Meanwhile, Horne had taken over from Auckland Geddes as President of the Board of Trade and stated the government's intention of returning the coal industry to private ownership in August 1921.[171] In May 1920, the Government took the first step towards decontrol of the mining industry when it decontrolled the inland distribution of coal. In early June, the Government abolished controls on wholesale and retail coal, with the intention that consumers should pay the real cost of the coal they consumed.[172]

On 15 June, the Government's position on the future of the coal industry was made clearer, with the introduction of the Mining Industry Bill, 1920. Part one of the Bill covered the Government's financial proposals to govern the industry until 31 August 1921, when the industry was to be returned to the colliery owners. Part two contained proposals for giving the miners a limited share in the management of the industry, and part

169 *Dean Forest Mercury* 7 May 1920.
170 May, *A Question of Control*, 239.
171 Supple, *The History of the British Coal Industry*
172 May, *A Question of Control*, 235-236.

three established the Miners' Welfare Fund to alleviate social conditions in the coalfields.[173]

Hands off Russia

The threat of escalation of British military involvement in more warfare united the labour movement in a campaign to end Britain's participation in the civil war in Russia. It was clear that British workers were not prepared to allow the country to be dragged deeper into this conflict. On 10 May 1920, London dock workers, with the support of Bevin, refused to load British armaments onto the *Jolly George*. The ship was bound for Poland, and the armaments were to be used by Polish forces in their invasion of Ukraine, which brought them into military conflict with the Red Army. The government linked the opposition to war with the threat of more industrial action at home. Its anxiety was fuelled by the impact of the somewhat hysterical reports emanating from Basil Thomson at the Home Office who, on 20 July 1920, reported that:

> extremists regard a miners' strike as merely a prelude to a general strike (and that) hotheads dream of seizing the government through a coup.[174]

The threat was given credence by the formation of the Communist Party of Great Britain (CPGB) on the 1 August 1920.[175] The CPGB managed to recruit a handful of activists in the Forest of Dean but there is no evidence that the CPGB had much influence within the FDMA or within the Forest of Dean coalfield at this time. Charles Fletcher was one of the first Forest miners to join the CPGB, having been a member of the British Socialist Party. Fletcher had been brought up in Muller Orphanage in Bristol and, as a teenager, had been sent to work on farms in the Forest, including Longley and Trow Green. He wrote articles on mining and industrial problems and was popular within the labour movement in the Forest. He left the CPGB a few years later.

173 Cole, *Labour in the Coal Mining Industry*, 130-136.
174 Desmarais, *The British Government's Strikebreaking Organization*, 124. Sir Basil Thomson (1861–1939) was a British intelligence officer, police officer, prison governor, colonial administrator and writer. In 1919, while remaining Assistant Commissioner (Crime) of London's Metropolitan Police, he was appointed Director of Intelligence at the Home Office, in overall charge of every intelligence agency in the United Kingdom. From 30 April 1919, he issued a fortnightly Report on Revolutionary Organisations in the United Kingdom from his offices in Scotland House.
175 Walter Kendall, *The Revolutionary Movement in Britain 1900-1921* (London: Weidenfeld and Nicolson, 1969) Chapter 11.

Poland

By August the Poles had been driven back by the Red Army, who then advanced towards Warsaw. Churchill was fearful that they would advance further westward and argued for British military intervention. On 5 August 1920, a National Council of Action was set up jointly by the Labour Party and the TUC to agitate against British involvement in Russia's civil war. It founded numerous local councils, including one in Gloucester organised by the Trades Council, and was supported by the FDMA. The National Council of Action warned the government:

> that the whole industrial power of the organised workers will be used to defeat this war.[176]

Lloyd George had been re-elected on the promise of no more war. The war against Russia had no democratic mandate, it was unconstitutional and was universally unpopular. Lloyd George had had his doubts about the intervention for some time and had already complained in November 1919 that the war had cost the government over 100 million pounds.[177] As a result, on 10 August, Lloyd George announced to parliament that there would be no military intervention by the British in Poland. He probably had little choice as the National Council of Action had the full support of the leadership of the trade union movement, including those on the right-wing of the movement. Jimmy Thomas, at a National Council of Action Conference on 13 August 1920, warned:

> If this country is dragged into another war, economically financially and morally, it will lead to such consequences that no one will be able to control them because I believe that giving effect to this resolution does not mean a mere strike. Do not be under any misapprehension that you are voting for a simple down-tools policy. It is nothing of the kind. If this resolution is to be given effect to it means a challenge to the whole constitution of the country.[178]

In the Forest of Dean, a local Council of Action was formed, bringing together Labour Party and trade union representatives from across the

---

176 Desmarais, *The British Government's Strikebreaking Organization*, 122.
177 Webb, *1919*, 141.
178 *Daily Herald* 14 August 1920.

district. The FDMA sent several delegates to the first meeting of the Council which was held in Parkend on 26 August.[179] This was replicated across the country and as a result, the government had little choice but to take heed. The success of the threat of direct action in influencing the Government's decision to limit its involvement in the Russian civil war bolstered the self-image of the labour movement. The general consensus within the movement was that labour stood at the threshold of momentous improvements in the status and power of the organised working class within British society.

Churchill was livid and admitted that the stance taken by the workers made the escalation of British military intervention in Russia almost impossible. His concern was that the right of the ruling classes to govern or wage war was under threat and resolved to undermine the power of the labour movement which he believed was infiltrated by communists.[180] In the end, the Red Army was defeated when it attempted to take Warsaw. By September it was in retreat and the crisis over armed intervention in Poland was over. An armistice was negotiated in October 1920.[181]

Warning to Miners

In mid-August, the Cabinet decided to resurrect the emergency statutory powers enacted during World War One to deal with industrial action and on 17 August 1920, a Cabinet meeting instructed the Treasury:

> to regard the situation arising out of a big industrial crisis, such as was threatened by an impending coal strike, as comparable to a state of war.[182]

The Cabinet authorised the Treasury to make financial provisions accordingly and Lloyd George announced that:

> If a Trade Union attempts to usurp the function committed to government by the whole body of the people, such a claim must be unhesitatingly resisted.[183]

---

179 FDMA Minutes 21 August 1920.
180 Renshaw, *The General Strike*, 73.
181 Geoffrey Swain, *Russia's Civil War*, (Stroud: The History Press, 2008) 131-132.
182 Desmarais, *The British Government's Strikebreaking Organization*, 122.
183 Ibid.

On 26 May 1920, 54-year-old Alfred Barnard was badly injured by a fall of dirt while working on a roadway at Lightmoor Colliery. On 10 July 1920, he died as a result of a haemorrhage to the spinal cord caused by the injuries sustained in the roof fall. His funeral was attended by his wife Julia and five children, Frank, Blanche, Maggie, Stanley and Harold.

This warning was explicitly directed at the miners, who had waited patiently for the report of the Sankey Commission in the spring of 1919 and had seen the government renege on its promise to accept its recommendations in the summer of 1919. This was then followed by the failure of the propaganda campaign, *Mines for the Nation*, launched at a special TUC conference in December 1919 and the rejection by a TUC conference in March 1920 of the MFGB proposal for a general strike. During this period the Forest of Dean miners had voted for a nationwide strike in support of their demands by a large majority on three separate occasions.

New Wage Demand

Forest miners were not interested in staging a coup, but they wanted substantial reform. They had become increasingly frustrated at the lack of progress in improving their working conditions and the lost opportunities in achieving their aim of public control of the mines with the hope that safety would come before profit. Five miners were killed in Forest pits in 1919, and four more would die before the end of 1920.[184] Many more would be seriously injured and some would never work again, while others would die premature deaths from lung disease.

At the same time, miners' earnings were just keeping up with the increase in the cost of living. Nationally the figures revealed that the cost of living had reached 152 per cent above the pre-war level by July 1920 and peaked at 164 per cent by the end of the summer.[185] For many miners, the issue of earnings had now become a pressing priority, and as a result, on 10 June an MFGB delegate conference decided to make a fresh wage

184 Tuffley, *Roll of Honour*.
185 Cole, *Labour in the Coal Mining Industry*, 141.

demand. At its annual conference on 6 July, delegates considered proposals by the MFGB Executive for a double-barrelled claim for an increase of two shillings per shift and a reduction in the price of coal of 14s 2d a ton which they felt was placing a significant burden on the broader community and contributing to inflation.[186]

On 10 July, the miners' demonstration at Speech House was poorly attended due to heavy rain. Hodges and Wignall were the main speakers and continued to pledge their support for the nationalisation of the mines.[187] However, they offered little in the way of a new strategy on how this could be achieved. Booth, Organ, Albert Wilding and Charles Luker represented the FDMA at the event and Organ summed up their feelings:

> At present, we toil in the mines, not for ourselves but for capitalist enterprise and gain. We want to see it that we risk our lives, not for those people, but that we might have justice in the interests of the community at large. Nothing would give more satisfaction to the miners of this country than to see the mines nationalised. That is what we are out for, and I contend that not only would that be a benefit to the miners themselves but it would be in the interests of every individual in the country. We also require to use every effort to turn out David (Lloyd George) and his crew and to return a government to power that is fit to be entrusted with reins of government who can see that this is a land fit for heroes to live in.[188]

Albert Wilding proposed a resolution demanding nationalisation and joint control by workers and the state which was duly passed. Booth informed the audience that there were now about 6,000 FDMA members in the Forest, which amounted to nearly all those employed in the mines, and argued they were strong enough to take on the government.[189]

Ballot for Strike Action

On 15 July, the MFGB presented its claim to the government. In response, the government was adamant in resisting both claims but hinted that a higher wage could be granted if the increase was linked to higher output.

186 Ibid.
187 *Gloucester Journal* 17 July 1920.
188 *Dean Forest Mercury* 16 July 1920.
189 Ibid.

The MFGB estimated that between 1 June 1920 and 1 June 1921 the industry would make a net profit of £66 million, assuming no change in demand, wages or prices.[190] Lloyd George, at a meeting held at the Board of Trade Offices on 26 July 1920, said:

I am not going to dispute that figure—I do not think it is very wide of the mark provided that we continue to export the same amount of coal and at the same prices.[191]

The importance of the export market at that time cannot be over-estimated. Whilst the average pithead price per ton to the domestic consumer was 33 shillings per ton, the pithead price per ton to the European consumer was 75 shillings per ton.[192] The government insisted they would continue to claim the money from the export market as a windfall for the treasury. In fact, this undermined the long-term viability of the British mining industry by allowing cheaper American coal to get a foothold in the European market.

On 29 July, the FDMA Executive agreed that their delegate to the MFGB conference on 12 and 13 August be mandated to vote in favour of strike action.[193] In the end, the conference agreed to organise a ballot on the issue, with a recommendation to vote for a strike in support of their original demands. In addition, the conference agreed that, if necessary, it would support a general strike to prevent the British government from continuing its intervention in the civil war in Russia.[194]

On August 21 an FDMA Executive meeting agreed to recommend that its members vote in favour of strike action in support of its demands.[195] On Sunday 22 August, Booth and Organ informed a mass meeting at Speech House that the cost of living was now running at 155 per cent above the pre-war level and pointed out that miners' wages had increased by only 125 per cent over the same period. They argued the men were entitled to a wage increase with no strings attached. A resolution was passed pledging those present to vote solidly for a strike.[196]

On 31 August 1920, the Forest ballot results were announced, with 5,132 for a strike and 388 against, meaning 92.97 per cent of Forest miners

190 MFGB Minute Book 1920 quoted in Griffin, *The Miners of Nottinghamshire*, 67.
191 Ibid.
192 Ibid.
193 FDMA Minutes 29 July 1920.
194 Cole, *Labour in the Coal Mining Industry*, 140-144.
195 FDMA Minutes 21 August 1921.
196 *Dean Forest Mercury* 27 August 1920.

were in favour of strike action.[197] The Forest miners polled so heavily that unrecorded votes were less than five per cent.[198] Nationally, the figures were 845,647 in favour of a strike with 238,865 against, meaning the two-thirds majority in favour of strike action required by the MFGB to call a strike was exceeded. As a result, notices were tendered to strike on 25 September.[199] In the Forest of Dean, the Craftsmen Association tendered notices at the same time in solidarity with the miners.[200] The next day a conference of the Triple Alliance agreed to give all possible support to the miners, but this did not amount to a declaration of a sympathetic strike.[201]

On 2 September, an MFGB national conference agreed the strike would start on 25 September. In response, Horne insisted there would be no reduction in the price of coal but said he was willing to refer the wage claim to arbitration and added that any wage increase should be contingent on an increase in output beyond an agreed figure or datum line. The big fear in the Forest of Dean was a return to local wage bargaining, and the Forest miners were firmly against the datum line as it would tie their wages to local productivity.

However, another factor strengthening the resolve of miners in the Forest of Dean was resentment against the treatment of disabled World War One veterans, some of whom were FDMA members and still finding it difficult to find suitable employment. At a meeting of the FDMA on 21 September 1920, it was agreed to send a letter to the employers insisting they honour the agreement with the government to employ five per cent disabled army veterans to carry out light duties in the collieries.[202]

In August 1920, the recommendation by the Sankey Commission that a welfare levy on coal output be introduced led to the introduction of the 1920 Mining Industry Act which established a mandatory requirement to provide educational, welfare and recreational facilities for miners and their communities. The levy was initially set at one penny a ton and resulted in the Miners' Welfare Fund which was administered by national and local Miners' Welfare Committees appointed by the Board of Trade, consisting of representatives of the colliery owners and mineworkers, with some independent members.

197 *Dean Forest Mercury* 3 September 1920. Earlier reports incorrectly stated that the Forest had the highest percentage in favour of the strike.
198 The *Western Mail* 30 August 1920.
199 Cole, *Labour in the Coal Mining Industry*, 144 -145.
200 *Daily Herald* 18 September 1920.
201 Cole, *Labour in the Coal Mining Industry*,144.
202 FDMA minutes 21 September 1920.

In September 1920, the employment prospects in the Forest of Dean remained good with only 21 men and 8 women officially registered as unemployed in the Lydney, Cinderford, and Coleford areas.[203] David Organ represented the miners on the Gloucester Employment Committee and it reported in December that, with one exception, they had succeeded to arrange the absorption of the disabled men who were in pre-war days employed in the mining industry. The one exception was a man who was so disabled that it was decided he should be trained in bespoke tailoring.[204]

Strike Suspended

In the meantime, the government produced some figures which revealed a sharp fall in profits in the coal industry over recent weeks. As a result, an MFGB special conference agreed to drop the demand for the reduction in the price of coal provided the issue was referred to a tribunal. Smillie had spent his life building the MFGB into one of the most powerful labour organisations in the world but he was concerned that a prolonged strike could destroy his union. As a result, at an MFGB delegate conference on 23 September, he desperately argued for arbitration by an impartial tribunal. Smillie was aware that the transport workers and the railwaymen were wary of being drawn into strike action when they had no influence on the negotiations between the miners and the government.

However, the delegates rejected this on a card vote of 545,000 to 350,000. This result meant that unless negotiations re-opened the strike would start on 25 September.[205] It was clear by now that the long term aims of the colliery owners and the government were identical. Both were making preparations for de-control in August 1921 and the introduction of district productivity deals based on laws of supply and demand. Therefore, it was no surprise that they remained in close contact throughout the negotiations. At the same time, an NUR special general meeting narrowly turned down a motion calling for a solidarity strike.[206]

Consequently, Lloyd George persuaded the MFGB to suspend the strike notices for a week to meet with the colliery owners behind closed doors in another attempt to thrash out an agreement which linked wages to output. This was a classic Lloyd George tactic in that it appeared to return the negotiations to the colliery owners even though the government

203 *Gloucester Journal* 18 September 1920.
204 *Gloucester Journal* 18 December 1920.
205 Arnot, *The Miners*, 255.
206 Bagwell, *The Railwaymen*, 455–458.

On 5 October 1920, Ernest Whitson was killed at Howbeech Colliery after he fell down a shaft. Whitson was born in Furnace Bottom, Blakeney in 1879, the son of a stonemason. After leaving school he obtained work as a coal miner. In 1904 he married Ann Wilkes and had five children: Thomas born 1902, Ruby 1904, Ernest 1906, Selina 1911 and Samuel 1917. Samuel was just four years old when his father was killed.

still formally held the financial control of the mines. The owners made an offer of one shilling a day, contingent on productivity beyond an agreed datum line. On Friday 1 October an MFGB delegate conference agreed to suspend strike notices for another fortnight to organise a ballot on the new offer.[207] On 2 October, an FDMA Executive meeting agreed to oppose any productivity deal, arguing that it was "fraught with dangers".[208] Reuben James told the *Daily Herald* that the Executive of the FDMA could not recommend that men accept the offer. The Princess Royal Colliery lodge went further and passed a motion condemning the MFGB Executive for even discussing output and the price of coal in relation to wages.[209]

The results of the ballot were announced on Thursday 14 October, revealing that nearly every single miner in the Forest had voted and the percentage against the new offer in the Forest was 86.28 per cent, with 4514 votes against the offer and 718 in favour. Nationally 78 per cent were against the offer, with 635,098 votes against and 181,428 for the offer. In addition, the craftsmen voted to support the miners in every way possible. The MFGB Executive had no choice but to issue strike notices.[210] Lloyd George thought that the time had finally come and, in September 1920, he wrote to Bonar Law that:

If the working classes are united against us, the outlook is grave and the gravity would be intensified if what I call intellectual liberalism unites with Labour against us. The great struggle which is coming must not be partisan. I have been thinking a good deal about the situation here, and I have become more and

207 *Gloucester Journal* 2 October 1920.
208 FDMA Minutes 2 October 1920.
209 *Daily Herald* 13 October 1920.
210 Cole, *Labour in the Coal Mining Industry*, 155 and *Daily Herald* 15 October 1920.

more convinced that the time has arrived for coming to grips with the conspiracy which is seeking to utilise Labour for the purpose of overthrowing the existing organisation of the time. This opportunity will show itself over the miners' demand. I think it would be a mistake if the fight had come sooner—the nation had not settled down, and the restlessness which affected the heart, the nerve and the blood of the people, was a dangerous element which it is well we should have given time to quiet. Now is the acceptable moment for putting everything to the test. We must show Labour that the Government mean to be masters.[211]

Datum Line Strike

In October 1920, the South Wales Enginemen, Stokers and Craftsmen Association voted to fuse with the SWMF.[212] The Forest of Dean craftsmen were not included in this arrangement and so set about forming their own independent organisation with the view to re-establishing links with the FDMA.[213] This would strengthen the hand of the miners during the dispute in the Forest of Dean.

The atmosphere in the Forest was tense as it was assumed the strike would be prolonged and bitter. A mass meeting was held at Speech House on Thursday 14 October where Booth informed the men that strike pay was one pound a week plus two shillings for each child. He requested that those who could afford it should forgo strike pay for the full period of the strike.[214]

The FDMA agreed to allow the craftsmen to carry on with pumping and essential repairs to prevent the flooding of the pits.[215] However, this was only to be carried out under the watchful eye of the pit committees and to be reviewed the following Tuesday. Booth pointed out that accidental flooding at Trafalgar colliery earlier in the year had led to a large number of men being laid off for several months and so flooding of the pits should be a last resort as it could lead to loss of jobs.[216]

On Saturday 16 October 1920, one million British miners went on strike and in the Forest the strike was solid. A mass meeting was held

---

211 Quoted by Jeroen Sprenger in http://www.jeroensprenger.nl/Triple%20Alliance/the-1919-railway-strike.html (Last accessed on 18 November 2019).
212 *Daily Herald* 11 October 1920.
213 *Dean Forest Mercury* 4 February 1921.
214 *Dean Forest Mercury* 22 October 1920.
215 The agreement allowed ostlers, stokers, pumpsmen and enginemen to continue working and in addition one onsetter and one banksman at each pit (FDMA Minutes 16 October 1920).
216 *Dean Forest Mercury* 22 October 1920.

on Tuesday 19 October when Booth warned that it could be a long hard struggle. It was agreed that installation of a pumping plant at Howbeach colliery should be allowed to continue.[217] This was because Howbeach had severe problems with water and needed to pump 1200 gallons a minute to prevent flooding which could then impact on nearby pits.

On Wednesday 20 October, a delegate conference of the NUR changed its mind and agreed that, unless the MFGB claims were granted or negotiations resumed by Saturday October 23, its Executive would instruct its members to cease work. This decision was conveyed to the MFGB Executive at its meeting held on 23 October, in a letter which reads as follows:

> That this Special General Meeting having carefully considered the position created by the Miners' Strike, and being satisfied their claims are reasonable and just and should be conceded forthwith, decides to instruct the General Secretary to intimate to the Prime Minister that unless the Miners' claims are granted or negotiations resumed by Saturday, October 23rd, which result in a settlement, we shall be compelled to take the necessary steps to instruct our members in England, Scotland and Wales, to cease work.[218]

Jim Jones, the branch Secretary of Cinderford NUR, informed the *Dean Forest Mercury* that the branch had passed the following resolution:

> We, the members of the Cinderford Branch of the NUR, extend our sympathy to our fellow workers of the Miners' Federation. We realise to the full extent the justice of their present demands, and hereby pledge our support to any measure adopted by the NUR calculated to bring the present fight to a successful conclusion. We strongly recommend a general "down tools" policy as the quickest and most efficient method of ending the present dispute.[219]

However, in Lydney, which was less of a mining town than Cinderford, a resolution to support the miners was only carried by a majority of one while a significant number remained neutral.[220]

217 Ibid.
218 Arnot, *The Miners*, 271.
219 Ibid.
220 Bagwell, *The Triple Alliance*, 116.

The government was panicked by the threat of the use of the Triple Alliance and immediately sent a letter to the MFGB asking to re-start negotiations, but at the same time prepared to rush an Emergency Powers Bill through parliament. The MFGB Executive agreed to ask the NUR to postpone its solidarity strike and representatives of the MFGB Executive met Lloyd George on Sunday 24 October, and by 28 October had come up with a provisional settlement.[221] This deal included an advance of two shillings a shift until January 1921 and, thenceforth, an increase or decrease in additional wages contingent on an increase or decrease in national output and the price of exports beyond or below a basic amount or 'datum line'.[222] The scheme would continue until a National Wage Board, made up of worker and owner representatives, met and reported on an agreed permanent scheme by 31 March 1921.

Hodges was instrumental in brokering this complex deal but was criticised by delegates from South Wales and the Forest of Dean for promoting a deal which few could understand and which linked wages to the price of coal. At a mass meeting the following Sunday morning, at Speech House, Organ argued:

> we are not very much in the know apart from what has been learnt from the newspapers and I confess that I don't fully understand the terms of the proposed settlement. One thing I do understand is that it will not give us what we have been fighting for.[223]

However, most members of the MFGB Executive believed that the National Wage Board would provide a forum to negotiate a national and permanent settlement on wages and conditions, something the MFGB had been campaigning for since its formation in 1888. As a result, the MFGB Executive organised another ballot but advised a return to work and an acceptance of the government's offer.

Wages and Output

In the resulting ballot a small majority voted in favour of continuing the strike, less than the two-thirds required to carry on with the strike, so an MFGB delegate conference agreed to accept the government's terms. In the Forest of Dean 1,961 voted for continuing the strike with 1,765

221 Cole, *Labour in the Coal Mining Industry*, 160.
222 Cole, *Labour in the Coal Mining Industry*, 160- 161 and Arnot, *The Miners*, 276-278.
223 *Dean Forest Mercury* 29 October 1920.

Table 3: Minimum Day Wage for a Hewer in the Forest of Dean, July 1912—March 1921[*]

Date	Pay Award	Calculation	Wage
July 1912	30% above 1888 rate	4s plus 30%	5s 3d
June 1914	5%	4s plus 35 %	5s 5d
February 1915	25%	4s plus 60%	6s 5d
July 1916	20%	4s plus 80%	7s 2d
September 1917	War Bonus 1s 6d	4s plus 80% plus 1s 6d	8s 8d
July 1918	War Bonus 1s 6d	4s plus 80% plus 3s	10s 2d
April 1919	Sankey Award 2s	4s plus 80% plus 5s	12s 2d
May 1919	Min. Wage Award	4s 7d plus 80% plus 5s	13 s 3d
April 1920	National Award 2s	4s 7d plus 80% plus 7s	15s 3d
November 1920	Datum Line Award of 2s (only up to January)	4s 7d plus 80% plus 9s	17s 3d
January 1921	Datum Line Award of 2s plus productivity bonus of 1s 6d	4s 7d plus 80% plus 10s 6d	18s 9d
March 1921	No Productivity bonus	4s 7d plus 80% plus 7s	15s 3d

[*]These figures are based on information taken from A. L. Bowley, *Prices and Wages in the UK 1914–1920* (London: Clarendon Press,1921) Chapter 10, J. W. F. Rowe, *Wages in the Coal Industry*, (London: King and Son, 1923), the *Dean Forest Mercury* and FDMA Minutes.

On 14 December 1920, at the age of 62, Oliver Hardwick was crushed by a water tank while working at Lightmoor Colliery. He died as a result of his injuries on 21 December 1920. Hardwick was born in 1858 in Paxford and married Martha Merritt in 1884. They had six children Lizzie, Eleanor, Lena, Charles, Elsie and Oliver, who had been killed in World War One.

against.[224] The ballots showed there was a deep hostility, particularly in the Forest of Dean, to any arrangement under which wages were related to output.[225] However, after seventeen days the men returned to work and the FDMA agreed to meet the colliery owners and establish a Joint Output Committee to monitor the levels of production.[226]

The hewers were the highest earners (see table above) with other grades earning less. To put these wage rates in context, in December 1920, the minimum wage of an agricultural labourer was 46s per week and the average wage of those employed in the railways was 73s per week.[227]

In November 1920, the temporary datum line award meant that the average national wage for a hewer had risen to 169 per cent above June 1914 levels.[228] At this time in the Forest of Dean, the average wage of a hewer had temporarily increased by 218 per cent. This was a higher percentage than most other districts because, since 1917, the Forest miners had received nationally agreed flat-rate awards starting from a lower standard rate compared to most other regions.

At the same time, the cost of living had risen to 176 per cent above June 1914 levels. However, the fundamental outstanding issue of the ownership of the mines remained unresolved. The *Jolly George* affair and the continued industrial conflict in the coalfields, convinced Lloyd George that the decisive struggle foreseen in 1919 had not been resolved.

224 *Dundee Courier* 4 November 1920.
225 Brace and Hartshorn were involved in secret negotiations with Government officials and Brace proposed the outlines of a settlement on which lines the strike was eventually resolved. These leaders acted contrary to their mandate and certainly contrary to the prevailing mood within the coalfields, and as a result, Brace and Hartshorn were forced to resign from their offices in the SWMF. Hartshorne was later re-elected as President of SWMF serving from 1922 to 1924.
226 FDMA Minutes 7 December 1920.
227 Bowley, *Prices and Wages*.
228 Supple, *The History of the British Coal Industry*, 153.

Emergency Powers Act

The government was now merely playing for time. The Triple Alliance had met repeatedly since the end of the war and passed several resolutions, but it had engaged in no specific action. Still, its mere existence and the threat that it would one day use its potential strength impacted on government policy and preparations were made to stockpile coal and open negotiations to import coal from abroad, if necessary.

The government was also intensifying its war in Ireland, where Churchill's Black and Tans were committing atrocities against the civilian population. On 25 October Terence MacSwiney, a member of Sinn Fein and Lord Mayor of Cork, died in Brixton prison. As a result, at the end of October 1920, the IRA embarked on a campaign of arson, bombing and assassination of prominent members of the government and military on the British mainland. The campaign involved numerous deaths and lasted until the establishment of the Irish Free State two years later. Although the British labour movement was highly critical of government policy towards Ireland, the Labour Party and the British trade union leadership were reluctant to support the campaign for full independence.[229] However, the war in Ireland only served to heighten the sense of siege felt by the ruling classes, some of whom feared 'dangerous forces' were at work and beyond their control.

On 28 October 1920, in readiness for war with the British working class, parliament passed the Emergency Powers Act which made permanent the dictatorial powers the government already possessed under the wartime Defence of the Realm Act.[230]

On 16 December 1920, Arthur Morgan reported to the board of Henry Crawshay & Co. Ltd. that he had met with the inspector of taxes and got him to agree to a manipulation of the accounting figures to wipe out their tax liability to the government. Similarly, he negotiated with the Mines Department to increase their standard profits by a variety of accounting means such as bloating the costs of pumping water, thereby limiting the amount the company paid out in excess profits into the pool.[231]

---

229 Geoffrey Bell, *Hesitant Comrades, The Irish Revolution and the British Labour Movement*, (London: Pluto Press, 2016).
230 Cole, *Labour in the Coal Mining Industry*, 201 -204.
231 Board Minute Book of Henry Crawshay & Co. Ltd. (O) 1919-1921.

Chapter Four

The Lockout

I am of the opinion that it would be well to go and have some fresh air and starve as to go and bury ourselves in a mine and starve there.

David Organ, President of the Forest of Dean Miners' Association, *Dean Forest Mercury* 1 April 1921.

During 1919 and 1920 the mining industry was still maintained under a system of control put in place to specifically meet the needs of the war economy. After the war ended the demand for coal was maintained because of a coal famine in Europe, which meant that the price for export coal was inflated. Coal sold on the domestic market was effectively being sold at a loss, the balance being made up out of the profits of the export trade. The state was receiving a large share of these surplus profits and could thus allow the colliery owners to receive large dividends while enabling miners to receive a living wage.

Depression

However, by the beginning of 1921 large quantities of German reparations coal entered the European market and impacted severely on the British export trade. In addition, British coal had to compete with cheaper American coal.[1] Also, the steelworks in South Wales, which had provided a market for Forest steam coal, were forced to close down because they could not compete with Belgian steel.[2] The depression did not just impact on the mining industry but spread throughout the economy. The sudden drop in markets for tin plate meant over five hundred workers at the Richard Thomas tinplate works in Lydney and Lydbrook were laid off after Christmas.[3] Lydbrook was particularly badly hit when the workers at the local cable works were put on short time with some of the women workers having to accept domestic service away from home.[4]

---

1 Supple, *The History of the British Coal Industry*, Chapter 5.
2 *Dean Forest Mercury* 14 January 1921.
3 *Gloucester Journal* 18 December 1920 and *Gloucester Journal* 8 January 1921.
4 *Gloucester Citizen* 15 January 1921.

At the end of 1920, there were clear signs of the economic depression deepening as the average price of export coal fell from £4 to about £2 a ton.[5] As a result, any gains in wages for miners under the datum line agreement were wiped out. Unemployment took a sharp leap in December, and short-time working began to spread. The government was conscious that a further collapse in the export market, resulting in a deepening of the depression in the coal trade, was just around the corner and predicted that soon their surplus profits would be reduced to a loss. The Mines Department recommended to the government that "there was no reason for the state to subsidise an industry in a period of depression" and the President of the Board of Trade, Robert Horne, made it clear to the colliery owners that he agreed.[6] The already serious situation was exacerbated by the government's deflationary policies.

The areas producing steam coal for export were hit particularly hard. In South Wales, where many Forest men worked, unemployment reached 20,000. In January 1921, the principal steam coal collieries in the Forest, Princess Royal, Cannop, Waterloo and Eastern, were still working full time although they had started stockpiling coal at the pitheads or just fulfilling long-standing contracts. However, the smaller steam coal collieries started laying men off. Harrow Hill colliery reduced its workforce from about 150 to 50. At Crown colliery, most of the men were laid off with the rest only working about two days a week. In addition, the house coal collieries were having problems selling their small coal which is typically used in manufacturing.[7]

In January 1921, the government announced it still planned to return control to the colliery owners in August. However, as a temporary measure, it provided a subsidy of seven million pounds to cover wages and to secure time for the MAGB to come up with a settlement with the MFGB. The owners continued to press the government for a continuation of the type of scheme implemented during the war, with a guarantee of standard profits, and warned they could not inherit the existing wage agreement without a subsidy. The MFGB were willing to accept wage cuts and even consider a profit-sharing scheme with the owners but argued for no return to district settlements. Both the owners and the MFGB were aware that exposure to unfettered market forces would require massive wage cuts.

By February, Lightmoor, Foxes Bridge and Waterloo were working half time, and Cannop was down to 3 or 4 days a week. There were now

5 Supple, *The History of the British Coal Industry*, 154.
6 Cole, *Labour in the Coal Mining Industry*, Chapter 9.
7 *Dean Forest Mercury* 14 January 1921.

On 8 February 1921, John Henry Taylor, aged 59, was killed at Crump Meadow Colliery by falling from the top of a cage while repairing pump work in the shaft. He left a widow and ten children.

about 300 unemployed miners in the Forest, but this was soon to be swelled by Forest born miners returning from South Wales, where the layoffs had continued. By the end of February, the number of unemployed South Wales miners had reached 50,000.[8] On 2 February 1921 Horne announced that he wanted to return control of the coal industry to the owners as soon as possible.

On 5 February a meeting of the FDMA Executive passed a resolution that requested a consolidation of wages which would incorporate the existing district percentages into a new 1921 standard, with the war wage and the Sankey wage as additions. The base rate was to be either reduced or advanced as a percentage as before.[9]

Soon afterwards, on 22 February, Horne called the miners' leaders and colliery owners into a conference and announced to them that decontrol would take place on 31 March. This news was a shock to both the MFGB and MAGB as it allowed just over one month for them to reach an agreement.

At this time, the colliery owners were still guaranteed a standard profit from a special fund or pool under the legislation enacted in 1917 and all the colliery companies were required to pay a contribution to the pool, based on tonnage produced. At first, the colliery owners pressed the government to maintain this arrangement until 31 August 1921. However, during backroom talks with the government, the MAGB was told the pool was quickly running out of surplus cash and soon would be in deficit. As a result, the MAGB did a deal with the government which guaranteed them the continuation of the standard profits they had received under the existing scheme until August, provided they dropped their opposition to de-control. The only way the owners felt that they could continue to guarantee their profits after August was through a considerable reduction in their labour costs.

8 *Dean Forest Mercury* 18 February 1921.
9 FDMA Minutes 5 February 1921.

The Pool

However, the MFGB continued to demand a National Wages Board to determine nationally uniform wages, paid out of a central profits pool to overcome the variation in productivity between individual pits and regions. Hodges proposed that a new pool system could work in a similar way as when the mines were under government control. As before, he proposed imposing a levy on every ton of coal raised to create a national fund to cover any losses by poorer collieries. In addition, he proposed a scheme whereby any excess profits would be shared between the miners and the colliery owners. He suggested that 90 per cent of excess profits should go to miners as wages and 10 per cent to the employers in addition to their standard profits. Finally, he proposed that a guaranteed wage be paid at a nationally agreed rate based on a new 1921 standard. Hodges persuaded Smith and the rest of the MFGB Executive to back his proposals and presented them to the employers who simply rejected them out of hand.[10]

By March 1921, the national rate of unemployment had reached over 15 per cent of insured workers, including 1,029 people in the Forest of Dean.[11] A reduction in the production of coal meant a reduced need for rail transport, leading to over 300 railway workers being dismissed from their jobs across the country. As a result, Charlie Cramp, the Industrial General Secretary of the NUR, issued a statement warning:

> there could be more job losses but this would not be done without the bitterest struggle they had seen in this country.[12]

On 1 March, a mass meeting of miners was held at Cinderford Town Hall, where Booth and Martin Perkins reported back from an MFGB meeting in London and outlined some of the options being put forward, warning that wages could be cut in half. Perkins was experienced enough to know what was around the corner and said at the meeting:

> We are up against the greatest tragedy in the mining industry that has ever been enacted.[13]

---

10 Thomas, *The Miners' Conflict with the Mineowners*, 29-42.
11 W. H. Fraser, *A History of British Trade Unionism, 1700-1998*, (Basingstoke: Palgrave Macmillan, 1999).
12 *Gloucester Citizen* 25 February 1921.
13 *Dean Forest Mercury* 4 March 1921.

In March 1921, the Forest of Dean Craftsmen appointed Jack Allen, an ex-official of the Scottish Miners' Association, as a full-time agent.[14] Allen immediately started to meet with FDMA officials with the view to overcome their differences and work together in the present crisis. Allen's Scottish colleague, Smillie, might have had the Forest of Dean in mind when he said:

> We will not if we can avoid it, I assure you, see the wages of the miners in one district of this country being reduced down to the starvation point or below starvation, while miners in other parts of the country more favourably situated are receiving fair remuneration for their labour.[15]

Smillie had done everything he felt was possible to make a case for the nationalisation of the mines over the last two years, but now his policy of negotiation by persuasion was in ruins. In the first three months of 1921, he desperately pressed the case against de-control in meetings with Horne, a man who had little knowledge of the mining industry and little sympathy for the miners' concerns.

Smillie was suffering from health problems and probably felt unable to continue to lead the miners with the prospect of a bitter industrial dispute on the horizon. He resigned at the end of March and returned to his miner's cottage at Larkhill in Scotland where he had begun his career. He was replaced by the existing Vice President, Herbert Smith. Horne wrote to the MFGB on 15 March to make clear to Smith that he could not accept the maintenance of a pool in any form arguing that:

> It would be not only contrary to the principles upon which we believe the commercial success of this country is based, but it would be disastrous to the coal industry itself.[16]

Two Weeks' Notice

On 8 March, the government Bill for de-control of the coal industry was put to the vote in parliament and passed with 277 in favour and 72 against.[17] On 11 March, the *Dean Forest Mercury* printed the following statement:

14 *Daily Herald* 28 April 1921.
15 Arnot, *The Miners*, 294.
16 Cole, *Labour in the Coal Mining Industry*, 191-192.
17 *Dean Forest Mercury* 11 March 1921.

De-control means that the loss (probably the heavy loss) on every ton of coal raised in the Forest of Dean under present conditions will no longer be borne by the Government (i.e. the taxpayers). The subsidy ends on March 31st, and the industry must then be self-supporting. Every pit will have to show a profit on every ton raised. A very short way out of the difficulty would be to raise the price of coal by 10s per ton. Everyone agrees this would be harmful to other industries. The nation wants cheaper coal.

Apparently, therefore, if local pits are to continue, wages must be reduced, and the owner must accept smaller profits. Wages in this coalfield must, apparently, be as they were before the war, lower than in other districts, owing to the special difficulties of the Forest coalfield, and the reductions proposed may be so seriously large as to bring the earnings of coalminers below the present cost of living.[18]

In mid-March, notices were posted on pits throughout the country giving two weeks' notice to end the existing contracts to all mine workers, including the craftsmen whose members were essential for maintaining the safety of the pits. On Monday 14 March, the Forest of Dean colliery owners posted notices up on the pit heads which included new rates of pay for both miners and craftsmen. The men were left in a state of shock by the proposed rates which amounted to nearly a 50 per cent cut in wages. The owners made it clear that the men would be locked out after 31 March unless they accepted the new conditions of employment.

In March 1921, the average wage for a miner in the Forest of Dean was 15s 3d per shift. The owners proposed reducing the minimum wage for a hewer to 8s 6d, or 6s 6d after deductions.[19] The rates for other skilled jobs, labourers and surface workers were less than this. The rate of inflation meant that, in real terms, Forest miners' rates of pay would be below their earnings in 1914. The owners proposed that wages in future should be controlled by District Conciliation Boards as was the case in 1914. The proposal to re-introduce district bargaining hit the miners in the Forest particularly hard.

In response, a mass meeting was held at Speech House on the morning of 13 March, where Booth informed the men that the MFGB

18 Ibid.
19 This was determined by the old standard of 4s 7d plus 35 per cent (the percentage addition in 1914), giving a new standard of 6s 2d plus 40 per cent giving 8s 6d.

was demanding a system based on a pool but that the colliery owners were against it in principle. The MAGB proposals would mean a considerable reduction in wages based on the individual ability of each colliery to pay. He went on to argue:

> With a much lower wage and short time, it would be impossible for them to live in decency and so far as there was every likelihood of the Forest being down considerably below subsistence level, it appeared to be the best thing for the whole of the men in the whole of the mines of the country to make a determined stand to put up a fight now and, if they were out for a time, it was better than to accept a wage which would entail slow starvation for months and months and probably for years.[20]

The men agreed and rejected the owners' offer and a message was sent to the MFGB informing them of their decision. Ernest Bevin and Booth addressed a meeting at Lydney picture house on the evening of Sunday 13 March. Bevin spoke for over an hour, warning that the country was facing a severe crisis. Booth pointed out:

> That the Forest of Dean provided ample illustration of the incapacity of the separate colliery undertakings to carry on, with its lack of machinery, old-fashioned plants and bad methods of production.[21]

District Settlements

The Executive of the MFGB met again on the morning of Friday 18 March before a delegate conference to consider a proposal from the MAGB for district settlements. The MAGB proposals included the abandonment of the pool and a return to district rates but accepted the introduction of a new scheme which allowed any excess profits to be shared between the owners and the workers. The exact ratio was subject to negotiation, but the Forest of Dean miners knew there would be little excess profit in the Forest pits, and without a national agreement, they would be asked to do the same work in worse conditions for less money than miners elsewhere in the country.

20 *Dean Forest Mercury* 18 March 1921.
21 Ibid.

Table 4: MFGB and MAGB Proposals in March 1921*

Miners' Demands	Owners' Offer
National Wages Board	District Wages Boards
National Pool	No National Pool and competitive free enterprise
New 1921 standard with flat-rate increases	The 1914 standard to remain with percentage increases
Standard Profits to be fixed at 10% of Wages	Standard Profits to be fixed at 17% of Wages
Surplus to be shared with 10% going to the owners as surplus profits and 90% to the miners as an increase in wages.	Surplus to be shared with 20% going to the owners as surplus profits and 80% to the miners as an increase in wages.

* Thomas, *The Miners' Conflict with the Mineowners*, 29.

Table 5: Wage Reductions Proposed by the Forest of Dean Colliery Owners for April 1921.*

Grade	Existing Wages	Owners' Offer	Reduction	Percentage Reduction	Real Value of Owners Offer at 1914 Prices
Hewers	15s 3d	8s 6d	6s 9d	43	3s 5d
Surface Labourers	12s 9d	6s 1d	6s 8d	52	2s 6d
Trammers	13s 3d	6s 8d	6s 7d	49	2s 9d

* Cole, *Labour in the Coal Mining Industry*, 197.

The discussion at the delegate conference was heated, with Hodges, Smith and the majority of the Executive seeking to recommend to their members that the pool be temporarily abandoned and that they should be empowered to make a settlement on a district basis. This proposal was supported by delegates from Yorkshire and Northumberland. However, many delegates, including Cook and Ablett, argued against this proposal. It was decided to refer back to the districts for a decision. The conference would then be reconvened on the following Thursday, 24 March, to make a judgement on the way forward.[22]

In addition, the MAGB proposed that in each district, a joint audit would ascertain the industry's profits by deducting from total sales: the standard wages; non-wage costs of production; and a standard profit equivalent to 17 per cent of the standard wages. The net excess profits, if any, would then be divided between wages and profits in the ratio 80:20. In the case when the ascertainment revealed an excess profit, a percentage addition would be made to the new standard wage of 8s 6d.

On 23 March, a meeting at Cinderford directed Booth to vote against the owners' proposal at the delegate conference and to argue that the MFGB should continue a campaign for a national wages board and pool.[23] However, at the conference on 25 March, some delegates from areas where productivity was high, such as Yorkshire, Leicestershire and Derbyshire, supported the proposal of accepting the owners' offer of district settlements. Under the owners' offer a hewer in areas like Nottingham would receive double the wage of one in the Forest of Dean.[24]

Most of the other regions, including the Forest of Dean, argued that the MFGB should fight back and demand the continuation of the type of scheme implemented during the war with a national wages board and nationally uniform wages paid out of a central profits pool to overcome the variation in productivity between individual pits and regions. The voting was 627 against and 241 for a temporary agreement meaning the attempt by Hodges and Smith to avoid the danger of a lockout was defeated.[25]

The MFGB Executive accepted this mandate and started making preparations for strike action. However, they were aware that they were negotiating in rapidly deteriorating conditions as coal stocks rose and coal export prices plummeted. The colliery owners, who would no longer receive a government subsidy, were determined to abandon any idea of

22 Arnot, *South Wales Miners*, 205.
23 *Dean Forest Mercury* 25 March 1921.
24 Cole, *Labour in the Coal Mining Industry*, 197.
25 Cole, *Labour in the Coal Mining Industry*, 155.

pooling of profits and insisted on district settlements. This was not a good time to go on strike. Hodges pleaded with the government to intervene and warned:

> As you are aware, the contracts of service between ourselves and the owners terminate on March 31, the owners having duly given notice to terminate such contracts. A Lock Out is, therefore, unavoidable unless the workmen are prepared to accept such terms of employment as would reduce them, in many instances, to very nearly the pre-war level of wages, with the cost of living at 141 per cent above pre-war prices. In our judgement, it would be a national calamity to have the trade brought to a standstill on Friday next.[26]

Hodges went on to plead for a temporary subsidy to avoid the crisis and added the MFGB would be willing to accept a reduction in wages based on the recent fall in the cost of living. Horne refused to accept any responsibility for the crisis, and it took five days for him to reply. In his response, he rejected a subsidy out of hand, arguing that it would only encourage other industries to request government support.[27]

Forest miner Frank Joynes knew the men had good reasons to oppose district settlements. As a boy, he started work in the iron mines and then worked at New Fancy colliery. In December 1915 he joined the army and spent the rest of the war on the Western Front. He was discharged in April 1919 and returned to New Fancy and later worked at Princess Royal colliery. Many years later he recalled:

> During the 1914-1918 war and for some time afterwards, the coal mines were under the direction of the government. When the government handed back the mining to private business in 1921, the coal owners called for a reduction in miners wages and a return to district agreements. District agreements, no less than wage reductions, were unpopular with miners. District agreements meant that men working in inferior pits received less money than men working in mines with richer seams. Naturally, the miners rejected both these proposals, whereupon the owners started the lockout.[28]

26 Ibid. 191.
27 Ibid. 192.
28 Phelps, *Forest Voices*, 63.

A Community Response

Many in the Forest of Dean feared that the government's strategy was to allow economic forces to take their toll, resulting in the closure of all the mines in the less productive districts. Therefore, the decision to fight back in the Forest of Dean was very much a response from the whole community. The district was already feeling the effects of the economic depression as layoffs and part-time working impacted on the mines. In addition, the closing down of the tinplate works in Lydney and Lydbrook increased the levels of unemployment and poverty.

The whole economy of the area was based on mining, and many of the other industries, including brickworks, timber suppliers, railways and docks were dependent on the business they did with mining companies. Nearly eighty per cent of the employable men living in Cinderford worked in the pits. If the pits closed, businesses would go bankrupt, property prices would plummet, and houses would become derelict and worthless as people left the area. Some of the smaller colliery owners and free miners would struggle to compete with larger concerns elsewhere and could be driven into bankruptcy.

Consequently, many working class people in the Forest believed this was a battle for the survival of the whole community and the miners discovered they had large sections of the local population on their side. The fightback involved miners, miners' wives, friends and relatives, the craftsmen, the buttymen and daymen, traders, shopkeepers, merchants, publicans, churches and chapels. In the past, there had been conflict between these groups. However, now all these groups came together to overcome their differences and unite to defend their community and families.

On Friday 25 March, at a well-attended meeting of craftsmen at Speech House, Allen informed the men their wages would be reduced in the same way as the miners. He pointed out that as they were not members of the MFGB, they were not subject to their decisions. However:

> He understood the feelings between the miners and the craftsmen had at times been far from pleasant, but he, as their agent intended to do all he could to promote a feeling of comradeship among all workers, and seeing that this forthcoming fight affected all mine workers he hoped if it were to be a fight they would all

fight shoulder to shoulder, irrespective of grade as members of the working class.[29]

The meeting agreed by a hand vote that, if necessary, they would stand and fight alongside the miners. Allen sent a letter to Booth informing him of their decision. Nationally the unions of other craftsmen issued instructions to stop work with the miners. On Monday 28 March, a mass meeting of Forest miners agreed to reject the 50 per cent drop in wages and to absent themselves from work on Friday. The sense of betrayal by the government and the determination to fight back were apparent in Organ's speech to the men.

> In my opinion, if there was a time in our history when we ought to feel like getting our backs up, then it was this time. The government which had betrayed and broken faith with us not for the first time told us that the National Wages Board should be in existence by the end of March. Instead of giving us assistance in that direction, the intention is to drive us back to district arrangements, practically the same as before the war. We as miners say we ought to have our wages regulated nationally with a practically uniform rate as far as possible throughout Great Britain. Sooner or later we have got to make a more strenuous fight than ever, and if so, it should be this time. The Federation has instructed the districts that no man should do any work whatever, and let every man who received a notice to come out, do so and let the owners and their collieries go where they choose. I am of the opinion that it would be well to go and have some fresh air and starve as to go and bury ourselves in a mine and starve there.[30]

A motion was passed to send a letter to the Craftsmen Association accepting their offer to stand with them and asking them to walk out on Friday with their fellow workmen.[31] The MFGB Executive met again on Wednesday 30 March and decided to seek the aid of the Triple Alliance. The issue of safety men and flooding was discussed. In the end, it was decided by a vote of ten votes to eight to recommend bringing the safety men out.[32]

29 *Dean Forest Mercury* 1 April 1921.
30 Ibid.
31 Ibid.
32 Cole, *Labour in the Coal Mining Industry*, 200.

In the past, it was normal that during a strike an agreed number of craftsmen would continue to work to prevent any long-term damage to the collieries. These men were called safety men and included pumpmen and stokers to operate the boilers which provided steam power for the pumps and men to inspect the timbers to minimise falls of rock. In response, the government announced that it would refuse to meet with the MFGB unless the safety men were allowed to go back to work.

In the Forest, the removal of safety men had already been decided by rank and file miners. The miners argued that the owners cared more for their pits than they did for their employees' families and as a result, the miners would put the welfare of their families above the property of the owners. On Wednesday evening, the FDCOA met with deputies and representatives of the craftsmen at Speech House. The craftsmen informed the owners they would not change their minds and would stand with the miners.[33] However, this had huge implications because of the exceptional risk of flooding which affected Forest pits, in particular, Cannop Colliery, which was one of the largest and most modern pits in the Forest.[34] The *Dean Forest Mercury* reported:

The danger of flooding in the Forest of Dean is particularly acute and might, owing to the geological lay of the district, become a disaster widespread and serious. Owing to the strata formation of the basin, if the workings of one undertaking are affected others in contiguity are quickly in peril also, and if the amount of pumping is ineffective, the whole coalfield in a very short time will be in a position of danger we would not like to contemplate.[35]

Lockout

On Thursday 31 March, one million British miners were locked out, including many war veterans and nearly 7,000 miners from the Forest of Dean. That evening, a meeting was held by the Craftsmen Association in Cinderford where they confirmed none of their members should go to work except for the men necessary to get the horses out of the pit.[36] A timeline of the events taking place over the next three months is given in the appendix.

33 *Dean Forest Mercury* 1 April 1921.
34 Ibid.
35 Ibid.
36 Ralph Anstis, *Blood on Coal The 1926 General Strike and The Miners' Lockout in the Forest of Dean* (Lydney: Black Dwarf, 1999) 93.

On the same day, the government declared a state of emergency and arranged for coal exports to be stopped, troops to be put on alert and the army reserve mobilised. More troops were ordered back from Ireland, Malta and Silesia and moved to the major coalfields.[37] Parks in London and elsewhere were used as camps for armed servicemen while troops were sent to Gloucester.[38]

On Friday 1 April a mass rally was held at Speech House where Booth gave a passionate speech attacking the government and the colliery owners. The meeting was also addressed by Allen who pledged the support of the craftsmen and the following resolution was passed unanimously:

> This joint meeting of miners and craftsmen of the Forest of Dean hereby pledge ourselves to stand shoulder to shoulder in this crisis, and demand from the powers that be full justice for the mining community. We further pledge ourselves to play our part in bringing into operation the original demands of the MFGB.[39]

Both organisations agreed to elect joint committees and organise combined mass meetings. The next day William Meredith, the manager at Lightmoor Colliery, and Trotter, the under manager, turned up to work at 5 am and were horrified to find that the craftsmen had joined the strike, although a few men were still raising the horses. Meredith wrote in his diary:

> Naturally, this placed us in a very precarious position ...We detailed overmen, inspectors and also certain clerks and officials to go to the various pumps which were naturally unattended, and do the best they could under the circumstances, and although this was attended with various mishaps and caused us great anxiety for the moment, they acquitted themselves with great credit.[40]

On Monday 4 April, the unemployment benefit offices in Lydney, which were already overworked with unemployed tin plate workers, were besieged by miners. Details were taken, but the men were informed that

---

37 Desmarais, *The British Government's Strikebreaking Organization*, 124 and Renshaw, *The General Strike*, 81.
38 *Dean Forest Mercury* 8 April 1921.
39 *Gloucester Citizen* 2 April 1921 and *Dean Forest Mercury* 8 April 1921.
40 Anstis, *Blood on Coal*, 93.

it would be unlikely they would receive the benefit because they were unemployed as a result of an industrial dispute. At one point, the police were called to establish order.[41] In fact, a test case was submitted to the Court of Referees sitting on 5 April and the Umpire decided that the miners were unemployed through trade dispute and therefore were not entitled to unemployment benefit.[42] This was despite the argument put forward by the miners that they had been locked out.[43]

On Tuesday 5 April, a well-attended meeting at Speech House heard speeches from Organ, Booth and Allen, urging the men to stand firm. Booth pointed out that the proposed wages for the Forest miners were the lowest in the country but added that miners in other areas, who were facing only small reductions, had joined the strike out of solidarity. The meeting was informed that a small number of Forest men were still working. As a result, the following motion was passed:

All men who have continued to work after 10 o'clock tonight in defiance of the resolution passed unanimously at last Friday's mass meeting to be expelled from the organisation and all men in both miners and craftsmen unions pledge not to work at any colliery in this district where any of these men are employed after the present crisis is over. Further that we picket collieries to carry into effect our resolution.[44]

Flooded Mines

In the Forest of Dean, the removal of the safety men was causing significant problems for the colliery owners because 15 million gallons of water had to be dealt with daily over the Forest coalfield. As a result, the managers recruited overmen, office staff, volunteers, friends and relatives to help stoke the boilers which supplied steam to the pumps.[45] This action meant that in all the major collieries except Cannop the pumps were kept working. At Norchard Colliery, Lord Bledisloe together with his son and heir and directors Robert Rawnsley Bowles and Brigadier General Tyler

41 *Dean Forest Mercury* 8 April 1921.
42 *Gloucester Citizen* 12 April 1921.
43 When a claim for benefit was disputed, it could be referred to the Court of Referees under the Unemployment Insurance Act (1920). A Court of Referees tribunal consists of an employers' representative, a workman's representative and an impartial chairman or umpire who must be a qualified lawyer.
44 *Gloucester Journal* 9 April 1921 and *Dean Forest Mercury* 8 April 1921.
45 *Gloucester Citizen* 4 April 1921.

from Clanna worked for a few hours as stokers as a publicity stunt. The *Daily Herald* reported that:

> It is suggested locally that the practice he was getting might be useful for a time when his Lordship had to earn a living.[46]

At Lightmoor colliery, the staff were having problems dealing with the failure of a large pumping engine, which were exacerbated by accidents to inexperienced staff and water rushing in from nearby pits where pumping had stopped. The pit was beginning to flood, but Meredith persuaded William Mountjoy, one of the enginemen, to secretly come into the pit and save the situation.[47]

At Cannop colliery, the management had successfully removed all the electrical equipment, but the mine was completely shut down. When open, it usually took 36 men pumping two to three thousand gallons a minute to keep the level of the water low, and so the colliery was now completely flooded and in danger of having to be abandoned.[48] At Howbeach colliery, where flooding was also a serious concern, development work had been brought to a stop and management were having to pump 1,200 gallons a minute. At Waterloo colliery, the management team led by Charlie Cooper, with the help of Cooper's son, a Bristol University student, and two Cambridge University students, had to pump 250,000 gallons of water per day.[49]

On Tuesday 5 April, a national conference of unions affiliated to the NTWF resolved to give the miners all the assistance in their

Lord Bledisloe.

46 *Daily Herald* 5 April 1921.
47 Anstis, *Blood on Coal*, 94-95.
48 *Dean Forest Mercury* 8 April 1921.
49 Information supplied by Steven Carter, grandson of Ron Carter who received a medal for his role in rescuing fellow miners during the flooding disaster at Waterloo in 1949.

power including strike action, despite the fact that in some parts of the country there was confusion over whether individual unions affiliated to the NTWF were required to ballot their members as agreed in June 1919. Three days later, a NUR conference voted unanimously to strike in support of the miners, provided the transport workers struck jointly and simultaneously with them. As a result, a nationwide solidarity strike involving all the main unions in the Triple Alliance and consisting of about two million workers was called for Tuesday 12 April.[50] On Thursday 7 April, James Wignall put the case for the Forest miners to parliament:

> [he] did not think there was a more law-abiding body of men than the miners of the Forest of Dean, and what was proposed would give them the hardest hit of any in the whole of the United Kingdom. When they realised that the average reduction in wages would be £1 16s 3d., the House would realise their indignation. That was a wage which would reduce them below the level of the average labourer in any industry one might name. When notice to terminate engagements was given there was no approach to any of the miners that they should continue to work on the old conditions. If the owners had been so anxious to preserve their property one would have thought that they would have published a statement when the notices were issued that they expected the safety hands to continue on the old conditions until a settlement had been arrived at. But no such step was taken.[51]

On Thursday 7 April, the Cabinet set up a special committee under the Lord Chancellor "to consider the use of all available troops and Reserves according to need".[52] On Friday 8 April, Lloyd George announced that he was calling up the reserves of the army, navy and air force. An appeal was launched for the enrolment of 80,000 special constables and another appeal for "patriotic citizens" to enlist in an emergency Defence Force. In some areas, machine gun posts were placed at pitheads.[53]

50 Cole, *Labour in the Coal Mining Industry*, 206.
51 *Western Mail* 8 April 1921.
52 Desmarais, *The British Government's Strikebreaking Organization*, 125.
53 Ibid.

Pit Ponies

On the propaganda front, the government released a statement that pit ponies were drowning in flooded mines. This information was untrue as in most pits the horses had already been brought to the surface. One exception was at Foxes Bridge colliery, where there were problems with the winding gear, and as a result, some men stayed on to help bring the horses up after the strike started.[54] It was very difficult bringing the ponies out of the pit in the cages and would only be done if the expectation was that the strike would last a long time. Harry Toomer remembers:

> I started work as a pony driver. There were some fifty ponies in this pit at this time, and some were lovely animals. For the most part, these ponies were very well cared for and we became very attached to our own particular animal. These ponies never saw daylight unless there was a strike.[55]

Harry Roberts remembered one incident:

> In the 1921 strike, the horses were brought up to the surface at Crump Meadow Colliery and turned out to graze into what is known as Crump Meadow Field, while the horses from Lightmoor grazed in the White Hart Fields. A horse got away from the field by the New Fancy and ran all the way in a mad gallop to a ditch in the Green by what was the Dog Inn in Victoria Street where it fell sideways and got wedged and unable to get up. A small crowd gathered, including children, and the pig-killer was sent for, and in a short time he arrived with a humane killer, and we all saw the struggling animal die.[56]

Some miners argued that the colliery owners cared more for their horses than they did for their men and this was no ordinary strike as they had been locked out. Other miners had developed political views that placed the root of the crisis within the capitalist system itself. This was the case for Harold Craddock, who was the second student to be sponsored by the FDMA to attend the CLC. In a letter to the *Dean Forest Mercury* Craddock argued that the capitalist class:

54 *Dean Forest Mercury* 8 April 1921.
55 Harry Toomer, Gage Library.
56 Anstis, *Blood on Coal*, 109.

Forest of Dean colliers with a pit pony.

has general ideas of lowering the workers' standard of life and the starvation of women and children so that they would be in a profit-making position again. It is for the working class to unite all the means at our disposal to sweep away the ruins of the present superstructure so that we build up a socialist state the world over, but for the common good of all. My comrades, we have suffered long enough the effects of capitalism, which will always be bound up with geographical, technical and other sectional advantages and disadvantages for workers. So, let us abolish the barriers of liberty the world over.[57]

Blacklegs

On Saturday 9 April, the government met with the Triple Alliance leaders and insisted that the safety men must be allowed to return to work before any negotiations could begin. On the same day, a well-attended meeting at Speech House with Booth, Allen and Organ on the platform, decided that the policy of withdrawing the safety men should continue, arguing it was an effective way of applying pressure on the colliery owners.

57 *Dean Forest Mercury* 8 April 1921.

Organ stated he was pleased that the Triple Alliance had decided to support the miners and would be joining the strike on Tuesday. However, he regretted that there had been a delay. Booth challenged the statistics put forward by the colliery owners concerning their profits and losses. He pointed out that some of the smaller collieries in the Forest had stated they were happy to pay their men a wage of 12 shillings a day and he said he did not understand why the large collieries were claiming they could not afford to do this.[58]

The issue of the handful of men, both craftsmen and miners, who were strike-breaking was discussed, and it was agreed that "it was up to the general body of men to exert their collective influence over them".[59] It was also agreed that the men should not be incited by the extra police that had been drafted into the district. Winifred Foley was only seven during the strike but remembers her father, Charlie Mason, confronting strikebreakers at Waterloo colliery near Lydbrook.

> I do remember once playing with older children watching for blacklegs going to work at Waterloo. We hid in the bracken, and when we saw them, we slipped away and told the men on strike in the village. They hurried off to meet the blacklegs and shout abuse at them.[60]

Princess Royal Colliery

The only place where there was any of trouble in the first week of the lockout was at Princess Royal colliery in Bream where management staff were pumping up to 3 to 4 thousand gallons a minute. About a week into the lockout, it was reported to a meeting of miners in Bream that some firemen and enginemen were helping out the management with pumping operations. As a result, a large crowd, composed of several hundred men, women and children, marched to the colliery and insisted the craftsmen stop work. Police were already at the pit head to protect the blacklegs. The *Gloucestershire Chronicle* reported that the situation was "ugly" and the crowd "somewhat threatening". However, after lengthy discussions with the manager, William Burdess, and chairman, Percy Moore, it was agreed that the firemen and enginemen would leave at six in the morning

58 *Dean Forest Mercury* 15 April 1921.
59 *Gloucester Citizen* 11 April 1921.
60 Anstis, *Blood on Coal*, 106.

Princess Royal strike breakers with police protection.

and not return.[61] The reporter for the *Gloucestershire Chronicle* went on to report:

> "We might as well stay at home and starve as go to work to starve," said one collier to me as he sat with a number of others on a seat at Parkend. The remark is typical of the men's attitude and it was brought home to me that they do not mean to accept the reductions put forth. This little group of which I write remarked with emphasis that 43s 4d a week was not a living wage and they could not see why they should get less per week than the agricultural labourers, who had many advantages the miners had not. I encountered another small group of men in the vicinity of Cannop mine, where they work. They were optimistic as to the pit's future and said they did not believe that it would take several months to get mine productive again. One of them spoke of the wages drop saying that the men would not have objected to gradual fall. As it was, they would rather go to the workhouse.[62]

61 *Gloucestershire Chronicle* 16 April 1921.
62 Ibid.

Hodge's Telegraph

The issue of safety men was causing problems for the MFGB Executive in their relations with other unions in the Triple Alliance and the government. In fact, in many other districts outside the Forest of Dean the safety men had continued to work. In the cases where the safety men had joined the strike, the MFGB issued advice that the owners be allowed to take measures to secure the safety of the pits by using managerial staff and volunteers. Allen suggested that students from the Royal College of Mining in London could be drafted in to carry out safety work. Booth had himself earlier consented to extra help being brought in.[63]

On Sunday, 10 April, Frank Hodges issued a telegraph to all districts instructing union members to allow pumping operations at the collieries to resume and insisting they refrain from interfering with the return to work of necessary safety men. In most districts, including parts of South Wales, miners obeyed this directive. There were a few exceptions such as Maerdy in the Rhondda.[64] In contrast, in the Forest of Dean rank and file miners decided to ignore the telegram despite the concerns of Booth. However, as a result of Hodge's telegraph, the government agreed to resume negotiations and met with the miners' representatives on 11 April, but with no compromise on either side, a deadlock ensued.

Realisation of Assets

Nationally, the tension was increasing, and as the build-up to the solidarity action gathered pace the leaders of the railwaymen and transport workers were starting to feel nervous about bringing their members out. As a result, they pushed the start date back to 10 pm on Friday 15 April. On Wednesday 13 April, Thomas announced that he had received applications from other unions, outside the Triple Alliance, to join the strike, including ASLEF.[65]

On Thursday 14 April Charles Cox, President of the Craftsmen Association and a carpenter at Princess Royal colliery, presided over a joint meeting of miners and craftsmen at Speech House. Cox informed the men he had received letters from several colliery owners insisting the safety men return to work to save their mines from flooding, including a letter from Captain Brazier Creagh and Arthur Morgan from Henry Crawshay & Co. Ltd. stating:

63 Ibid.
64 *South Wales Daily News* 11 April 1921.
65 *Dean Forest Mercury* 8 April 1921.

Triple Alliance ready to strike?

In the event of necessary assistance for the safety of Lightmoor, Trafalgar, Foxes Bridge and Howbeach and Eastern United Collieries not being immediately forthcoming, we shall call a meeting of the shareholders at the earliest possible moment and advise the abandonment of these collieries and realisation of assets.[66]

However, at a mass meeting at Speech House on Thursday 14 April, the mood among rank and file miners was one of no compromise, and a decision was made that no extra help would be allowed. At this point, the Forest of Dean was the only district where rank and file miners had successfully prevented safety men from going into all of the main pits.

A letter was sent to Creagh and Morgan informing them of their decision. In addition, a motion was passed resolving to firmly stick to the agreement made earlier that no member of the FDMA or Craftsmen Association should work in any of the collieries in the Forest of Dean during the period of the dispute. It was also decided to reject the suggestion by Booth and Allen that mining students be brought in to help out. It was announced at the meeting that a united demonstration of

66 *Dean Forest Mercury* 15 April 1921.

GET READY FOR ACTION!

Facts for Dock and Wete side Workers; Seamen and Firemen; Cooks and Stewards; Carters and Motormen; Cab, Tramway and Bus Men; River and Canal Workers; Warehouse and Distributive Workers; and Other Affiliated Grades and Sections.

Notice from NTWF in the *Daily Herald*, 9 April 1921.

miners, railwaymen and transport workers would take place in Lydney on Saturday morning to celebrate the action of the Triple Alliance.[67]

John Joynes, the manager at Cannop, warned: "Many of the places will never again be worked".[68] However, Booth and Allen had no choice but to accept the democratic decision of their members. The only men who expressed any doubts were some craftsmen from Eastern United who said they would go back if there was a significant danger of flooding at their pit.

God's Beautiful Sunshine

On Thursday evening, Booth attended an open-air mass meeting to galvanise local support from the other unions in the Triple Alliance at Gloucester Labour Club. The meeting was presided over by Arthur Holder, President of the local Triple Alliance Strike Committee and Gloucester NUR, who worked as a guard. Also present were Arthur E. Chandler, Cheltenham Station Master and NUR member, James Birt from Lydney NUR representing local railway workers and Arthur Munnoch, organiser of the National Union of Vehicle Workers, representing local transport workers. The *Gloucester Citizen* reported Holder's speech:

> They were met on the eve of the greatest industrial struggles that had ever been known in the history of this or any other country, and he desired all of them to realise the responsibility which lay upon their shoulders. It was of utmost importance that they should understand the position in which they were placed, and then to unite as one body to bring about a successful issue. The Triple Alliance was a stupendous machine. They had never tested it so far but he believed they would have the opportunity to do so

67 *Gloucester Citizen* 15 April 1921, *Western Daily Press* 15 April 1921 and *Dean Forest Mercury* 15 April 1921.
68 *Western Mail* 16 April 1921.

in the coming weeks, and it was up to them to see to it that the machine worked well.[69]

Booth described how the export of 24 million tons a year from Germany to France as part payment for the war indemnity had created a glut of coal in the market. This policy had led directly to a drop in demand for British coal in Europe by way of export and the consequent destructive impact on the British coal industry. This action, he argued, provided an excuse for the government to de-control the mining industry.

Booth appealed for the full support of the Triple Alliance. He argued the railwaymen and transport workers would soon find themselves in the same position, and it was not just a fight for the miners but the whole of organised trade unionism. Munnoch urged all railwaymen, dockers and transport, vehicle and tramway workers to stop work at 10 pm on Friday night as agreed by the Strike Committee.[70] Booth went home that night reassured that the Forest miners had the full backing of the leaders of the local railway and transport unions and their members. A letter from a Forest miner to the *Gloucester Citizen* published on Friday 15 April pointed out:

As an old Forester and collier of 45 years' experience. I have been very interested in the excellent reports you publish in your widely circulated newspaper. Much is being made of the splendid offer by the owners to the colliers all over the country of a slightly higher wage than paid in July 1914, and much has been made of the very difficult circumstances under which this offer has been made, but not one of your correspondents has mentioned this fact, or even seemed to have thought of it—that while the collier's wage ought to come down to pre-war levels, the cost of living (according to Board of Trade figures) remains 141 per cent above what it was in July 1914, and this fact is the crux of the whole business.

Now, Sir, while there are many things I do not know (I am like the blind man in the Scriptures) I know one thing — that the minimum wage of a coal hewer up to 31 March was 15s 3d a shift. If we had started work on 1 April, the maximum wage would

69 *Gloucester Citizen* 15 April 1921.
70 Ibid.

have been 8s 8d or 6s 7d after deductions. These are absolute facts. Then if we work three days a week, which we have been working since January, the most we are promised for a considerable time to come, would produce 26s less Is 9d stoppages for the union, unemployment, and insurance, which would leave 24s 3d to keep the home going. These facts, known to every collier in the Forest of Dean, have stiffened his back for this struggle. We have not entered upon the struggle without counting the cost; we know all about the depleted funds of our Union caused largely through unemployment, and we realise what it will mean to our families; but better die of starvation in God's beautiful sunshine than to go back to servile labour and semi-starvation caused by a wage that is not sufficient to keep a man, to say nothing about a family and a respectable home which the law expects us to do. These things I say will, unless much better terms are offered, make this struggle one of the worse known in the Forest of Dean for more reasons than one.[71]

Black Friday

There was no doubt the government backed the colliery owners, but it viewed a potential strike involving over two million workers with trepidation. On Thursday 14 April, the national leaders of the transport workers and the railwaymen met with Lloyd George who indicated there was room for manoeuvre on wages but not on the issue of district rates. Lloyd George had ascertained that Thomas was a weak link. He said in private:

Thomas is all for peace; he does not want a row to please Hodges. I have complete confidence in Thomas's selfishness.[72]

At the meeting, Lloyd George warned the NUR and NTWF leaders of dire consequences for their organisations if they took strike action. The same union leaders then met with the MFGB Executive and expressed concern about bringing out their members with the difficulties associated with picketing goods yards, transport depots, dockyards and miles of railway track.

71 *Gloucester Citizen* 9 April 1921.
72 Renshaw, *The General Strike*, 84.

Later that day, Hodges approached MPs independently in the hope of securing an interim solution based on temporary aid from the government. He was accompanied by Smith and Hartshorne and answered numerous questions from the MPs, including one on the issue of a temporary settlement on wages. However, in his response, Hodges's apparent willingness to consider a temporary agreement on wages, while leaving the question of a national wages board and a national pool to be determined at a later date, allowed Lloyd George an opportunity to create a division between the miners and other members of the Triple Alliance.[73]

The MFGB Executive were themselves split on Hodges' action, but in the end, a majority made it clear that they had to abide by the decision of their members that any agreement, temporary or not, must include a national wages board and a national pool with no hint of district settlements. In addition, they stated they expected their allies in the Triple Alliance to come out on strike at 10 pm the next day as arranged. Lloyd George saw his opportunity and immediately offered to meet with the MFGB Executive at 11 am to discuss Hodges' offer, which he argued included an offer to settle the wages issue on a district basis. The MFGB Executive refused, and this allowed the leaders of the other unions in the Triple Alliance an opportunity to reconsider their position.[74]

At 9 am on Friday, the NUR and NTWF leaders went back to Unity House, the headquarters of the NUR, and decided to withdraw their support, claiming frustration at the obstinacy of the MFGB in refusing to consider arbitration or a temporary settlement. Thomas was clearly very relieved and at 3 pm went outside to announce to the pressmen waiting at the door: "It's all over boys". [75]

On the evening of Friday 15 April, the local leaders of the transport and rail unions called a meeting at the Labour Club in Gloucester. The main speakers were Holder (NUR), Munnoch (Vehicle Workers), A. Lee (Dockers Union), H. Clark (NUR) and two Labour Councillors, W.L. Edwards and William Oxenham. Holder spoke first and the *Gloucester Citizen* reported his speech.

They had received no official information until 5 o'clock that day when a telegram arrived with the news that the strike was cancelled and instructions that all members should return to

73 This version of Black Friday is mainly taken from Cole, *Labour in the Coal Mining Industry*, 209-215.
74 Cole, *Labour in the Coal Mining Industry*, 209- 215.
75 Renshaw, *The General Strike*, 87.

work on Saturday morning for an indefinite time. In the absence of further information, they were not in a position to judge the actual state of affairs. As far as Gloucester was concerned, he had from the start had no fear that when the call came, it would rally around the standard. He was certain that had the fight continued a unanimous front would have been shown.[76]

All the other trade unionists present made it clear that they would be willing to strike in solidarity with the miners. Oxenham complained that "it was unnecessary that the Mayor and Chief Constable had brought police and soldiery into the city". The meeting ended with the singing of the Red Flag.[77]

However, it soon became apparent that local rail and transport workers on the ground were left in an impossible situation as solidarity broke down. Many wanted to strike in support of the miners, but their local leaders felt they had little choice but to advise their workers against walking out because going on strike in defiance of their national union policy would put their jobs at risk. The words of the *Daily Herald* published the next day reflected widely held views:

Yesterday was the heaviest defeat that has befallen the Labour movement within the memory of man. It is no use trying to minimise it. It is no use pretending that it is other than it is. We on this paper have said throughout that if the organized workers would stand together, they would win. They have not stood together, and they have reaped the reward.

In workplaces throughout the country Jimmy Thomas, Robert Williams and Ernest Bevin were accused of duplicity by many of their members. Hodges' intervention was seen as an act of betrayal by many rank and file miners. The event became known as 'Black Friday'. Despite Hodges' tactical cunning, he had been completely outmanoeuvred by Lloyd George. The government felt confident enough to suspend recruitment to the Defence Force, but both the volunteers and the army reserve remained mobilised.[78]

On 18 April a meeting was held in South Wales to review tactics in the aftermath of Black Friday and the collapse of the Triple Alliance. As

76 *Gloucester Citizen* 16 April 1921.
77 Ibid.
78 Desmarais, *The British Government's Strikebreaking Organization*, 125.

a result, the SWMF Executive Council, prompted by Cook and Ablett, recommended that all safety men be withdrawn.[79] The policy was readily endorsed by an SWMF coalfield conference two days later.[80]

Sombre but Determined

The demonstration arranged in Lydney, which was meant to involve the local members of the Triple Alliance, was abandoned. However, a large crowd including the Pillowell brass band turned up, and hundreds of people were milling around the streets in Lydney.[81] Most of the Pillowell brass band members were miners and included Horace Jones who was an FDMA Executive member and checkweighman at one of the Parkend pits. The mood was sombre, but speeches made it clear the miners were still determined to fight on alone. A meeting was arranged at Speech House for the Monday morning.

On Monday morning, a large crowd, consisting of miners, miners' wives and children, walked through the woods from West Dean to a rally at Speech House led by a large contingent of women and the Pillowell brass band. The Yorkley Women's Labour Party joined the march with their large red flag. The cry was "Are we downhearted?" and the answer was "No!"[82] Organ expressed his deep disappointment that solidarity action from the railwaymen and transport workers on Friday night did not happen. The *Dean Forest Mercury* reported his speech:

They would not, however, be deterred by the action the Triple Alliance had taken. He hoped some action would be taken which would show that they were going to stick to their guns and see the business through to the last ditch and they would not bend a knee until they were starved absolutely into submission. Then how much better off would the country be? Despite the expense they had gone to, the discontent which had been caused, and the names which had been given to them of 'rebels', 'Bolshevists', and

79 *Western Mail* 18 April 1921.
80 *Western Mail* 21 April 1921.
81 Pillowell Band was founded in 1889. The band's nickname at the time was "The Stompers". At the turn of the century, the band's practice room was the old chapel which then closed and was later bought by Pillowell and Yorkley Co-op Society. In 1903, it was decided to build a band room of timber and corrugated iron on a site at Captains Green, where the band room stands today. Sadly, a number of its members were lost during World War One but after the war, the band regained its strength and it still exists today. https://www.pillowellsilverband.com/band-history.html (Last accessed on 18 November 2019).
82 *Gloucester Journal* 23 April 1921 and *Dean Forest Mercury* 22 April 1921.

a lot of other 'ists' and 'isms', let them stick to it; let them not be led astray. Under the proposals which had been made, they could not possibly live, and seeing they could not live while at work, they might as well enjoy God's sunshine and not descend and get coal, and let someone else live on their backs all the time.[83]

Voices from the crowd shouted out "it was the leaders that let us down" and "the only change from our side is that we are firmer and more bitter". Miners' wives had started attending lodge meetings and now were playing a significant role in the strike and urging the men to stay solid.[84]

Booth spoke next and reminded the audience that from the time of the Chartists the political process had failed the working class and that industrial action built around their organisation was the way forward. The *Dean Forest Mercury* reported:

> If it so happened that the miners went down, then it surely followed that the railwaymen would go down too. He regarded it as certain the Triple Alliance was dead as a doornail ... The interests of the working class transcended the interests of the executive bodies that composed the Triple Alliance. The working classes must look out for another organisation, and it might be in the form of syndicalism, or on some other lines. The working-class consciousness would express itself in an organised form. Don't let them despair over the breakdown of the Triple Alliance. The solidarity of the miners could win. If they could stand together, they could get through this successfully. [85]

Allen argued that it was not the transport workers or the railwaymen that had let them down but their leaders. All three men received applause throughout their speeches. Reuben James reported he had found out from the secretary of the Lydney branch of the NUR that he had received a message from the railway centre at Derby as early as 11 am on Friday morning implying that the NUR leaders had decided to abandon the strike much earlier than they stated. A resolution was passed to support the continuation of the strike and to suspend judgement on Hodges.[86] In

---

83 *Dean Forest Mercury* 22 April 1921.
84 A meeting of the Executive of the MFGB at the end of April received a large number of resolutions passed by meetings of miners' wives and daughters urging their men to stand firm.
85 *Gloucester Journal* 23 April 1921 and *Dean Forest Mercury* 22 April 1921.
86 *Dean Forest Mercury* 22 April 1921.

South Wales, a resolution was passed demanding the resignation of Hodges and the removal of safety men in all the pits across the country, and rioting took place in Scotland.[87]

Poaching

Historically Forest miners have hunted for game on the estates and farms of the landed gentry surrounding the Statutory Forest and in the Forest itself.[88] As a result, throughout 1921, the magistrates were busy prosecuting colliers caught for poaching. On Tuesday 19 April, forty miners from West Dean with dogs and ferrets raided a rabbit warren at Hagloe Park belonging to Edward Mortimer Clissold.[89] Consequently, local miners Albert Edmunds, Albert Turley, Walter Turley, Charles Norris, Edgar Norris, John Tay and Reuben James were arrested by the local police.[90] When spoken to, one of the defendants, a World War One veteran, said:

> If old Clissold isn't satisfied with this, he will have to lose more. We went out and fought for such as he. The rabbits are as much ours as his!

The defendants were brought before the magistrates and found guilty of day poaching and fined £2 each. A few weeks later Albert Edmunds and Reuben James were up in court for stealing chickens. Edmunds was sent to prison for three months of hard labour, but James was found not guilty.[91]

Threat to Close Collieries

At a board meeting of Henry Crawshay & Co. Ltd. held on 21 April 1921, Morgan reported that he had met with Allen and a deputation of craftsmen at Abbotswood House, warning them that if they continued to withdraw the safety men then there was a danger the Directors would wind up the company. In addition, Morgan announced that the Directors of Foxes Bridge colliery had already agreed to call an Extraordinary General Meeting on Tuesday 3 May to discuss winding up their company. Morgan said they would have to follow suit. The other Directors agreed:

87 *Daily Herald* 20 April 1921.
88 Ian Wright, *Walter Virgo and the Blakeney Gang*, (Bristol Radical History Group, Bristol, 2013).
89 Clissold was a member of Gloucestershire County Council, Chair of Awre District Council and a JP.
90 It is unclear if this was Reuben James, the ex-President of the FDMA. It is more likely it was another Reuben James who was living in West Dean and was a miner and a world war one veteran.
91 *Gloucester Citizen* 29 June 1921.

Forest of Dean colliers.

that Foxes Bridge having taken the lead, we have no choice but to follow on the same lines.[92]

Creagh proposed that similar notices be sent out to their shareholders, inviting them to meet at the Wellington Hotel, Gloucester, on 4 May for the purpose of proposing the desirability of winding up the company. The proposal was passed unanimously. At the same meeting, the manager of Eastern United reported that the clerical staff were managing to keep the colliery functioning. In complimenting these staff, Creagh said:

> Their energy, endurance and cheerfulness were wonderful and they had put their regular men in the shade.[93]

Standing for the Original Demands

On Friday 22 April, Booth attended a national delegate conference of the MFGB with a mandate from his members to argue:

> That provided a national wages board and a national pool, as understood in the settlement of the 1920 strike, be guaranteed,

92 Board Minute Book of Henry Crawshay & Co. Ltd. Ltd (O) 1919-1921.
93 Ibid.

we are prepared to take a uniform reduction in wages, such reductions to be consistent with the decreased cost of living.[94]

The conference received reports from all the districts and they overwhelmingly agreed to stick with their original demands. However, many delegates vented their anger at Hodges, and it was reported that:

> there poured forth a stream of repudiations of the treachery of all those who took part in Black Friday and declared that we look to you again to proclaim your intention of standing for the original demands.[95]

However, despite the efforts of Ablett and other militants, the tactic of withdrawing the safety men as a national policy was not re-introduced. The Forest men were becoming even more isolated and their money was running out. Strike pay of 10s a week for adult men, 5s for youths and 1s for boys, with an addition of 1s 6d per child, was paid out for the first three weeks to FDMA members, but now the union's funds were exhausted.[96] The craftsmen had no funds to pay out strike pay as their organisation was new. However, the Forest miners shared out the money they received from the MFGB with the craftsmen. Nearly all the miners' organisations across the country were now insolvent. Families were beginning to run out of food.

On 22 April, a meeting was held in Cinderford, consisting of representatives of the local churches and chapels, to raise funds to provide meals for the children of miners.[97] The religious organisations' relief fund in Cinderford was chaired by George Rowlinson and included members who were colliery owners. The organisers gave strict instructions to the volunteers to only provide food for children of school age.[98] In addition, the FDMA negotiated credit with the local Cooperative Society and other shops who were invited to a meeting on Monday 25 April at Speech House to discuss arrangements for the introduction of a credit coupon scheme.[99] The key element in the ability of the miners to stay out was the role of women in fundraising, organising soup kitchens and feeding the children.

---

94 *Dean Forest Mercury* 22 April 1921.
95 *Gloucester Journal* 23 April 1921.
96 *Dean Forest Mercury* 22 April 1921.
97 Ibid.
98 *Dean Forest Mercury* 6 May 1921.
99 Ibid.

Feeding the children at Bilson School, 1921.

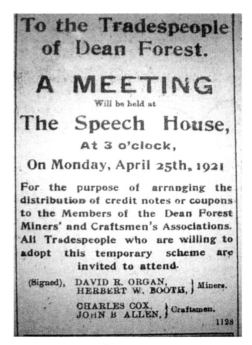

To the Tradespeople of Dean Forest.

A MEETING

Will be held at

The Speech House,

At 3 o'clock,

On Monday, April 25th, 1921

For the purpose of arranging the distribution of credit notes or coupons to the Members of the Dean Forest Miners' and Craftsmen's Associations. All Tradespeople who are willing to adopt this temporary scheme are invited to attend.

(Signed), DAVID R. ORGAN, } Miners.
HERBERT W. BOOTH, }

CHARLES COX, } Craftsmen.
JOHN B ALLEN, }

1128

Notice of coupon meeting.

Coal Embargo

On the 22 April, the Executives of the NTWF and the NUR met and decided to place an embargo on the handling of imported coal, and the NUR instructed its members to refuse to move coal from colliery sidings.[100] On Sunday 24 April, a meeting at the picture house in Lydney attracted several hundred people to hear Charlie Cramp, the General Secretary of the NUR, attempt to justify his Executive's failure to support the miners. Francis Yeatman, chair of the Parish Council and Treasurer of the Forest of Dean Labour Party, chaired the meeting and he was joined by Organ, George Powell and Charles Howells from the Dockers Union and Edwin Rennolds, William Parslow and James Birt from the NUR. There were a large number of miners present in the audience and the atmosphere was tense.

Cramp assured the meeting that Black Friday would always be remembered as such. However, he argued that railwaymen were far more vulnerable than miners in a strike because they were more isolated and susceptible to blacklegging. He added that if any of his members lost their jobs as a result of going on strike, then they would be blacklisted from the railways. However, this only created a suggestion from the audience that if that was the case, they needed a decent trade union. He went on to say that if the call for solidarity action had been adhered to, then the response would have been magnificent. This statement produced shouts from the audience questioning why it was called off. Cramp argued that Hodges had been set up by the MPs and after he made the mistake of making a new offer, they had no choice but to call the strike off.

Cramp gave a commitment that his Executive would instruct his members not to handle any imported coal. He said he had already ordered his members to refuse to handle any coal from Forest pits or assist in its removal. He stressed that they should not become divided and there was tremendous sympathy for their plight. At this point, he was challenged from the floor by a miner who shouted out: "By still continuing to work, I suppose?" Cramp was then bombarded with more questions and comments from the floor, but he refused to say which way he voted at the crucial Triple Alliance meeting. An angry voice shouted out: "He has not told us anything". At this point Rennolds from the local NUR made it clear that his members in the locality disagreed with the behaviour of their Executive:

100 Cole, *Labour in the Coal Mining Industry*, 222.

Ninety-eight per cent of the Forest of Dean railwaymen were ready, and were ready now to come out and aid the miners. As a local engine driver, he should now refuse to take his engine into a colliery yard.[101]

Similarly, George Powell explained that one hundred per cent of local dockers at Lydney were willing to strike with the miners and refuse to handle coal. He went on to explain that he expected that his union would be sending £10,000 to help out with relief for mining families. This offer only created a response from a miner who said they wanted a solidarity strike, not charity.[102] Organ finished up by saying "all the same he was sorry that Mr Hodges had set up a situation that now faced them".[103]

Rally

The collapse of the Triple Alliance strike altered the nature of the dispute in the coalfield and now the miners prepared to dig in for a protracted test of endurance. All the resources of the mining community in the Forest of Dean were tapped into a collective endeavour. The Co-operative Societies, the chapels, the Labour Party and women's organisations came together to sustain the body and soul of the mining community, which was entirely dependent upon the community's resources. For single men, often in lodgings and with no access at all to outdoor poor law relief, their dependence upon these resources was total. A meeting of the women's section of the Pillowell and Yorkley ward of the Forest of Dean Labour Party passed the following resolution.

We extend our warmest sympathy to, and agreement with the women of the coalfields who are standing so magnificently by their men in their struggle against low wages and the threat to their standard of life. We also condemn utterly the government's disloyalty to the undertakings which it has given from time to time during the last two years and call upon them to secure without further delay a settlement of the dispute on the lines propounded by the Miners' Federation. We express our wholehearted opposition to the military measures so hurriedly and wastefully taken by the Government under the threat of a further extension

101 *Gloucester Journal* 30 April 1921.
102 *Dean Forest Mercury* 29 April 1921.
103 *Gloucester Journal* 30 April 1921.

of the dispute and declare that such preparations are a deliberate provocation of order and incitement to the workers to adopt methods of force.[104]

On Monday 25 April, a meeting was held at Speech House to discuss arrangements for the distribution of credit notes to members of the FDMA and Craftsmen Association. Allen explained the general outline of the scheme and explained that the coupons be issued weekly for a period up to one month and that the two associations had agreed to settle the account at some future date. Cinderford, Pillowell and Bream Co-operative Societies had already volunteered to join the scheme. A number of other retailers were present and agreed to throw their lot in with the miners in the hope that they would be repaid when the dispute was over. The dispute was now impacting on the whole Forest community, and the future of local businesses depended on its success.[105] A meeting of the FDMA Executive held on 27 April agreed that arrangements be made for the printing of coupons of 7s 6d for full members, 3s 9d for half members (part-time workers) and 1s per child.[106]

In addition, a relief committee was formed, with its headquarter at Cinderford Town Hall, to accept donations and arrange for the distribution of food. The chair of the committee was Enos Taylor who was a locked out miner and represented Foxes Bridge colliery on the FDMA committee.[107]

On the afternoon of Monday 25 April, the largest rally yet was held at Speech House with three brass bands from Cinderford, Pillowell and Yorkley. Processions were held along all the main roads to Speech House. Women made up a significant proportion of the assembly, and the Yorkley Women's Labour Party had their red flag flying. The main speakers were Cox and Allen from the Craftsmen Association and Organ and William Vedmore from the FDMA. Booth was in London at an MFGB delegate conference. Reports were heard from delegates from all the main pits, all of whom said their members were still solidly behind the strike.[108]

William Vedmore worked at Parkend Royal Colliery and represented the pit on the FDMA Executive Committee and had been a delegate at the recent MFGB conference on Friday 22 April. He reported that the

104 *Dean Forest Mercury* 29 April 1921.
105 Ibid.
106 FDMA Minutes 27 April 1921.
107 *Dean Forest Mercury* 29 April 1921.
108 Ibid.

conference had passed a resolution in support of Hodges and condemned the actions of the other two members of the Triple Alliance. Allen made the point the colliery owners had made huge profits during World War One when coal was in such high demand:

> The owners had done very well during the war, and I suppose it would not be a bad thing for them to extend a little charity to get over this period. The men would live longer, if they had to starve, enjoying God's sunshine than they would at 8s 6d a shift for it would not provide energy sufficient for their work to be done.[109]

In fact, the Sankey Commission revealed that owners' profit had risen by over 200 per cent during the war in contrast to miners' wages which had risen by about 100 per cent, just about keeping up with the cost of living.[110] Allen pointed out a request had been made to the Forest school managers to put in force legislation to provide free school meals for miners' children. In addition, he announced that Eastman's butchers from Cinderford would be making a distribution of bread during the week.[111]

In late April, Francis Yeatman, chair of the Parish Council, called a meeting of leading members of the community in Lydney and Aylburton to elect a committee to help deal with the distress in the area. The Directors of Richard Thomas and Company donated £50 to help relieve the distress of 400 unemployed tin plate workers in Lydney.[112] Lord Bledisloe donated some firewood from his Lydney Park Estate. Yeatmen, who was elected chairman of the committee, said: "his Lordship's beneficence was very much appreciated". [113]

However, Bledisloe was not so keen on those in distress poaching rabbits on his land. In August, Frank Legge, an unemployed Aylburton tin worker, was fined 10 shillings for trespassing in search of rabbits on Lydney Park Estate.[114] According to Harry Roberts, some families were forced to leave the area:

> Some men took their families out of the Forest to get work in another part of the country. One man, in particular, took his wife and children to work for the Crittal Window Company at

109 Ibid.
110 Ibid.
111 *Gloucester Journal* 30 April 1921.
112 *Gloucester Citizen* 28 April 1921.
113 *Gloucester Journal* 7 May 1921.
114 *Gloucester Journal* September 1921.

Braintree in Essex. Others went to Cheltenham to work on the railways, one went to Wolverhampton, and others to Yorkshire.[115]

Government Offer

On 26 April, the government put forward an offer of a £10 million subsidy to allow reductions in wages to be made gradually, but still insisted on district settlements and no pool.[116] On Thursday 28 April, Booth attended another national delegate conference of the MFGB with a mandate to continue with the strike. A card vote resulted in all the districts except Northumberland voting to reject the government's offer.[117]

Booth reported back on the details of the delegate conference to a mass meeting of miners and craftsmen at Speech House the next day, explaining there was little possibility of a settlement. He pointed out that the miners in the more productive districts such as Yorkshire and Leicestershire could easily return to work and negotiate an acceptable local deal but remained out on strike in solidarity with the more deprived districts like the Forest of Dean.

Booth explained that the MFGB Executive had now fully exonerated Hodges and that the failure of the Triple Alliance lay with the NUR and the NTWF who had tried to blame Hodges. However, he pointed out that the leaders of the NUR and NTWF were not solely to blame as he had discovered there were piles of resolutions from NUR and NTWF branches refusing to come out in sympathy with the miners or demanding a ballot first.[118]

He went on to explain that the meeting had to decide if they supported the decision of the delegate conference, warning that to continue the strike would mean much distress and suffering. In response, a resolution approving the action of the delegate conference was enthusiastically carried.[119] A resolution from the women of the Coleford and District section of the Labour Party:

pledged themselves to do everything in their power to assist the miners in their struggle, and call upon the miners to stand until victory is won.[120]

115 Harry Roberts, *Memoirs*, Gage Library.
116 *Daily Herald* 27 April 1921.
117 Cole, *Labour in the Coal Mining Industry*, 225.
118 *Dean Forest Mercury* 29 April 1921.
119 Ibid.
120 Ibid.

On the same day, a mass meeting of the Craftsmen Association at Speech House agreed to seek affiliation with the MFGB through the FDMA. On Saturday afternoon a meal of cold beef and bread was provided at Lydney Assembly rooms for 500 children of locked out miners and unemployed tin workers. The money had been raised through friendly football matches. On Monday 2 May, a special meeting of the Forest of Dean Council of School Managers passed a resolution calling on the Education Authority to provide meals for those children attending an elementary school whose education was suffering as a result of hunger. Members of the Council of School Managers included locked out miners Martin Perkins and Enos Taylor.[121]

Internationalism and Fraternity

The day before, a well-attended May Day rally at Speech House began after the arrival of a large procession from West Dean headed by the Berry Hill Silver Band. The meeting was chaired by Organ and speakers included Wignall, Booth, Allen and Yeatman. Booth suggested the men try and ignore the propaganda campaign in the press, which was being funded by the MAGB and the Federation of British Industry. He warned them that if they accepted the government's offer of a temporary subsidy they would be back in the same place as they were now when it ran out after a few months. He went on to press the case for internationalism arguing that:

> they could not have national or international peace until the whole of the miners throughout the world acted as one body, and as it had taken years of agitation and suffering in Great Britain to build up the Miners' Federation, so it would take years of agitation and struggle to build up an international body.[122]

Allen related the story of an attempt by a local minister to ask for funds from one of the local colliery owners to provide food for hungry women and children. Allen said the colliery owner refused to give a penny and went on to blame the Craftsmen Association for causing the hunger by refusing to work.[123] The women present again called upon the miners to stand firm. Yeatman explained he belonged to the fraternity of tradespeople

121 *Gloucester Citizen* 30 April 1921 and *Dean Forest Mercury* 29 April 1921.
122 *Dean Forest Mercury* 6 May 1921.
123 *Gloucester Citizen* 2 May 1921.

in the Forest of Dean and it was his duty, honour and privilege to stand with miners celebrating May Day. He argued:

> this fight was one waged on behalf of the whole industrial working class, and if the colliers went down, they would go down too.[124]

On Wednesday 4 May, a joint shareholders' meeting of Foxes Bridge and Company and Henry Crawshay & Co. Ltd. held in Gloucester passed the following resolution:

> In consideration of the uncertainty of continuing to conduct the company's collieries on a remunerative basis brought about by the governments mishandling of the coal industry and the apparent indifference of the miners as to its future, we hereby confer on our Board of Directors full powers to act at their discretion, and if necessary, take steps to wind up the Company.[125]

At about this time, Booth discovered that a small mine at Leechpool on Lord Bledisloe's estate, worked by a free miner, Simeon James, with about a dozen hands, was still working.[126] On 7 May, Booth attended the colliery and got an agreement from James that no more coal would be raised until the end of the dispute.[127]

Coal Embargo

On Saturday 30 April, Bristol dock workers walked out on strike in solidarity with the miners after they were asked to unload a Bristol steamship, carrying general cargo but burning German coal, which had arrived overnight from Antwerp.[128] However, a ballot was held the following Tuesday resulting in the men returning to work.[129] On Wednesday 4 May, Wignall spoke in the House of Commons warning the government of the consequences of attempting to import coal under

---

124 *Dean Forest Mercury* 6 May 1921.
125 *Gloucestershire Chronicle* 7 May 1921.
126 Lydney Park Estate is not part of the Statutory Forest and so is not subject to free mining rights under the 1838 Dean Forest Mines Act. However, Lord Bledisloe allowed free miners to work the reserves provided they paid him royalties. The James family ran a successful mining operation there for many years before it was taken over by Don and Gilbert Kear. Thanks to Jonathan Wright from Clearwell Caves for providing this information.
127 *Dean Forest Mercury* 6 May 1921.
128 *Western Daily Press* 2 May 1921 and 3 May 1921.
129 *Western Daily Press* 4 May 1921

the Emergency Powers Act, arguing that the dispute up to now had been relatively peaceful. He warned:

certainly, there would be resistance to anything in the nature of importing coal by refusing to handle it.[130]

In some ports, rank and file dockers had already refused to handle the coal and successfully prevented it from being unloaded. In other ports, the coal had been unloaded using blackleg labour. In Glasgow for example, on Saturday 7 May, the Scottish Union of Dock Labourers broke with the policy of the NTWF and called its members out on strike. On the same day, wage reductions were imposed on merchant seamen, leading to a well-supported general strike at the docks in Glasgow which lasted for over a month.[131] In response, the military was called in to guard blackleg labour and on 7 May, the following statement was issued by the NTWF:

The Federation anxious to assist the Miners' Federation of Great Britain to promote a satisfactory settlement of the existing lockout have instructed all sections engaged in loading, discharging and manning of all ships conveying coal from abroad to Great Britain to refuse in any way to work this foreign coal.[132]

Outcropping

One extra source of income for striking miners came from small-scale opencast mining of the outcrop, where a seam of coal comes to the surface. The coal was accessed by digging by hand and was hefty work as it sometimes involved removing soil to a depth of twelve feet. Desperate to raise extra cash, some miners had started outcropping at Woorgreen, Delving Wood, Crab Tree Hill and Cockshutt. According to the *Gloucester Citizen* at Woorgreen "the scene resembled a well-mined battlefield". On Thursday 5 May, a steam locomotive from Quedgeley drawing two trailers was loaded with twelve tons of house coal and sold in Gloucester for £2 a ton. Another customer during that week was East Dean Rural District Council whose stock at the waterworks pumping station was near to exhaustion.[133]

130 *Gloucester Citizen* 5 May 1921 and *Dean Forest Mercury* 6 May 1921.
131 *Gloucester Citizen* 7 May 1921.
132 *Northern Whig* 9 May 1921.
133 *Gloucester Citizen* 7 May 1921.

Outcropping was common during miners' strikes, and the unions were usually not concerned if the coal was for the miners' use. However, in this case, there was clear profiteering and the majority of locked out miners could not allow a few to take financial advantage of the situation. As a result, the FDMA posted notices instructing the men that all outcropping must stop by Saturday.[134] Harry Roberts reported that another source of coal was in the mounds of colliery waste:

> The unemployed miners soon got to work digging over the dirt mounds for small coal. One area turned over was the edge of a wood by Crump Meadow field, the Monkey Wood, and it was here where a heap of ground about a hundred and fifty-foot square, three-foot-high, covered with grass, was dug over for the coal contained in it. It must have been part of the Crump Meadow dirt mound, and the proportion of coal to dirt was good. It was an offence against company rules to send up even small quantities of dirt with coal, so if a shovel contained only a handful of dirt and the rest of it coal, it would either be thrown into the gob or brought out to be tipped. Consequently, the dirt mounds contained a good proportion of coal. The men with picks and shovels turned over the dirt and picked up each individual lump of coal by hand to fill the sacks to be taken away by wheelbarrows or horse and cart.[135]

> At seven years of age, I went to Crump Meadow where coal was being got. My two uncles who had got a large heap of coal recognised me and put a large shovel full of coal into my sack and sent me on my way, I half carried and dragged my burden home.[136]

Fight to the Bitter End

By now, some families had run out of money and food. The FDMA arranged that from Monday 9 May each union member would get a voucher, but this was not enough to feed a family. The state of affairs was exacerbated by a large number of Forest miners who had migrated to work in pits in South Wales and now returned to the Forest, often hungry and

134 Ibid.
135 Anstis, *Blood on Coal*, 105.
136 Harry Roberts, *The Tar Castle*, Gage Library, 7.

dependent on family members. This added to the burden of local attempts to provide relief to those without food. The churches managed to raise about £500 in an attempt to provide a daily meal for at least 1500 miners' children. Clearly, this was also inadequate.

At the monthly meeting of Monmouth Board of Guardians, some colliers and their families presented themselves for relief, arguing they were on the point of starvation. Some of these men had fought in World War One. The families were represented by Tom Liddington, a Labour West Dean District Councillor from Viney Hill and former member of the British Socialist Party. However, single men had no entitlement to relief outside of the workhouse and one of the Guardians, T.W. King, said:

> If this is a land fit for heroes to live in, are we going to put men in the workhouse after they went out and fought for us?

Fortunately for the applicants with families, a member of the Board of Guardians, Charles Luker, who was a locked-out miner and member of the FDMA Executive, argued for a temporary loan. As a result, several families were lent 15s and 2s 6d for each child to help them out until they were issued with traders' coupons.[137]

Six Weeks

The miners had now been locked out for nearly six weeks. On Monday 9 May, Organ, Booth and Allen attempted to raise morale at another mass meeting at Speech House. Booth reminded the men that they were out for six weeks in 1912 and had won a guaranteed minimum wage.[138] Organ argued:

> They were now approaching the testing time. If they had grit in them, they must show it. They were bound to win if they stuck it a little longer and then fight it to the bitter end and so finish it off.[139]

Lloyd George's recent speech at Maidstone was severely criticised for making no concessions and insisting the government would oppose a national pool. The meeting expressed appreciation for the support of

137 *Dean Forest Mercury* 6 May 1921.
138 *Dean Forest Mercury* 13 May 1921.
139 *Gloucester Citizen* 9 and 10 May 1921.

religious bodies for organising relief committees and for the Co-operative Society and traders for supplying credit backed by the union. The meeting agreed that they would only go back to work when forced into submission by starvation. Rumours that the MFGB Executive wanted to organise a national ballot were condemned from the floor:

> We have had our ballot. We don't want to go back until there is an agreed settlement.[140]

A motion was passed committing every Forest trade unionist to refuse to work the outcrop coal except for domestic purposes. Reuben James said he had heard of a couple of lorries arriving at Bream and taking coal from some small workings. He had enquired and was told they would stop if others did likewise.[141] On 10 May, a meeting of the FDMA Executive voted to allow the craftsmen to affiliate to the MFGB and the FDMA, provided there would be no transfer of membership or funds for twelve months and the organisations to remain separate until then.[142]

On 12 May, the miners were shocked by the announcement from Lord Bledisloe in the *Gloucester Citizen* that he was going to move a resolution at the next director's meeting on 18 May to close down Howbeach for good. Bledisloe argued the pumping operations were proving expensive and the change in the economic climate meant that further investment in development was too risky.[143] On 13 May the *Gloucester Citizen* reported:

> The Executive of the NUR announced on 13 May that it had instructed its members to refuse to handle imported coal no matter what purpose it is intended. They further instructed their members not to handle any coal that was handled or loaded by blackleg labour.[144]

Hunger

On Saturday 14 May, a meeting of Cinderford Cooperative Society discussed the deteriorating situation regarding distress and hunger in the district. Enos Taylor, who was chairman of the central distress fund,

140 Ibid.
141 Ibid.
142 FDMA Minutes 10 May 1921.
143 *Gloucester Citizen* 12 May 1921.
144 *Gloucester Citizen* 13 May 1921.

reported that it had spent £350, of which £100 came from Cinderford Cooperative Society and the rest from private traders and individuals. Several other members of the Cinderford Cooperative Society committee were locked out miners. The meeting agreed to offer £500 to the distress fund.[145]

The next meeting of miners at Speech House, held on 14 May, was the smallest since the start of the lockout. Booth, Organ, Allen and Charles Cox were the main speakers. The meeting was the second that week, and there were no new developments to report. A resolution was passed to reject an appeal from a coal merchant in Hereford to supply small consignments of coal to run bakeries, gas works and infirmaries in Herefordshire. A resolution was passed attacking Bledisloe for his proposal to close down Howbeach.[146] Booth reported on a statement from a woman who held shares in a local colliery and also owned houses in the Forest that she rented out to families of miners in which she said:

I have miner tenants that are better off than I am in many ways, for not a single wish in their simple lives has gone ungratified. They have beautiful cottages and many of them have little farms.[147]

This statement caused a great deal of laughter and Booth reminded the audience of the recent report made by Mr L.G. Lyne, the Sanitary Inspector to East Dean Council, which described the poor state of housing in the Forest of Dean.[148] The issue of outcropping was raised again, and it was noted that it was an irritant and causing bad feeling. A strong resolution was passed:

calling on all workmen so engaged to cease operations, or stronger measures would be taken to bring about a cessation of these activities.[149]

The *Dean Forest Mercury* reported that the government had gone to the expense of putting propaganda posters up on hoardings throughout the Forest encouraging the men to return to work. The paper added that there was not a single poster that had not been defaced or destroyed.[150] On Sunday

145 *Dean Forest Mercury* 20 May 1921.
146 Ibid.
147 Ibid.
148 See chapter one.
149 *Gloucester Journal* 21 May 1921.
150 *Dean Forest Mercury* 20 May 1921.

15 May, the Lydney churches reported they had raised £300 for the distress fund and helped out 70 families. The committee stated they had not been able to get into contact with some of the more desperate cases.[151]

On Friday 20 May, a meeting was held at Bilson Green in Cinderford and chaired by Jesse Hodges (Snr) who expressed concern about the working of the outcrops which meant that some men were doing better than others. The sale of the coal for profit infringed communal values and solidarity and Hodges argued if coal was being sent out of the district it could prolong the struggle. Booth said there was no objection to the men getting coal for themselves, but he appealed to the men not to sell to intermediaries or supply coal for commercial purposes. The meeting reported that there were rumours that a handful of non-union men were working at Eastern United. The men then marched to Crab Tree Hill to speak to men working the outcrop and persuaded them to stop. It was significant that neither Allen nor Cox attended the meeting or sent an apology. [152]

A meeting of miners and craftsmen was held at Speech House on Monday 23 May. However, the number of miners present was less than usual. It was clear that morale was low and the government had the upper hand.[153] The issue of outcropping at Woorgreen came up again. As a result, at the end of the meeting, a group of men and women accompanied by the Pillowell brass band walked over to Woorgreen where they discovered a lorry being loaded with coal. Some of the out-croppers were confronted and there was an argument. Men and women from the Speech House meeting scattered the coal with the result that outcroppings were discontinued and the lorry left empty.[154]

On 23 May, after the campaign by the members of the Forest of Dean School Board, Gloucestershire County Council agreed that miners' children be given a free school meal. As a result, a midday meal was provided for children at 19 different sites, amounting to about one thousand meals a day.[155] Forest miner Ted Gwilliam recalls:

I remember very well the children during the 1921 strike having to go to Five Acres School to have their dinner which was soup.[156]

151 Ibid.
152 *Dean Forest Mercury* 20 May 1921.
153 *Gloucester Citizen* 23 May 1921.
154 *Dean Forest Mercury* 27 May 1921.
155 *Gloucester Citizen* 23 May 1921, *Gloucestershire Chronicle* 28 May 1921 and *Dean Forest Mercury* 27 May 1921.
156 Anstis, *Blood on Coal*, 106.

Pillowell Recreation Ground. The photograph was taken during the levelling of the ground by the local community during the lockout.

The summer of 1921 was very hot and some miners took advantage of the sunshine to do work for the community. Lord Bledisloe owned large tracts of land around his country estate just outside Lydney. In 1919, he gave a piece of land to the inhabitants of Pillowell to create a recreation ground. During the lockout, a group of local miners devoted themselves to levelling the ground and creating an open space for children and a field for sport and leisure activities for the community of Pillowell.[157]

New Offer

On Friday 27 May, the government announced another offer based on an arrangement to subsidise a gradual scaling down of wages until they reached an economic level that the industry was capable of sustaining and, in addition, proposed arbitration on a permanent scheme. However, the government made it clear there would be no pool, and any agreement

157 The People of Pillowell, *Pillowell* (Yorkley: Yorkley A&E, 2017) 12.

would be done on a district basis. Lloyd George also warned both parties that if they could not agree then he would introduce legislation to enforce compulsory arbitration. On the 28 May, the MFGB decided to refer the offer to the districts for their views.[158]

On Monday 30 May, a meeting of miners and craftsmen at Speech House, supported by the Pillowell brass band, discussed the government's proposals.[159] Allen was not able to attend due to an "unspecified indisposition". Booth and Organ warned the meeting that the poor conditions in the Forest of Dean would mean the economic level would be so low that they would never get a living wage. It was decided that a full response would be agreed upon at a mass meeting arranged for the following Thursday. Organ said he hoped they would turn the proposal down and stick with the original MFGB demands. At that point an exchange took place between Organ and a woman in the crowd who shouted:

"We will have them, Mr Organ",
Organ replied, "You are prepared to go on then Mrs Jones?"
She replied, "Ah! That I be."[160]

Sharpness

Trouble continued throughout May and early June. A considerable number of men around the country were suspended for refusing to handle coal and there was conflict in the majority of ports. Foreign coal was being imported into a majority of the British ports, some sixty in all, including the Thames, Mersey, Clyde, Forth and Humber ports, Southampton, Bristol and Sharpness. The quantity of foreign coal imported during May was 450,162 tons.[161]

Forest coal was regularly transported over the Severn railway bridge to Sharpness docks and, as a result, the Sharpness dockers, local railway workers and Forest miners had strong connections. On Saturday 4 June, the *Gloucester Journal* reported that Sharpness dockers were refusing to handle imported coal. Some railwaymen had alleged that blackleg labour had been employed to unload a cargo of coal from Belgium. The men contacted the NUR headquarters and were advised by Cramp not to handle the coal. As a result, three Sharpness shunters and Arthur Holder, President of the local

158 Cole, *Labour in the Coal Mining Industry*, 229.
159 *Gloucester Citizen* 30 May 1921 and *Dean Forest Mercury* 3 June 1921.
160 *Dean Forest Mercury* 3 June 1921.
161 *Hansard* 13 June 1921 Vol. 143 14-15.

Triple Alliance Strike Committee, were suspended. Consequently, other guards refused to work the train and were also suspended. In the end, inspectors carried out the work under police protection.[162]

The high level of suspensions on the railways, now standing at 72 men nationally, and the use of blackleg labour on the docks meant that the government could keep the supplies of coal on the move. As a result, on 31 May, the NUR and NTWF lifted the embargo on handling imported coal.[163] In spite of this, Glasgow dockers remained on strike in solidarity with the miners.[164]

Pressure on the Craftsmen[165]

Neither Allen nor Cox had attended the last two mass meetings and it was clear to everyone something was going on. Over the last few weeks, Allen had become aware that there were rumblings of dissent among some of his members. As a result, he was caught between a rock and a hard place as he was committed to representing his members and having to accept their democratic mandate, while at the same time honouring the agreement that he had made with the FDMA.

At the start of the lockout, the decision to join the strike had been made by Allen and his Executive after consulting the membership in a hand vote. The craftsmen then agreed with the FDMA to elect joint committees to meet, discuss tactics and organise mass meetings together, while accepting that each organisation could manage their affairs independently. They agreed to keep each other informed of any developments and consult with each other over any decisions which would impact on each other's organisation. In fact, very early on during the dispute, the craftsmen applied to re-join the FDMA and MFGB.

However, bringing out the safety men in the Forest of Dean had far more severe consequences than for most other areas of the country. As a result of the flooding, Allen had been subject to severe criticism from the colliery owners and their supporters in the press who claimed that he was the sole cause of all the trouble by bringing his members out and putting the pits at risk. They blamed him rather than his Executive and his members or even the FDMA and miners. Consequently, he had to deal

162 *Gloucester Journal* 4 June 1921.
163 *Gloucester Journal* 4 June 1921.
164 *Daily Herald* 03 June 1921.
165 The account of these events involving Allen and the craftsmen is dealt with in detail in *Dean Forest Mercury* 10 June 1921 when it reported Allen's explanation for his actions in response to recent events at a mass meeting of miners on Monday 6 June.

with threats and abuse and shoulder this burden alone. Now he feared he was in danger of losing the support of some of his members who had become critical of his leadership.

Some of the concerns felt by the craftsmen had legitimacy. Unlike the miners, the craftsmen did not have the opportunity to express their views through a full ballot. In addition, except in the case of Cannop colliery, the managers, volunteer labour, overmen, colliery inspectors and office staff had successfully kept the pumps going. Some craftsmen felt this undermined the main reason for withdrawing their labour, which was to apply extra pressure on the colliery owners to get a quick settlement. In addition, they claimed that this was hindered by the MFGB decision to ask their members not to picket or interfere with the voluntary labour who were now doing their jobs.

Over the last two weeks the colliery owners, led by Arthur Morgan, had approached some craftsmen whom they identified as weak links in the solidarity shown by the miners and the majority of the craftsmen. Morgan set about trying to break this solidarity by attempting to persuade a few craftsmen to go back to work. He informed the craftsmen that they had brought in skilled labour from Bristol to run the pumps in the Crawshay pits. Then Morgan approached a member of the craftsmen's Executive and told him that unless the craftsmen returned to work within a week, they would lose their jobs, and they would retain the services of those they had employed from Bristol.

Allen claimed he first heard about this when he started receiving anonymous letters warning him about the approaches the colliery owners were making to his members. At first, he ignored them, but became concerned when one letter said:

Watch, Carefully. A certain colliery owner and colliery manager are going to make overtures to get some of your members to return to work. Destroy this letter.[166]

After Allen received the anonymous letter, he phoned Morgan and asked him if he had made overtures to members of his Executive. Morgan said that was none of his business but warned that he had better come and see him.

166 *Dean Forest Mercury,* 10 June 1921

Allen then discovered that Charles Morgan, the manager at Eastern United colliery, had made contact with a member of his Executive and persuaded him to organise a meeting of craftsmen at Ruspidge on 30 May. Allen was not informed about the meeting but decided to attend, which was the reason for him missing the Speech House meeting on the same day. When he arrived, he found that the meeting was well attended and that Charles Morgan was warning the men that they had employed some "very efficient men from Bristol" to operate the pumps. Charles Morgan repeated the threat that if they did not return to work within a week, they would lose their jobs and they would keep the Bristol men on permanently. Allen was now in no doubt that there was a deeply laid plot to induce a section of men from all over the Forest of Dean to return to work.

That evening, he decided to go and see Arthur Morgan at his home at Abbotswood House. He took along Leonard Morgan, a member of the Craftsmen Executive, as a witness. At the meeting, Arthur Morgan told Allen he had been approached by some craftsmen about a return to work and now he wanted to negotiate the terms and conditions with him. Allen claimed that he refused to discuss this any further and left after half an hour.

The atmosphere in the Forest was tense as rumour fuelled rumour. Some miners became suspicious of Allen's loyalty after hearing a rumour he had accepted a lift home from Charles Morgan in his car after the Ruspidge meeting. The situation was exacerbated when he did not inform Booth and the FDMA Executive about these events. However, Booth was aware something was going on as Allen had not attended the meetings at Bilson Green on 20 May nor at Speech House on 30 May. Some miners then told Booth that they had seen Allen and Leonard Morgan coming out of Abbotswood house on Monday evening. When Thomas Etheridge, the full-time paid Financial Secretary of the FDMA, asked Allen the next day if he had been at Abbotswood House, he denied it.

On Wednesday 1 June, Booth heard a rumour that the craftsmen had made an application to go back to work at the Crawshay controlled pits of Lightmoor, Eastern United, Trafalgar and Foxes Bridge. As a result, Booth summoned a meeting of the FDMA Executive who expressed concern, particularly as a small number of the craftsmen were still FDMA members.

The miners were now becoming more isolated, strike money had run out and they were thrown back onto their own resources, becoming more dependent for help from within their communities. Despite this, a meeting of the representatives of the whole of the coalfield was held at Speech House on Thursday 2 June to discuss the government's recent offer when:

> it was unanimously decided to send a message that the Dean Forest workmen, totalling about seven thousand hands, had entirely rejected the scheme.[167]

On 3 June, the MFGB Executive met and reported that every district had pronounced against acceptance, with the result that Lloyd George threatened to withdraw the offer of the ten million pounds subsidy made in April.[168]

Rumours

On Saturday 4 June, the *Gloucester Journal* reported rumours that the Craftsmen Association had opened negotiations with the local colliery owners to arrange a return to work.[169] As a result, the meeting of miners and craftsmen at Speech House on Monday 6 June was very tense. Booth confronted Allen about his failure to attend the recent meetings and the rumours that the craftsmen intended to return to work.

Allen responded that there was no compulsion to attend meetings and that his obligation was to the craftsmen. He insisted on their right to manage their affairs independently and went on to argue that the recent offer from the government made to the MFGB only concerned the miners, which created problems for his members because they did not know where they stood. However, Allen agreed that the two unions had a responsibility to collaborate and no partner should take separate action without consulting the other. He accepted that if there was an attempt by the craftsmen to return to work the FDMA should be consulted. He went on to acknowledge the miners had given some of the MFGB strike money to the craftsmen and expressed his appreciation. He said that he was fully aware of the kind of underhand methods used by the owners of the collieries because while he was working in Cumberland the colliery owners had sent the police around to raid his house.

Booth was not convinced Allen was telling the whole truth and raised the issue of the visit to Abbotswood House and his initial denial

167 *Gloucester Citizen* 2 June 1921.
168 Cole, *Labour in the Coal Mining Industry*, 230.
169 *Gloucester Citizen* 6 June 1921.

to Etheridge that he had been there. Allen responded by insisting he had not denied it to Etheridge, that he was at Abbotswood house, but denied he was there negotiating a return to work. Leonard Morgan confirmed Allen's version of events. In the end, a vote of confidence was passed for Allen, Leonard Morgan and Etheridge. Finally, Allen said he hoped this unpleasantness would not produce any disunity in their ranks. A request by Lord Bledisloe to provide 12 workmen to dismantle Howbeach Colliery was discussed and turned down.

Final Ballot

The Forest miners were becoming increasingly isolated and in danger of being divided. The MFGB Executive were desperately trying to come up with a settlement that was acceptable to all sides and hoped their members could be persuaded to reconsider their position. The government's and owners' offer was extended to include a new standard minimum wage based on the wages paid in 1914 with a minimum of a 20 per cent increase on the 1914 base rate. However, there would be no pool and wages were to be determined locally.[170]

A national delegate conference of the MFGB met in London on Friday 10 June to discuss the terms of the offer. Over two hundred delegates representing 958,000 members attended the meeting. A motion was passed to ballot all members on the offer. However, a motion to advise members to reject the offer was defeated, and so no recommendation would be made on the ballot paper. It was agreed that a two-thirds majority would be needed to continue the action.[171] The delegates were warned that if the ballot rejected the offer Lloyd George would remove his proposal of a temporary subsidy.

At the meeting at Speech House on Monday 13 June, there was a concern that Allen was absent again. In his opening address, Organ gave his opinion that they should reject the offer. However, he warned the men:

They had got to bear in mind if they rejected the terms it would mean they must be starved into submission.[172]

Booth advised that it was MFGB policy to make no recommendation and that the rank and file workmen should have a free vote. He made it

170 Cole, *Labour in the Coal Mining Industry*, 231.
171 Ibid. 232.
172 *Dean Forest Mercury* 10 June 1921.

clear that it was up to them if they wanted to continue with the strike. He said:

> They had to face the fact that neither the government nor the owners had given way, and that was the serious aspect of it. In spite of the extraordinary solidarity with which the struggle had been conducted by the miners, they were in this position—that the government and the mine owners had deviated very little from the position they took up at the end of March last, and due significance had to be given to that fact.[173]

Nevertheless, the meeting cast a vote unanimously against the settlement on the terms offered.[174] The ballot took place on Thursday 16 June, and the papers reported that they were confident that the Foresters would maintain their militant reputation.[175] Allen told the *Dean Forest Mercury* that the craftsmen did not run a ballot because if it came up with a different result, then that would only create deadlock and conflict. He added he did not attend the last meeting because he was away for the weekend.[176]

The result of the national ballot was announced on Saturday 18 June, resulting in a majority in favour of staying out with 180,724 in favour of accepting the colliery owners' terms and 435,614 in favour of continuing the fight.[177] In the Forest of Dean, a larger majority voted in favour of continuing to stay out with 5,222 against accepting the colliery owners' terms and 659 for the terms. This result was the highest in percentage terms, at 88.79 per cent, compared to all the other districts. In the past, ballots had been organised at the pitheads but this time they were organised at each individual lodge. This meant that every miner had an opportunity to vote even if they were not at work on the day of the ballot. As a result, the turnout of votes cast, at 98 per cent, was the highest of all districts, meaning nearly every miner in the Forest of Dean voted.[178] Lloyd George, true to his word, withdrew the offer of the subsidy.[179]

The rules of the MFGB were ambiguous, as it was unclear if they required a two-thirds majority of the votes cast or of the total membership

173 Ibid.
174 *Gloucester Citizen* 13 June 1921.
175 *Gloucester Citizen* 16 June 1921.
176 *Dean Forest Mercury* 24 June 1921.
177 Cole, *Labour in the Coal Mining Industry*, 232.
178 *Dean Forest Mercury* 24 June 1921.
179 Cole, *Labour in the Coal Mining Industry*, 232.

to continue the strike. This was the case in the first instance, but not in the second. As a result, the MFGB was split over how to proceed, with the militants arguing that the Executive should accept the result and intensify the campaign. However, Hodges and Smith argued that they had no choice but to accept the government's offer.

The End

In the Forest, at a mass meeting on Saturday 18 June, gratitude was expressed by Booth and Organ at the huge turnout for the ballot and the commitment of the Forest miners to continue the fight. On the negative side, Booth pointed out that a significant minority of miners in other districts had voted to accept the employers' offer. On the positive side, Booth went on to say that some areas like Yorkshire still had a majority in favour of continuing the struggle despite the fact they would get a far better deal in a district settlement than areas like the Forest.[180] However, in other parts of the country, such as Nottingham and Cannock Chase, some miners were beginning to return to work.[181]

Allen was still having problems with the colliery owners targeting his members. At a meeting of West Dean craftsmen at the Miners' Arms in Whitecroft chaired by Cox, Allen reported that on 21 June, the manager of Eastern United, Charles Morgan, had set up a meeting at Eastern United with five stokers from the pit who were members of the Craftsmen Association and encouraged them to return to work. He added that he immediately called a meeting of the craftsmen from Eastern to prevent a return to work. The meeting was well attended but only one of the five stokers put in an appearance and he refused to give out any information about the meeting with Charles Morgan, claiming he was sworn to secrecy. However, another craftsman reported that Charles Morgan had made a verbal offer that if the craftsmen returned now, they would receive the same rate of wages they were paid in March.[182]

The West Dean craftsmen agreed that they viewed this as an attack on their organisation and an attempt to break the solidarity between themselves and the miners. As a result, they resolved to arrange a demonstration with other branches of the Association at Eastern United at 5am on Monday 27 June to attempt to dissuade the men from returning to work. Allen reported that a meeting of the Cinderford branch of the

180 *Dean Forest Mercury* 24 June 1921.
181 *Western Morning News* 20 June 1921.
182 *Dean Forest Mercury* 24 June 1921.

Craftsmen Association would be arranged at the Town Hall for Saturday 25 June to build support for the demonstration.[183]

It is unclear if the craftsmen's demonstration took place, but a miners' meeting was held at Speech House later on Monday and Allen did not attend. Organ reported that the MFGB Executive had resumed negotiations and it was rumoured that they had dropped the demand for a pool and a national wages board. He expressed concern that the MFGB Executive appeared to be backing down only nine days after the ballot had resulted in a majority of miners in the country voting to stick to the original demands. He argued any new settlement should be put to a ballot. It was no surprise that morale was low and the meeting was poorly attended.[184]

Thirteen Weeks

On the same day, Monday 27 June, the MFGB Executive in London decided to advise a return to work on the basis of district settlements. The MFGB Executive was reluctant to call a ballot, fearing rejection by rank and file miners, so the decision was referred back to the district executives advising that acceptance was the only alternative to the collapse of the MFGB. On the morning of 1 July, the FDMA Executive met and passed the following resolution:

> That we advise our men not to accept the agreement submitted for the settlement of the present dispute, provided, however, in the event of the majority of miners in the country voting in favour of a resumption of work on Monday next, under the terms of the agreement, we as a District Executive pledge ourselves to negotiate with the Forest owners, to obtain the best possible rates of pay in accordance with the agreement.[185]

Later that day a meeting of Forest miners at Speech House, presided over by Organ, unanimously rejected the terms of the settlement by a hand vote but agreed that if the country as a whole supported the settlement, they should negotiate with the local colliery owners for the best terms obtainable. However, resentment was expressed that there had been no ballot. Booth reported that the situation was tragic, with the Forest miners

183 Ibid.
184 *Gloucester Citizen* 27 June 1921 and *Dean Forest Mercury* 1 July 1921.
185 FDMA Minutes 1 July 1921.

facing the possibility of being the lowest paid in the country. On top of this, the FDMA had a debt of £27,000, mainly to the Co-operative Society and local traders.[186] A telegram was sent to the MFGB in London confirming the rejection of the settlement.

The MFGB Executive met in London on the same day to hear reports from the various districts. The majority of districts, including the large ones, voted in favour of accepting the terms of the settlement with card votes showing 832,000 in favour and 105,000 against. The only districts against were the Forest of Dean, Bristol, Lancashire, Kent and Somerset.[187] A telegram was sent by Hodges and Smith to all the districts:

> Overwhelming vote in favour of resumption of work. Workmen to return without delay.[188]

Forest miner, Frank Joynes later expressed his bitterness:

> During the 1921 strike, we got no pay, no money, nothing. Thirteen weeks, and at the end of it, I had nothing. Nothing, Nothing!

Joynes's workmate added:

> Yes, if you owned your own house, in them days you could yut this! (He thumped the stone wall of the Miner's Arms in Sling). Yes, could yut this for all they cared. If it hadn't been for our bacon on the wall, we'd starved.[189]

The Forest men had been locked out for 14 weeks and either returned to work disillusioned and resentful or were forced into unemployment and poverty. They had to accept a deal which involved scrapping national agreements and a wage reduction which left them worse off in real terms than in 1914. This hit the miners in the Forest hard and by January 1922 the day rate for a skilled hewer in the Forest was down to the minimum rate of 7s 7d. Along with Bristol, this was the lowest rate in the country; in contrast, the rate for a skilled hewer in Nottinghamshire was 17s 4d. However, by the middle of 1922, the wages in all districts except Nottinghamshire fell

186 *Dean Forest Mercury* 1 July 1921 and *Western Morning News* 2 July 1921.
187 Cole, *Labour in the Coal Mining Industry*, 234.
188 Arnot, *The Miners*, 331.
189 Phelps, *Forest Voices*, 63. Yut is Forest dialect for eat.

to their district minimums. In August 1922, even the wage for a skilled hewer in Nottinghamshire was down to approximately 11s a shift.[190]

During the next three years, the effect of Black Friday was to undermine the morale of workers across all industries as employers used the lockout to break any resistance. Trade unionists could only fight defensive actions as six million workers suffered wage cuts. In the following years, railway workers, transport workers, tin workers and agricultural workers in the Forest of Dean all faced wage cuts.

In August 1921, the control of railways was returned to private ownership. The 1921 Railways Act instituted the compulsory amalgamation of the numerous large and small railways into four existing companies, including Great Western Railway, but did not enable workers' participation in their management. Although the Act did not take effect until 1 January 1923, many of the mergers took place in 1922. It did not take long before the railway companies started chipping away at the terms of the national agreement as wages were reduced, workers put on short time and some laid off. [191]

In the immediate aftermath of Black Friday trade union membership in Britain slumped dramatically from 8.3 million in 1920 to 5.6 million in 1922. Membership of the MFGB fell by 22 per cent from 957,610 in March 1921 to 744,464 in March 1923.[192] The situation in the Forest was catastrophic for the FDMA; by May 1922 the membership had dropped to 1,300 and it still had a debt of £24,000.[193]

The Agreement

The agreement reached between the MFGB and the colliery owners on 1 July 1921 provided a new principle for the determination of earnings, linking them to the ratio of profits to wages. The terms of the National Wages Agreement of 1921 laid the foundations of wage structures in the industry until the Second World War.

In summary, for an initial period of three months, up to 30 September, the government provided a subsidy (limited to £10 million) which was used to restrain the speed at which wages were reduced. Over the longer run, a standard wage was established in each district, defined as the current base rate on 31 March 1921 plus the district percentage in force in 1914,

190 Cole, *Labour in the Coal Mining Industry*, 241, *Nottingham Evening Post* 14 January 1922 and Griffin, *The Miners of Nottinghamshire*, 112-113.
191 Bagwell, *The Railwaymen*, Chapter 16.
192 Arnot, *The Miners*, 339.
193 R. Page Arnot, Interview with John Williams, 1961, Richard Burton Archives.

both of which were determined locally, as described below. In addition, the agreement provided for a minimum wage determined by the relevant standard wage for the grade plus 20 per cent. Finally, men for whom the resultant wage led to poverty were to be paid a locally determined subsistence allowance as necessary.

The base rates ranged from the agreed rate for piecework in a particular pit, or even seam, to district-wide rates for whole categories of day-wage workers. The added percentages depended on the profitability of all the mines in the district, established by a joint audit. In each district, the audit would ascertain the industry's proceeds by deducting from total sales the standard wages, non-wage costs of production, and a standard profit equivalent to 17 per cent of the standard wages. The result of this ascertainment, if any, would then be divided between wages and profits in the ratio 83:17. If there were insufficient funds to pay profits, the deficiency would be carried forward to set against possible future surpluses. The system was to be overseen, and unresolved details settled, by a National Board, with equal membership of miners and owners, and a neutral Chairman

In the Forest of Dean, the base rate for a hewer on 31 March 1921 was 4s 7d and the district percentage in force in 1914 was 35 per cent, giving a district standard for a hewer of 6s 2d.[194] Adding the 20 per cent gave a minimum wage for a hewer in the Forest of Dean of 7s 5d which exceeded the wage rates of June 1914 (5s 5d) by about 40 per cent, as against a 92 per cent increase in the cost of living.[195]

Figures presented by the Forest of Dean colliery owners claimed that their profits lagged behind those of Bristol and Somerset and were close to zero. If this was the situation, miners in the Forest would be the worst paid in the country. In addition, the stipulation that if there were insufficient funds to pay profits then the deficiency would be carried forward to set against future surpluses meant that Forest miners could be reduced to minimum rates for the foreseeable future. This turned out to be the case.

Booth reported that the FDMA would have to employ auditors and it would be an incredibly complex task to ascertain the profits of the sixty-eight separate coal mining companies operating in the Forest, some of which employed only a few men. In addition, only four companies were members of the FDCOA which meant there would need to be complex negotiations to determine rates of pay at each pit and with no district pool some collieries may have to close.[196]

194 FDMA Minutes 1 July 1921.
195 That is 6s 2d plus 20 per cent.
196 *Dean Forest Mercury* 1 July 1921 and *Dean Forest Mercury* 8 July 1921.

Chapter Five

A Glimpse of the Knife

You cannot forget things that have been your entire life for many years. The insult of a moment, Willie, is hard enough to forget but when men have to endure the insult of being idle, degraded and useless for years on end, not only is it impossible to forget that, it becomes an act of faith to cherish the memory of it every moment one lives, because one's duty as a human being from that time on is to fight against the possibility of that insult being levelled against oneself or against others again. You're young, Willie. You only caught a glimpse of the knife that went right through our bodies.

Gwyn Thomas, The Dark Philosophers.[1]

In the weeks after the lockout, some miners were told they were not needed, and others were offered only two or three days work a week. Harry Toomer described the system:

You had to listen for the hooter every night and every pit had its hooter and everybody knew their own pit's sound of hooter. And if there was no work the next day, they would give loud blasts on the hooter for minutes on end—no work tomorrow … that was called a play day.[2]

Nationally unemployment in the coal industry rose to 20 per cent, and 125,000 miners were no longer needed.[3] On Monday 4 July, at one Labour Exchange alone, Lydbrook, over 300 men registered as unemployed with more registering the following day.[4] Some of these men had returned from South Wales, adding to the queues. However, the government announced that men unemployed as a result of damage to their pits or as a result of an industrial dispute could not receive unemployment benefit. An additional burden resulted from the government's decision to extend the time from

1 These are characters in a short story called *The Dark Philosophers* by Gwyn Thomas, in *The Sky of Our Lives*, London: Hutchinson,1972) 120.
2 Harry Toomer, Gage Library.
3 Supple, *The History of the British Coal Industry*, 168.
4 *Dean Forest Mercury* 8 July 1921.

Walter Peart was killed on 12 August 1921, when he was 30 years old, as a result of a fall of coal which fractured his spine, leg and arm. Peart was born in Wigan in 1889, the son of a coal miner. He had lost his elder brother James to typhoid in 1890 and another older brother, Sidney, was killed at the Princess Royal colliery in 1909. Peart also lost three other siblings who died when they were toddlers.

In 1911, he was working at Princess Royal colliery as a labourer and married Harriett Lee at Parkend Baptist chapel in July 1915. They had three children Ethel, Elise and Dorothy.

In November 1915, Peart joined the Worcester Regiment as a volunteer but was discharged from the army in May 1917 due to ill health or injury. After he recovered, he returned to work at Princess Royal. His third daughter, Dorothy, was born in October 1920, ten months before her father's death.

Walter Peart.

Over four hundred people attended his funeral, and large numbers of people lined the streets of Bream on route to the churchyard. Peart was described in the *Dean Forest Mercury* as "a very quiet man and much loved"

three to six days before providing unemployment benefit. Booth spent much of his time over the summer months supporting his members in their attempt to make claims for benefit.

The only alternative for people not entitled to unemployment benefit was means-tested outdoor relief, claimed from the local Board of Guardians under the Poor Law. In the Forest of Dean, the Westbury Board served East Dean, and the Monmouth Board served West Dean.[5] Claiming Poor Law relief would have been very humiliating for unemployed miners, some of whom were World War One veterans. In any case, relief was usually refused by the relieving officer, who claimed the rules stated they could not offer relief to those who were unemployed as a result of an industrial dispute. In one case at Westbury, Booth pleaded with the Guardians to provide boots for children so they could attend school, but this was also refused. The Monmouth Board of Guardians agreed to offer relief for those in extreme distress as a loan.[6]

Return to Work

About 50 per cent of Forest of Dean miners returned to work on Monday 11 July. In most pits, it was five weeks before the haulage roads were cleared of rubble from roof falls and equipment damaged due to flooding was repaired or replaced. The concerns about the flooding at Cannop causing permanent damage proved to be unfounded and once the craftsmen got the electrical equipment re-installed and the pumps running again some coal could be mined. However, one estimate stated that it would be six months before the mine could get back to full production, which meant the majority of the men would remain unemployed until the repair work could be completed.[7]

In addition, Howbeach was now closed for good, and the 250 men laid off before the stoppage were finding it difficult to get work elsewhere. The steam coal collieries Eastern, Harrow Hill and Waterloo were all working part-time. In contrast, Princess Royal was back to close to full employment and full production within a few days of the return to work, although this did not last as the demand for steam coal subsided.[8]

5 In 1842 the main part of the extra-parochial area of the Forest of Dean was divided, for Poor Law Act purposes, into two townships of East Dean and West Dean. A rough line was drawn in a diagonal direction from Lydbrook to Ayleford to form the boundaries. East Dean was attached to the Westbury-on-Severn union and West Dean to the Monmouth union. In later years the boundaries were often changed and parts of these two townships were added to various adjoining parishes.
6 *Dean Forest Mercury* 8 July 1921.
7 *Dean Forest Mercury* 15 July 1921.
8 Ibid.

THE COAL CRISIS.

Relief for Starving Women and Children.

JOINT COMMITTEE.

Trades Union Congress Parliamentary Committee:	The Labour Party Executive Committee:	The Parliamentary Labour Party:
E. L. POULTON	W. H. HUTCHINSON	J. R. CLYNES, M.P.
A. PUGH	CHARLES DUNCAN	TOM SHAW, M.P.
MARGARET BONDFIELD	J. RAMSAY MACDONALD	JOHN HODGE, M.P.
C. W. BOWERMAN, M.P. SECRETARY.	ARTHUR HENDERSON, M.P. SECRETARY.	H. S. LINDSAY, SECRETARY.

The "Daily Herald" Save the Miners' Children Fund;
GEORGE LANSBURY.

TO THE LABOUR MOVEMENT.

The miners' fight has drawn to a close, but widespread hunger and distress will continue to prevail long after work is resumed. This will be the most difficult period for the women and children, and as the re-opening of the mines will quickly tend to a revival of employment generally, we urgently appeal to all sections of the organised Labour Movement to render what assistance lies in their power to give, whether in the form of donations, loans, the provision of food and other necessaries of life, or by taking collections at all Labour Public Meetings, in order that the terrible effects of the long-drawn-out struggle may be mitigated as far as is practicable.

For thirteen weeks, the miners have fought against the attempt to reduce the workers' standard of life, and have offered stout resistance to the greatest combined onslaught ever delivered upon any section of organised workers.

The conflict was deliberately occasioned by the action of the Government in decontrolling the Coal industry on March 31st instead of on August 31st, and by the coal-owners who announced a series of wages reductions that were universally condemned as staggering and excessive.

Since the opening of the conflict on April 1st, the coal-owners and the Coalition Government have been reinforced on a gradually increasing scale by the forces of distress, hunger, sickness and starvation. It is now generally known that the miners' organisation had less financial resources at their disposal for maintaining their members than the Government has since spent on feeding the population with "Messages to the Nation" and other propaganda.

How hundreds of thousands of miners and their families have been able to offer such sustained resistance to the forces of organised capitalism is a mystery. Their splendid heroism, their quiet and unflagging fortitude, their remarkable capacity to sacrifice and endure, their inspiring devotion to the workers' cause, and their unbreakable spirit of solidarity have not been surpassed by any body of people in the long annals of industrial history, and their epic struggle will never be forgotten by the Labour Movement.

One of the men laid off from Howbeach colliery in December 1919 was colliery clerk William Richards from Parkend. Richards served in the army during the war when he was gassed twice resulting in permanent damage to his health. He returned home in 1919 and, after being laid off from Howbeach, he travelled the country seeking work. He then returned to the Forest of Dean, and for a short period, obtained manual work at the Cannop Stone Company. However, his health deteriorated further, he was admitted to Gloucester hospital on 13 June 1921 and died at the end of August 1921 at the age of twenty-six.

On 31 August 1921, Sir Francis Brain, aged 67, died at his private nursing home in Clifton in Bristol, where he owned a substantial property in Stoke Bishop. According to his probate returns, he left £233,000 to his wife and daughters. In terms of today's money, this would be equivalent to approximately 10.2 million pounds. Most of this was earned in the years 1914–1918. The probate figure does not include inheritance from his properties held abroad, including in Australia and Ireland.

The Miners Annual Demonstration day at Speech House in July 1921. Top row fourth from left is Herbert Booth, Front row second from left is James Wignall MP, third from left is Ernest Bevin and fourth from left is David Organ.

The annual miners' demonstration on 9 July was held on a sunny day and well attended, although the mood was sombre. The main speakers were Organ, Wignall and Bevin. Wignall argued that his priority was to work politically through parliament but explained this was a challenging task due to the small number of Labour MPs.

Bevin admitted Black Friday was a tragedy and went on to explain that one of the reasons for the failure of the Triple Alliance was that the NTWF consisted of a number of separate unions, all with different constitutions, which made organising strike action a complex task. He went on to argue the case for industrial unionism which he believed would bring all workers within the same union structure, making organising industrial action easier. The miners gave him a fair hearing but not surprisingly he had to put up with heckling during question time.[9]

Temporary Subsidy

On Tuesday 6 September, at a well-attended meeting of miners at Cinderford town hall, Booth gave details of how the wages for July, August and September were calculated. He explained how they were based on the ascertained profits in the district for March, which was 33 per cent, plus an extra amount from the government subsidy which was gradually reduced over the three months.

In addition, Booth informed the men that the FDMA subscription rates had been raised to 1s 6d a week to help pay off the coupon debt. He added they had already paid off £3,000 of the £27,000 debt and emphasised they needed to honour it as the tradesmen had been very generous and not even charged interest.[10]

The minimum day rate for a hewer in July, August and September 1921 was based on the ascertainment for March (6s 2d plus 33 per cent giving 8s 3d). The additions from the government subsidy were 5s for July, 4s 6d for August and 4s for September, giving figures of 13s 3d, 12s 9d and 12s 3d respectively.

John Ballinger's standard wage over three days was 14s 7d. (3 x 4s 10½d). Ballinger was probably a surface worker or a labourer. The government subsidy for September was 4s a day giving 12s and the percentage ascertainment for March was 33 per cent of 14s 7d giving 4s 9d. The deductions are for national insurance (unemployment and sickness)

9 Ibid.
10 *Dean Forest Mercury* 9 September 1921.

PRINCESS ROYAL COLLIERY CO. LTD.
BREAM, GLOS.

No. *526* Name *R. J. Ballinger*

Description and Stall No.

Pay ending 2 4 SEP 1921 192

	T.	C.							
Cutting	...	...							
Yardage	...	...							
"	...	...							
Timber Sets	...	...							
3 Days	...	...	4/10½		14	7			
"	...	...			12	0			
"	...	...							
Percentage	...	...			4	9			
" 12%	...	...							
Allowances & Day Work	...								
" "	...								
War Wage	...	...							
Sankey Wage	...	...							
Increased Wage	...	...							
2nd ditto	...	...				1	11	4	
Less—									
Health Insurance	...				5				
Unemployment ditto	...				7				
Explosives	...	...							
Sick Club	...	...			1			2	
General Accident	...								
National Savings	...								
			£			1	9	4	

PAID

John Ballinger's wage slip.

Table 6: Wage Rates in the Forest of Dean Coalfield in 1921.*

Date	Face Worker (Hewer)	Trammer	Surface Worker
January 1921	18s 9d	16s 11d	16s 3d
March 1921	15s 3d	13s 5d	12s 9d
July 1921	13s 3d		
August 1921	12s 9d		
September 1921	12s 3d	10s 5d	9s 9d
October 1921	9s 10d	7s 9d	6s 11d
November 1921	7s 5d	5s 10d	5s 3d

* *Dean Forest Mercury* 4 November 1921.

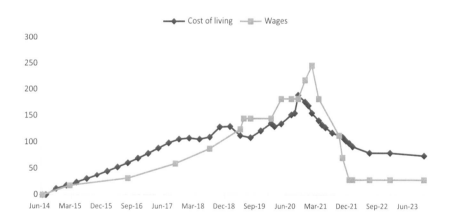

The vertical column for the two graphs gives:
(1) the cost of living index which was sourced from the *Labour Gazette* which calculated the cost of living index as the percentage above the figure in June 1914.
(2) the percentage increase of a hewer's wage above 5s 5d, the wage in June 1914.
The peak in wages at the end of 1920 was a result of the temporary datum line award of 2s plus productivity bonus of 1s 6d awarded at the end of the year.

and the sick club would be to cover hospital and doctor's fees. His wages would soon be reduced further by the removal of the government subsidy. Therefore, it is no surprise that, in 1922, he left the industry and moved to France and obtained work as an horticultural officer for the Imperial War Graves Commission based near Arras.[11]

The October rate for a hewer was 6s 2d plus 58 per cent based on the ascertainment for August, but down to the minimum by November.[12] The piecework rates were also down to the minimum, and the buttymen were struggling to earn any more than the minimum day rate themselves. One estimate gives the buttymen receiving on average 5s to 10s more a week during the 1920s than the hewers they employed.[13] The minimum wage prevailed in the Forest coalfield for eleven out of 12 months in 1922. Eric Warren remembers:

> Two butty men would take the main headings and two butty men would take the stalls off the main heading. The butty men were paid so much for coal got out and so much per yard for rippin' the roadways and they were responsible for payin' the men. The minimum wage was seven and ninepence per day, less stoppages and the butty men would share out. If not enough coal was got, the company guaranteed the butty men seven and ninepence per day.[14]

In 1922, at the age of 14, Percy Bassett started on the screens at New Fancy colliery and was paid 9d a day. He then worked as a hodder at 11d a day before being promoted to work on the pumps at 2s 6d a day.[15]

Bob Nailing

In periods when the trade was slack, there was a temptation for the buttymen to take most of the work for themselves and the daymen were the first to be laid off. In the Forest, this was called 'bob nailing'. During the next few years, resentment against the butty system grew, particularly as it mainly benefited the colliery owners. In the end, even the buttymen realised the system was unfair and were happy to see it abolished. Harry Barton remembers:

11 Sungreen, Stuart Ballinger and the Stuart Ballinger family archive.
12 FDMA Minutes July to November 1921.
13 Cyril Hart, *The Industrial History of Dean* (Newton Abbott: David and Charles, 1971) 240.
14 Phelps, *Forest Voices*, 50.
15 Percy Bassett interviewed by Ms Parfett in May 1983 in Blakeney, Gage Library.

Now when I was about 17, my grandfather who was a 'Butty-man' with my father, he retired when he got old, he got the coal dust on his lungs. And father said to me one day he was going to take me in with him as a 'butty', so I was a butty. That was all right by me because we paid the men who were working for us and we shared the money out between us afterwards ... Whatever was left over I shared between my father and me, that was the butty system. I don't think it was (a good system) because those men were as good a workman as I was or my father. But it was just the system involved and it was a system that the old men of the Forest of Dean used years and years ago.[16]

The butty system operated in most of the Forest deep pits up to the end of the war and into the 1920s, particularly in the house-coal pits. However, as a result of campaigns against the system, it was gradually replaced by an arrangement where the piece work earnings were shared out equally between the men in the team.[17]

Consequently, the FDMA was able to negotiate independent agreements through collective bargaining which included a detailed price list, day rates for different grades of workers and other issues such as variations on shift pay. The first pits to abolish the butty system were Princess Royal and Cannop. In spite of this, there were still buttymen employed at the Eastern United colliery up to 1938. It would take the threat of strike action at the pit to finally rid the Forest of the system.

Women's Protest

The temporary subsidy meant the reductions in wages were not fully implemented until October 1921. However, by the Autumn most of the mines were only working two or three days a week, partly because they could not compete with cheaper coal from elsewhere. In September, the women's section of the Pillowell Labour Party passed a resolution:

that we the miners' wives of the Forest of Dean strongly protest against the proposed reduction of our men's wages and declare our inability to live on the wages existing at the present time—

16 Harry Barton, Gage Library.
17 This was called the share out system and is the type of agreement that miners negotiated in the South Wales pits earlier in the twentieth century. See B. L. Coombes, These Poor Hands, the autobiography of a miner working in South Wales, (Cardiff: University of Wales, 2002).

much less after another reduction. At present, the majority of men are only doing two shifts a week, making it impossible to provide the necessaries of life, especially where there are large families. We appeal to all miners' wives affected by this proposed cut in wages to stand with us by our men as in the recent Lock Out and send in their protest to the *Daily Herald*, the working man's friend.[18]

Some miners chose to migrate to districts where the pay and conditions of work were better. As a result, Jesse Hodges (Jnr, born 1907) decided to leave the Forest and settle near Castleford in Yorkshire where members of his extended family had previously migrated. Harry Barton was another miner who left for Yorkshire. Harry Roberts remembered that many:

families left the Forest in that period between the two coal strikes in the 1920s to find work in coal mines in Yorkshire, Coventry and Kent, never to return.[19]

Evictions

The number of evictions of miners from their homes rose considerably in the Autumn of 1921. The *Dean Forest Mercury* of 30 September provides details of three cases from one sitting of Littledean magistrates on 23 September.

On 5 September, notice was served on Ernest Nail, a collier, to quit his home. The property belonged to Mrs Malcolm who was represented in court by her solicitor W.W. Whitman and by her agent Frank Bathe. Nail owed 32 weeks rent amounting to £8/15s, but had paid the full amount after the notice was served. However, Whitman argued that in legal terms this was too late. Nail had no legal representation and could not challenge this. He was married with seven children and had no place to live if evicted. He had been living in the house for seven years and claimed the property was in a bad state of repair. The magistrates granted an order to quit the property within six months.

At the same sitting, Simeon Jones, the owner of the small mine mentioned earlier, made an application to evict Allan Meek, a collier, from his cottage on Ruardean Hill on 13 June. The rent was 3s 9d a week, and

18 *Daily Herald* 30 September 1921.
19 Harry Roberts, Cinderford, *A Town Built on Coal*, Gage Library, 95.

Meek was in arrears of £2 12s 6d. Jones was represented by his solicitor but Meek had no legal representation. Meek said he had been out of work from January to July, and his wife was in a hospital, but he admitted being behind with his rent. The magistrates granted an order to quit within three months.

Emily Phelps made a similar application to evict collier George Hall from his home in Dancing Green. A notice to quit had been served on 30 June when he was 18 weeks in arrears with a rent of 2s 6d a week. Hall wrote to the court:

> I am writing to tell you I am sorry I can't attend court as my wife is ill and going to be operated on tomorrow, and I am sure I can't lose a day's work to come, as we are only doing three days a week. I can't afford it. I have two children. If the court will allow me, I will give possession within 21 days.

He went on to explain that he took the rent to Mrs Phelps three times but she refused it, saying she needed the house to store fruit and the only way to get him out was to refuse rent. The court gave an order to quit within 29 days.

The Crawshays

In early October, miners working for Henry Crawshay & Co. Ltd. heard rumours that the Directors of the company were proposing to break away from the terms of the recent national agreement. Initially, the proposal only concerned their house coal collieries: Lightmoor, Trafalgar and Foxes Bridge. This proposal meant that they would no longer accept a joint audit or pay the wages determined by the District Board. Members of the Executive of the FDMA met with the Directors in the offices at Lightmoor and appealed with them not to go down this route. However, the Directors insisted they would have no interference in their affairs from outside auditors.[20] One can only speculate about their reasons for this, but it is possible they did not want a close examination of Morgan's creative accounting. On 8 October the FDMA Executive passed the following resolution:

20 *Dean Forest Mercury* 14 October 1921.

The Executive, having met on this occasion, after careful consideration, cannot accept the proposal of the Henry Crawshay Group to break away from the terms of the agreement.[21]

As a result, on 10 October, the FDMA called a mass meeting on Bilson Green, addressed by Booth, Martin Perkins and Enos Taylor. Booth reported that Captain Brasier-Creagh had argued that the company was no longer making any profits and their shareholders were receiving no dividends. Booth informed the men that Creagh had argued that the company needed to reduce the cost of production and sell the coal at a cheaper rate to compete with other districts.

He explained to the men that the Directors were proposing to give the shareholders a guaranteed ten per cent on their capital investment but were offering a minimum wage of 7s 5d a day for a hewer. After payment of wages, meeting of costs and paying dividends, any extra money would be split between the shareholders and the workers. Creagh insisted that they would close down their pits rather than accept a joint audit or a national agreement.

Perkins reported that the Executive of the FDMA had pleaded with the Directors not to take such drastic action, arguing it could lead to cut-throat competition between employers in the Forest of Dean and elsewhere. During the week, the company had reduced the cost per ton for their house coal by 5s. The *Dean Forest Mercury* speculated that this could result in a price war leading to even lower wages.[22] Perkins told the men that it was the view of the FDMA Executive that they reject this proposal.

The next day, another mass meeting was held on Bilson Green. Booth reported that the FDMA had now negotiated a temporary agreement with the Crawshay Directors to pay the October and November district rates as agreed by the District Board based on the joint audit of the other colliery companies in the Forest of Dean. The October rate for a hewer, determined by the District Board to be paid by the other colliery companies in the Forest of Dean, was 9s 10d a shift. It was agreed the men would return to work the next day at this rate.[23]

A further mass meeting was held on Bilson Green on Thursday 20 October when the men agreed that they would insist the company abide by all the terms of the recent national agreement. However, as the notices

21 FDMA Minutes 8 October 1921.
22 *Dean Forest Mercury* 14 October 1921.
23 Ibid.

put up by the company had been postponed until the following Monday, it was agreed they would continue working.[24]

Another mass meeting of all the miners employed by Henry Crawshay & Co. Ltd. was held on Bilson Green on Monday 24 October. The company now included Eastern United colliery in their proposal. Taylor and Booth reported that they had now negotiated an agreement that in future wages would be paid at the district rate for the foreseeable future.

Booth said the issue of wages had been temporarily resolved, but he believed the company would reject any notion of a joint audit or national agreement and insist on a guaranteed ten per cent return to the shareholders. The FDMA Executive had agreed that they could not advise the men to work outside the terms of the national agreement as it could adversely affect their wages in the future. However, Booth accepted they had no resources to fund a strike and one miner at the meeting spoke:

> of the signs of destitution among the men and children even now being observed, and the small hope of assistance while they were idle. He was as angry as anyone could be against the masters, and he had stood up before, as he was ready now, to stand up for principles but they had to face the position from another serious standpoint—the health and even lives of their children.[25]

Taylor proposed that they resume work under protest with the view of organising a ballot on the issue and this was accepted. There is no record of a ballot taking place. The Forest of Dean Joint District Board met on 3 November at Speech House and as a result of the joint auditor's report wages were fixed at the minimum rates for November giving a minimum rate of 7s 5d a shift for a day rate hewer. The November rates were based on the joint ascertainment for September as agreed by the accountants auditing the colliery owners' books for each party. The only consolation was that the rates could not drop further.[26]

The price of steam coal continued to fall, and Norchard was now only working two or three shifts a week. At the end of November, the shareholders of Norchard Colliery, headed by Lord Bledisloe, called a meeting and invited all the workers from his colliery. He warned them that unless productivity improved, they would have to close the colliery due to competition from cheaper steam coal from South Wales. Bledisloe

24 *Dean Forest Mercury* 21 October 1921.
25 *Dean Forest Mercury* 28 October 1921.
26 *Dean Forest Mercury* 4 November 1921.

changed his mind and, a few days later, informed the *Dean Forest Mercury* that he would endeavour to keep the pit open.[27]

Unemployment

From November 1920, the new Unemployment Insurance Act covered 12 million workers. In December, there were 700,000 unemployed insured workers in Britain. However, by June 1921 that figure had risen to 2,171,000.[28] In the summer of 1921, there were 50,000 unemployed miners in South Wales out of a total of 250,000. A large number of Forest of Dean miners who were working in South Wales returned home, swelling the ranks of the unemployed in the Forest. Despite this, the population of the Forest of Dean fell after 1921 as people moved away to get work in other areas.[29]

The Unemployment Insurance Act 1920 allowed a weekly cash payment of 15s for unemployed insured men and 12s for unemployed insured women for up to 15 weeks. The benefit was funded in part by weekly contributions from both employers and employed.[30] Unemployment benefit for those on short time required a six-day qualifying period and, provided the claimant was out of work for more than three days, they would get 2s 6d a day. The depression of 1921 set the tone for the inter-war years when the average rate of unemployment was 14 per cent of the insured workforce.[31] The persistence of high levels of unemployment undermined the basic principle behind the 1920 Act which was that claimants received unemployment benefit as a right for a limited period.

By September, many miners were only working two or three days a week. Many of those out of work were refused unemployment benefit because it was deemed that their unemployment was a result of an industrial dispute. Some presented themselves at Westbury and Monmouth Boards of Guardians asking for relief but, as a rule, the most the Guardians could offer was a temporary loan.[32]

In response, a committee of the unemployed was formed in West Dean to provide solidarity and support for those forced into poverty. The

27 *Dean Forest Mercury* 2 December 1921.
28 C. L. Mowat, *Britain Between the Wars, 1918–1940* (Methuen, 1955) 126.
29 Victoria County History of Gloucestershire, *A History of the County of Gloucester: Volume 5, Bledisloe Hundred, St. Briavels Hundred, the Forest of Dean, Forest of Dean Settlement*, 300-325.
30 Under the Act every male adult worker had to pay 4d a week, his employer the same amount and the State added 2d a week.
31 S. Glynn and J. Oxborrow, *Interwar Britain* (Allen and Unwin, 1976) 144-5 Table 5.1.
32 *Dean Forest Mercury* 23 September 1921.

Table 7: Unemployment among insured workers in the Forest of Dean.

Date	Cinderford Area	Coleford Area	Lydney Area	Newnham Area	Total
September 1920[a]	29 in total for Cinderford, Coleford and Lydney				29
January 1921[b]	107	66	264	26	463
February 1921[c]	210	156	484	42	892
March 1921[d]	268	184	527	50	1029
April 1921[e]	588	162	562	43	1355
May 1921[f]	455	180	586	44	1265
June 1921[g]	520	205	598	50	1373
July 1921[h]	1708	730	1015	253	3706
September 1921[i]	567	159	217	118	1061
October 1921[j]	2122	912	642	47	3723
November 1921[k]	2233	473	999	142	3847

a—*Gloucester Journal* 18 September 1920. b—*Gloucester Citizen* 18 January 1921. c—Gloucester Citizen 22 February 1921. d—*Gloucester Citizen* 19 March 1921. e—*Gloucester Journal* 16 April 1921. f—*Gloucester Citizen* 10 May 1921. g—*Gloucester Citizen* 14 June 1921. h—*Gloucester Journal* 16 July 1921. i—*Gloucester Journal* 24 September 1921. j—*Gloucester Citizen* 19 October 1921. k—*Gloucester Citizen* 24 November 1921.

Coleford and West Dean Unemployed Committee's main objectives were to support the unemployed in obtaining unemployment benefit or relief at the Board of Guardians and to lobby the authorities for work schemes for the unemployed with rates of pay based on trade union conditions of work.

Two of the main organisers of the committee were Tom Liddington and William Hoare, who was now back home having finished his course of study at the CLC. Similar unemployed committees had sprung up throughout the country, and many were affiliated to the National Unemployed Workers Movement which was set up by the newly formed CPGB. Hoare was among the most vocal in the campaigns against poverty and unemployment, as the broader community rallied around to provide support. Hoare had been involved in the industrial dispute at Norchard in 1918 mentioned earlier and now worked at Princess Royal.

The figures refer to those who are in receipt of unemployment benefit and therefore are insured workers. The figures do not include most women (uninsured), children, the elderly, the disabled, striking miners, miners unemployed as a result of an industrial dispute and unemployed uninsured workers. The statistics are complicated by the fact that some unemployed workers from West Dean area, which included Princess Royal and Norchard collieries, signed on at the Lydney Employment office. Unemployment among miners was comparatively low in August and September because, when the miners returned to work after the lockout, coal was needed to replenish stocks. However, the demand for coal was only temporary and, as the depression deepened, unemployment grew.

According to the 1921 census, the population of East Dean (including Cinderford and surrounding settlements) was 20,494, West Dean (including Coleford and surrounding settlements) was 17,431, Lydney and surrounding settlements was 9,842 and Newnham, Westbury and Awre 4,029.[33] The overall population of the town of Cinderford was 7,224, many of whom were now unemployed.[34]

By the Autumn many miners were working short time. If they were out of work for more than six days, they were able to claim benefit and so some were included in the above statistics. However, a miner who worked, for instance, only six days in six weeks may not have been entitled to a single penny of benefit, simply because he could not show the necessary waiting period.[35]

Guardians

The Guardians struggled to cope with the demand for relief. The chair of the Monmouth Board, aristocrat Lady Mather Jackson had little idea of the distress existing in the Forest of Dean but some board members were shocked at the state of destitution of some of the miners claiming relief. Most believed they should not let women and children starve, although some, such as William Burdess, the under manager at Princess Royal

33 *Gloucester Journal* 27 August 1921.
34 Victoria County History of Gloucestershire, *A History of the County of Gloucester: Volume 5, Bledisloe Hundred, St. Briavels Hundred, the Forest of Dean, Forest of Dean Settlement,* 300-325.
35 *Gloucester Citizen* 19 October 1921. Some of the people who were still unemployed had exhausted their benefit and were now not registered. As a result, they were advised to retain their names on the register and some continued to do this. Other unemployed applications were refused benefit because they were not considered to be genuinely seeking work, not formerly insurable or otherwise not able to comply with the conditions for receiving benefit. Most of these did not continue to register. The number of miners claiming benefit who were also working short time in October 1921 was 1500 in Cinderford, 680 in Lydney and 470 in Coleford.

Table 8: Some cases heard before Monmouth and Westbury Boards of Guardians in September 1921

Board of Guardians	Applicant	Dependents	Unemployment Benefit	Decision
Monmouth[a]	Unemployed miner.	Wife and six children.	Claim for unemployment benefit rejected.	A loan of 25s a week.
Monmouth[b]	Miner earning 30s a week part-time.	Wife and six children.	Claim for unemployment benefit rejected.	A loan of 6s a week.
Westbury[c]	Unemployed miner.	Wife and six children.	In receipt of 15s a week unemployment benefit.	A loan of 20s a week.
Westbury[d]	Destitute single man who worked at Lightmoor before the lockout.	None.	Claim for unemployment benefit rejected.	Offered a place in the workhouse.
Westbury[e]	Unemployed miner from SouthWwales with family living in the Forest.	Wife and two children.	Claim for unemployment benefit rejected.	A loan of 25s a week.

a—*Dean Forest Mercury* 23 September 1921. b—*Dean Forest Mercury* 23 September 1921. c—*Gloucester Journal* 24 September 1921. d.—*Dean Forest Mercury* 21 October 1921. e—*Dean Forest Mercury* 18 November 1921.

colliery, were less sympathetic and relief was usually refused to miners who had been involved in the lockout. Among the twenty-five Guardians on the Monmouth Board were Forest of Dean Labour representatives Charles Luker, Tom Liddington and Ellen Hicks, who spoke up on behalf of the miners by arguing for a system of loans.

William Burdess.

The chair of the Westbury Board was Sir Russell Kerr, a local aristocrat and staunch Conservative. George Rowlinson, the ex-FDMA agent, sat as an independent and Frank Ashmead, an official of the FDMA, was a Labour representative. Rowlinson pointed out that the Board received no money from the central government and all the money available had to be raised from the local rates. At Westbury, the clerk ruled the board could only offer relief for two weeks at a time for those in extreme distress. Otherwise, applicants could be offered a loan or a place in the workhouse.

The board argued that many local miners were getting two or three days work a week and earning 25s but not claiming relief. A miner from South Wales listed in the table responded:

> There are thousands who are living in a state of privation, although they are at work, and if they would give me only two or three shifts a week at the colliery, I shall have to share their fate. As it is, I am absolutely destitute, without the assistance I have had, I am not going to see my wife and children starve. They can put me behind bars before that shall happen, and that is a terrible thing for a man to say who has always led a straight life and who has references from South Wales of many years standing.[36]

He went on to explain that he was planning to walk back to South Wales to pursue his claim for unemployment benefit.

36 *Dean Forest Mercury* 18 November 1921.

Work Schemes

On Tuesday 13 September, a demonstration of 3000 men, women and children marched with banners from the Market Square to the workhouse in Gloucester demanding work or maintenance. As a result, Gloucester Council, with the aid of a grant from central government, provided relief work, such as stone breaking and road works, for about 400 men, while paying a basic maintenance allowance of 15s for a single adult, 30s for married couples, 5s for each of the first four children and 2s. 6d. for each remaining child.[37] In September, the police baton-charged marches of the unemployed in Bristol and other major cities and this was repeated at Trafalgar Square in October, resulting in the death of one of the demonstrators.[38]

On Saturday 1 October, a public meeting was organised by the Coleford and West Dean Unemployed Committee in Coleford. The main speakers were Tom Liddington, Reverend John Putterill and Charles Drake. Putterill was ordained as a deacon and now worked as a curate at Coleford. He had worked in the East End of London and unusually for an Anglican curate he was a supporter of the communist cause. His speech mixed religious metaphors with communist idealism.

> The capitalist system depended on unemployment and those who owned made slaves of those that did not. The position of the workers of this country was that of the Israelites in Egypt—they were absolute slaves—and if they wanted their freedom, they would fight for it. [39]

Charles Drake, a long-standing councillor on Coleford Urban Council, put forward the following resolution which was passed unanimously:

> That this meeting of the unemployed men in Coleford and West Dean calls upon the local authority to bring pressure to bear on the government to introduce schemes of a socially useful character to meet the needs of the situation, the costs to be defrayed by grants from the National Exchequer and not to fall upon local rates.[40]

37 *Gloucester Journal*, Saturday 17 September 1921 and *Gloucestershire Chronicle,* Saturday 24 December 1921. The adults had to work alternate weeks and in December the allowances were reduced.
38 *Western Morning News* 9 September 1921 and *Times* 5 October 1921.
39 *Dean Forest Mercury* 7 October 1921.
40 Ibid.

The following Thursday, 6 October, a delegation of unemployed miners and quarry workers lobbied the West Dean Rural District Council to introduce work schemes for the unemployed. William Hoare, the chairman of the deputation, said the unemployed of the district would prefer relief in the form of work and wages rather than depend on unemployment benefit of 15s a week or relief from the Guardians, which could lead them into semi-starvation. The council responded positively and committed themselves to endeavour to do everything in their power to gain government funding for work schemes.

On Friday 14 October, Hoare led another deputation of unemployed miners from West Dean to place demands in front of the Monmouth Board of Guardians, which was chaired by Lady Mather Jackson. The deputation had to walk from Coleford and, as a result, was late. At first, the Board were reluctant to see them but the Labour members of the board, Liddington, Luker and Hicks, argued that it would be a wasted journey for hungry men if they were refused an opportunity to present their case. Hicks who lived in Coleford informed the meeting that she had:

seen men walking about hungry. There are men in the district who have not enough to eat.[41]

Liddington said the men could not wait for another month and in the end the Board agreed to hear the deputation's representatives. Hoare spoke on behalf of the men, arguing they needed adequate maintenance until the government could implement its work schemes and said:

Are you aware that while the grass is growing the horse is starving? ... they had been forced to come there to seek maintenance till such time as schemes were put into operation. They were unemployed through no fault of their own—they considered the present situation was due to the utter breakdown of the capitalist system.[42]

Hoare said maintenance should be a living wage and they said they would take any work provided it was paid at trade union rates.[43] The Board

---

41 *Dean Forest Mercury* 14 October 1921.
42 Ibid.
43 The unemployed committee presented a case that a living wage should be 15s a week for a married man plus 15s a week for a wife plus 7s 6d per child and house rent up to 10s weekly. Single men and single women to be paid £1 weekly plus extra for dependents as for married men.

members responded by arguing that the rates would be set nationally and would be considerably below trade union rates. Some of the miners said they would rather starve than ask for relief. In the end the Board passed a motion urging the government to fund a scheme repairing roads and developing waterworks in the West Dean area. They added that relief would be awarded at the usual rate and according to merit. A member of the deputation ended the discussion by saying, "we want work, we don't want doles".

On 15 November, Wignall joined a deputation from East and West Dean District Councils and Coleford Urban Council in a visit to London to lobby the relevant government departments.[44] On 9 December 1921, the *Dean Forest Mercury* reported that Sir Percival Marling had complained about the sight of unemployed ex-servicemen hanging around the towns and villages of Gloucestershire. He suggested that the government should introduce work schemes for the unemployed to get them off the street.[45] Discussions on a variety of schemes for the unemployed in the Forest of Dean took place over the next two years, but none were ever implemented.

Hunting for Game

In the Autumn of 1921, there was an increase in poaching among miners who sought to provide food for the table by hunting for game, which they believed was their customary right. Arthur Morgan, managing director of Henry Crawshay & Co. Ltd., became very concerned about the amount of poaching taking place in the woods around his mansion at Abbotswood and insisted the police patrol the woods at night. As a result, on 17 October, John Joiner and Albert Beard, both colliers, were caught poaching with a gun in Abottswood. They were fined one pound each and the guns confiscated. They claimed they had no food in their houses for their families.[46]

This event was not an isolated incident. Charles Wilkes, William Wilkes, Thomas Hart, Frank Hobbs, Ivan Bevin, Austin Pound, Stephen Dixon, William Walden, Horlick Marfell, Arthur Tomkins, Tom Hoskins, Edward and William Reid, Fred Manning, Samuel Wilkes, Fran Markey, Harry Harvey, Sidney Morgan, Alfred Davies, John Duffield, William Williams, Arthur Stallard and Joseph Hale were all up before the magistrates for poaching in the Forest of Dean area during 1921. The fines

44 *Dean Forest Mercury* 8 October 1921.
45 *Dean Forest Mercury* 9 December 1921.
46 *Dean Forest Mercury* 4 November 1921.

varied from £1 to £2.[47] It is very likely that this was just the tip of the iceberg as most miners were very experienced hunters and only a few ever got caught.

Bankruptcies and Debt

One of the problems facing miners was lack of funds to pay their income tax from the previous tax year's earnings when their wages were higher. As a result, proceedings were taken against a large number of men at the magistrates' courts across the Forest. On Tuesday 6 December, 218 miners were brought before the local colliery owner, Thomas Deakin, the chairman of the magistrates at Coleford Petty Sessions. He issued orders to pay within eight weeks. Deakin complained that for a considerable time the miners had been able to earn good money, and it was only the less prudent who had not paid their tax on time.[48]

It was not just mining families facing unemployment, poverty and debt, as the depression impacted on the majority of the workplaces in the Forest of Dean including the quarries, railway and forestry as more and more workers were laid off. Some of the traders who had provided coupons feared they would never get their money back and some were forced into bankruptcy. These included Alfred Field a fruiterer and part-time collier from Cinderford and William Hughes a grocer from Lydbrook.[49]

Betrayal

In December 1923, Hodges was elected as the Labour MP for Lichfeld and joined the first Labour Government, under the leadership of Ramsay MacDonald, in which he was given the office of First Lord of the Admiralty. MFGB rules stated that its permanent officials could not serve in parliament and, as a result, he was forced to resign as Secretary of the MFGB, being replaced by the far more radical Arthur Cook from the Rhondda district. In May 1924, Hodges was invited to the Rhondda to play at Ton Pentre golf club in a game with the Duke of York who later became King George VI. However, his period in government was short owing to his defeat in the general election of October 1924.

As a result of his role in the events leading up to Black Friday, Hodges' reputation among some rank and file miners was permanently besmirched

---

47 Reports in the Gloucester papers from January 1921 to December 1921.
48 *Dean Forest Mercury* 9 December 1921.
49 *Gloucester Journal* 26 November 1921.

John Marfell was born in 1866 in Ruardean. He married Annie in 1890 and had three children. He started work in the mines when he was 14 and then continued working as a miner for the rest of his life. On 16 September 1921, he had an accident at Eastern United and injured his back. He continued to suffer from pain but returned to work a few weeks later. On the morning of 7 December 1921, he walked into his garden and attempted to cut his throat and then shot himself with a gun. He was found by his son Ernest but died a few hours later.

Victor George Jones was born in Parkend in 1891. He was killed by a roof fall on 8 December 1921 at Hopewell in Wimberry colliery which was owned by his father.

Joseph Carpenter was born in Cherhill, Wiltshire in 1853. He initially gained work as a policeman in Cheltenham. He married Elizabeth Maggs in 1883 and went on to have four daughters and one son. After 1901, he moved to Drybrook and gained work at Crump Meadow colliery where he worked as a timberman. On 9 December 1921, he was crushed between two pieces of timber at the colliery and died in Gloucester hospital of peritonitis and shock two days later.

and, on 19 March 1925, the FDMA Executive wrote a letter to the MFGB protesting at Hodges' appointment to the office of Secretary to the International Miners Federation.[50] During the 1926 General Strike, when the miners were locked out again, he supported the return to work organised by George Spencer from Nottingham who had set up a company union in opposition to the MFGB.[51]

Hodges' final break with the labour movement came with the launching of a successful business career. In 1926, Hodges was appointed a member of the Central Electricity Board. He soon became a director of a number of companies, including Securities Management Trust, a subsidiary to the Bank of England established to finance inter-war industrial reconstruction.

50 FDMA Minutes 19 March 1925.
51 Renshaw, *The General Strike*, 88.

Hodges' move to the other side was confirmed when he became a Director of Rockwood Collieries in Leicestershire. He also served as chairman of the Glasgow Iron and Steel Company and became a good friend of the Conservative Prime Minister, Sir Stanley Baldwin.

Hodges died on 3 June 1947 at Ruthin Castle, Denbighshire, the same year the mines were nationalised. Wales's conservative newspaper, the *Western Mail*, described him as one of the foremost leaders in industry. To many of his erstwhile colleagues in the labour movement, however, he remained someone who, through self-seeking opportunism, betrayed his early promise and joined the other side. His probate lists him leaving £133,000 to his wife and daughter which would be worth about £5.5 million today.[52]

The other leading personalities associated with Black Friday gradually deserted the labour movement or moved to the right. In 1931, Jimmy Thomas was expelled from the Labour Party and the NUR for joining Ramsay McDonald's National Government.[53] Robert Williams was expelled from the Communist Party for his role on Black Friday and re-joined the Labour Party the following year. He gradually drifted to the right-wing of the labour movement and was critical of the miners during the 1926 Lock Out. He committed suicide in 1936.

Ernest Bevin founded the Transport and General Workers Union in 1922 bringing together the small unions affiliated to the NTWF into one large industrial union. Bevin became the General Secretary of the new union and advocated pragmatic collective bargaining. However, he withdrew his support for the miners during the 1926 General Strike, leaving them isolated and defeated once again.

Arthur Morgan continued as Managing Director of Henry Crawshay & Co. Ltd. and was instrumental in persuading the company's shareholders to invest in the Forest coalfield by sinking a shaft at Bilson to create Northern United colliery. He died of a heart attack in 1936 leaving

52 Ancestry and This is Money https://www.thisismoney.co.uk/money/bills/article-1633409/Historic-inflation-calculator-value-money-changed-1900.html
53 Jimmy Thomas was appointed Secretary of State for the Colonies in the incoming Labour government of 1924 under Ramsay MacDonald. In the second Labour government of 1929, Thomas was made Lord Privy Seal with special responsibility for employment. He became Secretary of State for the Dominions in 1930 and retained that position in Ramsay MacDonald's National Government (1931–1935). For the first few months of the National Government in 1931, he also served as Colonial Secretary once more. Thomas served as Secretary of State for the Colonies again from 1935 until May 1936, when he was forced to resign from politics. It was revealed that he had been entertained by stock exchange speculators and had dropped heavy hints as to tax changes planned in the budget. This would have made some of his new friends very wealthy to the detriment of the ordinary worker.

£123,093 to his daughter. This would be equivalent to over £8.6 million in today's money.[54] Thomas Deakin, who had complained that bankrupt miners had been able to earn good money, died in 1935 leaving £56,780 to his sons, equivalent to over £4 million today.[55]

The only recommendation of the Sankey Commission to directly benefit the Forest of Dean mining community was the 1920 Mining Industry Act, which placed a levy on every ton of coal raised to be used for welfare and educational facilities. The first significant local grant from the resulting Miners' Welfare Fund was £6,000 donated to the Forest of Dean Mining School which was opened in November 1925.[56] Other facilities which benefited from the Fund were the Bream Miners' Welfare Hall which was opened in 1927 and Cinderford Miners' Welfare Hall which was opened by Frank Hodges in 1930.

Halls and playing fields administered by local committees in other parts of the Forest also received grants from the Miners' Welfare Fund, such as the recreation grounds at Viney Hill, Ruardean, Cinderford and Coleford as well as memorial halls such as those at Ruspidge and Blakeney. The Dilke Memorial Hospital also received funding and the welfare of miners' wives was eventually acknowledged with the funding of pit head baths at Cannop colliery in 1930 and Princess Royal colliery in 1941.[57]

Eventual nationalisation

The Craftsmen Association struggled to maintain its membership and honour the debt to local traders. At a meeting of craftsmen in Cinderford in February 1923, Allen protested that there were only two craftsmen at Lightmoor colliery paying dues to the Association.[58] At another meeting of craftsmen in early August 1923, Allen complained that the conditions for stokers working on furnaces in hot weather under galvanised roofs were worse than the Black Hole of Calcutta and yet they were only being paid a minimum wage of 5s 10d a shift compared to 8s 2d elsewhere.[59] Allen did his best to re-build his union but failed and, later in 1923, had to resign his post due to lack of funds.

54 Ancestry and https://www.thisismoney.co.uk/money/bills/article-1633409/Historic-inflation-calculator-value-money-changed-1900.html
55 Ibid
56 *Gloucester Journal* 7 November 1925.
57 *Gloucester Journal* 20 December 1930 and *Dean Forest Mercury* 26 September 1941.
58 *Dean Forest Mercury* 23 February 1923.
59 *Gloucester Citizen* 9 August 1923.

John Williams, Noah Ablett and Frank Hodges (left to right).

In early 1922, a demoralised Booth resigned his post and returned to Nottinghamshire where he was elected as a checkweighman at Annesley Colliery. After the defeats of 1921 and then of 1926, he moderated his views and developed a more pragmatic approach to industrial relations. Booth continued to be involved in union politics and in 1945 was elected General Secretary of the Nottinghamshire Area of the National Union of Mineworkers. He retired a few years later in 1950 and died in 1978.[60]

In May 1922, Booth was replaced as agent for the FDMA by John Williams a miner from Kenfig Hill who was secretary of the Garw district of the SWMF when Hodges was the agent. When Williams arrived to take up the post, he was shocked to discover:

> the conditions under which the miners worked was truly appalling. The wages in this coalfield were the lowest in the country. I found men working at the pit-top for four shillings a day at one colliery.[61]

60 Griffin, *The Miners of Nottinghamshire*, Volume 2, 39.
61 R. Page Arnot, Interview with John Williams, 1961, Richard Burton Archives.

In the inter-war years nationalisation in the form of state control remained a central demand of the MFGB. However, there was no more talk of workers' control as the optimism generated by the Sankey report in 1919 evaporated. Williams, like Booth, was influenced by syndicalism and continued to use the tactics he had learnt in the South Wales coalfield to help rebuild the FDMA with Organ and other members of his Executive. Williams remained the agent for the FDMA through the 1926 Lockout, the 1930s depression and the Second World War. In 1947, the mines were nationalised by the post-war Labour government and brought under state control.

In 1955, the NUM negotiated a national day wage agreement which provided a uniform rate of pay for all grades of workers in the country, except those on piece rates. In 1966, the National Power Loading Agreement aimed to bring an end to piece work and introduce a national uniform wage rate for face workers, craftsmen and power loading operators. However, at first the rates were dependent on the district productivity, with areas like Nottingham and Kent receiving the highest rates.[62] It was not until the end of 1971 that parity was established at £30 a week. However, by this time the National Coal Board had closed all the deep mines in the Forest of Dean, deeming them to be uneconomic.

62 B.J. McCormick, *Industrial Relations in the Coal Industry* (London: Macmillan, 1979).

Conclusion

The crisis of 1921-2 had curbed the progress of working-class strategies centred on political radicalism and industrial militancy. Undermining their base, it paved the way for the ascendancy of a labourism already increasing in appeal, based on parliamentary reformism and constitutional collective bargaining. The dramatic increase in unemployment, the retreat of trade unionism and reverses for key groups of workers marked the significance of 1921. It knocked the stuffing out of workplace activists and workplace organisation, decimated union membership, arrested syndicalist tendencies and ensured that the weak CPGB was born in unpropitious circumstances. But discontent and resistance continued. They found new hope in the industrial upturn and the swing to the left in the unions between 1924 and 1926 — a significant disjuncture. The miners' defeat of '21 was not so severe as to preclude the struggle of 1926, although certainly weakened it.[1]

The struggle in 1921 was as much about dignity, status and independence as about wages and hours. It was the realisation of a long-expected confrontation between the working class and its enemies, on the outcome of which labour's hopes depended. The demand for a living wage in the form of a profits pool and wages board entailed some degree of mediation and control over economic forces and so recognised that the status of the miner was not just one of economic cost. The introduction of district wage agreements meant the Forest miner's life was again to be governed by the vagaries of the unpredictable market. This meant the standard of life of a miner, and that of the community around him, would be determined by the impersonal laws of supply and demand, personified by impenetrable ascertainments by accountants over which miners had little control.

In 1919, rank and file miners in the Forest of Dean were confident that change was possible and were willing to use industrial action to achieve their aim of joint control of the coal industry. However, the economic conditions of the post-war period meant that the miners' demands were unachievable without radical change in the whole economic and social structure of society.

1 John McIlroy , Alan Campbell and Keith Gildart (Editors), *Industrial Politics and the 1926 Mining Lockout: The Struggle for Dignity*, (Cardiff: University of Wales, 2009) 301.

From 1914 to 1920, the leaders of the Triple Alliance believed they could gradually improve the living and working conditions for their members with little awareness that all the gains of the post-war period would be swept away and the working class would be forced back into poverty and unemployment. After Black Friday, G.B.H. Cole said about the leaders of the Triple Alliance:

> These leaders, more from lack of foresight and imagination than from any other cause, took things easy or busied themselves with small affairs when they should have been straining every nerve to prepare for the coming struggle. The result was that the slump towards the end of 1920 took them altogether unprepared. As they had no policy for taking advantage of favourable conditions, they had none for bearing up against unfavourable conditions. And, conscious of their own helplessness and lack of ideas for dealing with the situation, and of the panic which was laying hold of them, they attributed helplessness and panic to the rank and file in an even higher degree.[2]

The 1921 defeat had its roots in the commitment of the MFGB leaders to constitutional means while refusing to take the opportunity to force through their demands in 1919 by industrial action. The historic compromise which led the miners down the road to the Sankey Commission revealed the industry was poorly organised and the distributive side of the trade was in a state of chaos. The commission highlighted the contrast between the wretched living conditions of many mining families on the one hand and the excessive wartime profits and royalties earned by the owners and landowners on the other. However, the MFGB leaders continued to procrastinate, and in the end, the government was able to stifle the demand for joint control and the potential for radical change. Finally, the miners were defeated by the political skills of Lloyd George and the acquiescence of the leadership of the broader trade union movement, including the Triple Alliance.

The miners' demands had been set out clearly by their leaders at the Sankey Commission and many in the general public believed they were justified, reasonable and achievable. However, in the end, the Forest of Dean miners' dream of a prosperous, modern and well-funded coal industry which provided safe working conditions and a living wage for its workers

2 Quoted by Sprenger, The Triple Alliance.

Table 9: Results for ballots on strike action carried out by the FDMA 1919 — 1921.

Date	Total Votes	Votes for a Strike	Votes Against a Strike
February 1919	4,174	4,020	154
April 1919	5,824	393	5,431
April 1920	4,684	3,508	1,176
August 1920	5,520	5,132	388
October 1920	5,232	4,514	718
November 1920	3,726	1,961	1,765
June 1921	5,881	5,222	659

was in tatters. Once handed back to its aristocratic owners, profit-seeking entrepreneurs and shareholders, the realisation of this dream was out of the question. Hodges later admitted they missed their chance in 1919. In his book, *My Adventures as a Labour Leader*, written in 1925, Hodges says of the miners' preparations for the nationalisation struggle of 1919:

> everything was in trim for the most smashing blow that had ever been delivered at the system which had governed the coal industry since its inception.[3]

Hodges was correct, but in the end, he sided with the political establishment and those trade union leaders who did not trust their members. The Forest miners had consistently voted to take strike action in support of their demands from 1919 onwards but when their voice was eventually heard it was too late. In April 1921, there was unemployment, short-time working and stockpiles of coal at the pitheads. This was the worst time possible to go on strike and without the support of the Triple Alliance, they did not stand a chance.

The miners went from a position in 1919 when the debate was about workers control or nationalisation, to a situation in 1921 where they were in dire poverty. Smillie was fully aware that the agenda of the ruling classes was to crush militancy within the labour movement and was frightened the MFGB could be destroyed in a long-protracted strike. He was

3 Hodges, *My Adventures*, 80.

concerned that defeat could lead to the loss of the many gains the MFGB had achieved in his lifetime. In addition, most of the MFGB Executive, as well as the Triple Alliance leaders, believed that the trade union movement must never, in the words of Jimmy Thomas, become "more important than the state as a whole".[4] This conviction was illustrated in an account Smillie later gave of his meeting with Lloyd George in 1919 to Nye Bevan. In his book, *In Place of Fear* published in 1952, Bevan described the meeting and quotes Lloyd George's warning to Smillie and Smillie's response:

> Gentlemen you have fashioned in the Triple Alliance of unions represented by you a most powerful instrument. I feel bound to tell you that in our opinion we are at your mercy. The Army is disaffected and cannot be relied upon. Trouble has already occurred in a number of camps. We have just emerged from a great war, and the people are eager for the reward of their sacrifices, and we are in no position to satisfy them. In these circumstances, if you carry out your threatened strike, you will defeat us. But if you do so, have you weighed up the consequences? The strike will be in defiance of the government of the country and by its success will precipitate a constitutional crisis of the first importance. For, if a force arises in the state that is stronger than the state itself, it must be ready to take on the functions of the state or withdraw and accept the authority of the state. Gentlemen, have you considered and if you have, are you ready?

> "From that moment on", said Smillie, "we were beaten and we knew we were".[5]

In the period 1919-1921, there was little evidence of political forces seeking to overthrow the state in the Forest to Dean. However, the Forest miners had a history of militancy based on their particular tradition of independence, custom and practice, natural justice and democratic principles which had elements of syndicalism and socialism and which offered an alternative way to organise society. The miners in the Forest of Dean were confident they could win, they were organised enough to fight, and some were prepared to consider an alternative way to organise society. Martyn Ives has argued:

4 Ives, *Reform, Revolution and Direct Action*, 43.
5 Aneurin Bevan, *In Place of Fear* (Great Britain: Simon and Schuster, 1952) 20.

that in 1919 there was a conjuncture of factors which rendered the situation profoundly unpredictable, and pregnant with alternative possible outcomes. To contemporaries who felt themselves to be standing at the threshold of a new society, the defeats of the future were barely conceivable.[6]

Faith in industrial militancy alone was not enough to bring victory, and the defeat of 1921 was catastrophic for the Forest of Dean mining community. The syndicalist challenge with its demand for workers' control could not respond to economic depression in the coal trade. Harry Roberts remarked years later that the government and mine owners had been fully prepared for the lockout and believed the miners never stood a chance because:

the mine owners had the foresight to stock up many hundreds of tons of coal alongside their individual railway spurs, and from time to time trucks would be loaded for the normal deliveries out of the area.[7]

Certainly, it was the worst time to take on the government and, having missed the opportunities in 1919, far too late. For the government, the timing could not have been better for such a confrontation. The depression in the coal trade and the season of the year combined to keep disruption to a minimum. Furthermore, the Government was concerned with broader industrial issues than just the industrial relations in the coal industry and needed to bring to an end a movement that had even challenged its right to fight a war. The government believed the unrest was political and so its response was political. As a result, they conspired with the colliery owners to defeat the miners, resulting in a disaster for the whole trade union movement.

In the Forest of Dean, the large number of votes for strike action and the decision to flood the pits made by rank and file miners imply that the defeat cannot be simply put down to poor leadership by Booth and the FDMA Executive. Under the influence of syndicalism, Booth was keen to encourage the Forest miners to use their industrial muscle but very aware that in April 1921 they were in a weak opposition and expressed caution in his speeches to his members. In the end, he had little choice but to support the mandate of his members who wished to fight to the bitter end. In his study of this period in South Wales, Edward May argues:

6 Ives, *Reform, Revolution and Direct Action*, 7.
7 Harry Roberts, *The Tar Castle*, 7

The militant optimism of the period allowed and encouraged miners to look beyond the horizons offered by existing institutions and traditions. This optimism and the possibilities it entertained evaporated in the aftermath of the lock-out of 1921. The triumphalism of the owners and the class bitterness they engendered ensured, however, that the militancy remained.[8]

The general strike and miners' lockout which followed in 1926 are often thought of as the high points of inter-war industrial militancy. However, in many respects, they were just an echo of the more insurgent militancy of the 1919-1921 period.[9] In 1926, David Organ and John Williams led the Forest miners into battle again.[10] Women were at the forefront of the strike, not only organising soup kitchens, but this time confronting the blacklegs and sometimes ending up in court. It was a long, hard and bitter struggle.

Most of the men mentioned in this pamphlet ended up being blacklisted after the 1926 Lockout. These included Harold Craddock, David Organ, Richard Kear, Fred Warren, Albert Meek, William Hoare and many more. Jesse Hodges (Jnr) returned to the Forest in the late 1930s and in 1983 said:

I have left too much of my blood in the mines to ever want to go back down, and I would not wish it on anybody ... It was a pity it was ever discovered. I don't believe God meant for a man to grovel in the bowels of the earth and to leave blood on coal ...They are still doing it now dying day by day, coughing their lungs up from it. Then I look back to the days of my youth to days in the mines, to the grovelling in the bowels to earth and to the terrible work, the hard work, the sores, the bleeding, crying, the parents saying "I can't help you son." … I think this as I look back; I would not mind going back to those days if, there was equality for all, and we could live the life without having to grovel. In those days Spring was Spring, Summer was Summer, and Autumn was Autumn, and Winter was Winter—we knew them all. We could tell them apart. This is what I say as I have said before, the cuckoo has left us—he doesn't want us.[11]

8 Edward May, *A Question of Control*, 9.
9 Ives, *Reform, Revolution and Direct Action*, 1.
10 Anstis, *Blood on Coal* and David M. Organ, *The Life and Times of David Richard Organ*.
11 Jesse Hodges (Jnr), Gage Library.

Appendix One: Timeline of 1921 Lockout in the Forest of Dean

Date	Event
Thursday 31 March	Miners and craftsmen locked out
Thursday 31 March	State of Emergency declared
Friday 1 April	Mass meeting at Speech House
Monday 4 April	Unemployment Benefit Offices under siege
Monday 4 April	Collieries start flooding
Tuesday 5 April	Court of Umpires decides locked out miners are not entitled to unemployment benefit.
Tuesday 5 April	Mass meeting at Speech House.
Tuesday 5 April	NTWF resolves to support miners with strike action.
Thursday 7 April	Wignall presents the miners' case in parliament.
Friday 8 April	Demonstration outside Princess Royal colliery
Friday 8 April	NUR resolves to support miners with strike action
Friday 8 April	Triple Alliance calls for a nationwide strike of its members on Tuesday 12 April
Friday 8 April,	Reserves of the army, navy and air force called up.
Friday 8 April,	Appeal launched for the enrolment of 80,000 special constables.
Saturday 9 April,	Triple Alliance leaders insist the safety men return to work.
Saturday 9 April,	Mass meeting at Speech House resolves the policy of withdrawing the safety men to continue.
Sunday 10 April	Frank Hodges sends a telegraph ordering the safetymen to return to work.
Monday 11 April	National negotiations resume.
Monday 11 April	Triple Alliance pushes the strike start date back to 10 pm on Friday 15 April.

Date	Event
Thursday 14 April	Craftsmen receive a letter from colliery owners requesting they return to work.
Thursday 14 April	Mass meeting at Speech House refuses the request to allow the safetymen to return to work.
Thursday 14 April	Mass meeting with local Triple Alliance leaders at Gloucester Labour Club.
Friday 15 April	Black Friday.
Friday 15 April	Meeting of local Triple Alliance leaders at Gloucester Labour Club calls off strike.
Monday 18 April	Mass rally at Speech House.
Tuesday 19 April	40 poachers arrested.
Wednesday 20 April	SWMF Executive calls for a national policy of removing the safety men
Thursday 21 April 1921	Morgan threatens to wind up Henry Crawshay & Co. Ltd.
Friday 22 April	Booth attends national delegate conference with a mandate to stay out.
Friday 22 April	Delegate conference rejects a national policy of removing the safety men. Safety men remain out in the Forest of Dean.
Friday 22 April	Strike pay runs out.
Friday 22 April	NTWF and the NUR place an embargo on the handling of imported coal and the removal of coal from colliery sidings.
Sunday 24 April	Lydney meeting with Charlie Cramp from the NUR.
Monday 25 April	Food coupons distributed at Speech House.
Monday 25 April	March and rally at Speech House.
Tuesday 26 April	Government offers £10 million temporary subsidy.
Thursday 28 April	Delegate conference rejects government offer with support from Forest of Dean.

Date	Event
Friday 29 April	Mass Rally at Speech House approves decision made at delegate conference.
Saturday 30 April	Bristol dockers walk out in solidarity with the miners.
Sunday 1 May	May Day rally at Speech House.
Wednesday 4 May	Foxes Bridge & Co. and Henry Crawshay & Co. confer on their Board of Directors the power to take steps to wind up their Companies.
Wednesday 4 May	Wignall warns the government of the consequences of attempting to import coal under the Emergency Powers Act.
Thursday 5 May	Outcroppers load a train with twelve tons of coal and sell it in Gloucester for £2 a ton.
Saturday 7 May	NTWF instructs members to refuse to handle imported coal.
Monday 9 May	FDMA members now receiving a voucher worth 3s 9d a week and 1s a week for each child.
Monday 9 May	Mass rally at Speech House
Friday 13 May	NUR instructs members to refuse to handle imported coal
Saturday 14 May,	Cinderford Co-operative Society donates £500 to the distress fund.
Saturday 14 May	Mass meeting at Speech House.
Sunday 15 May	Lydney Churches donate £300 to distress fund.
Friday 20 May	Mass meeting at Bilson Green to protest against commercial outcropping.
Monday 23 May	Mass meeting at Speech House and demonstration against commercial outcropping.
Monday 23 May	Gloucestershire County Council agrees to provide free school meals
Friday 27 May	New government offer includes gradual scaling down of wages.

Date	Event
Saturday 28 May	MFGB refers offer to districts.
Monday 30 May	Mass meeting at Speech House recommends rejection.
Monday 30 May	Sharpness dockers and railwaymen refuse to handle imported coal leading to suspensions.
Monday 30 May	Meeting of craftsmen at Ruspidge
Monday 30 May	Allen meets Arthur Morgan at Abbotwood House.
Tuesday 31 May	NUR and NTWF lift embargo on imported coal.
Thursday 2 June	Meeting of Forest miners rejects government's offer.
Friday 3 June	MFGB announce every district had rejected the offer.
Saturday 4 June	Newspapers report rumours that craftsmen may return to work
Monday 6 June	Mass meeting at Speech House. Allen denies rumours.
Friday 10 June	MFGB delegate conference recommends a ballot on the offer.
Monday 13 June	Mass meeting at Speech House recommends rejection of the offer.
Thursday 16 June	Ballot takes place.
Saturday 18 June	Forest of Dean rejects the offer by a large majority.
Saturday 18 June	Nationally about two-thirds reject the offer.
Saturday 18 June	Lloyd George withdraws offer of a temporary subsidy
Saturday 18 June	Mass meeting at Speech House.
Monday 27 June	MFGB Executive advises a return to work but final decision referred back to the district Executives
Friday 1 July	FDMA Executive advises rejection of offer.
Friday 1 July	Mass meeting at Speech House rejects the offer by a hand vote.
Friday 1 July	MFGB Executive instructs miners to return to work.

Appendix Two: FDMA Executive Committees

The FDMA executive committee in 1919.

Name	Role	Colliery	Home and year of birth
Elected district officials			
Herbert Booth	Agent	FDMA Employee	Cinderford 1886
David Organ	President and Checkweighman	Norchard	Oldcroft 1876
Gilbert Jones	Vice President up to 14/05/19		Yorkley 1897
Leonard Douglas	Vice President		Lydbrook 1879
Charles Luker	Secretary	Crown	Whitecroft 1886
Henry Watson	Treasurer		Berry Hill
Thomas Etheridge	Clerk	FDMA Employee	Cinderford 1897
Richard Kear	Auditor	New Fancy	Oldcroft 1876
Ambrose Adams	Auditor and Checkweighman	Crump Meadow	Ruspidge 1859
Delegates from pit lodges			
John Harper	Timberman	Waterloo	Ruardean 1867
William Bradley	Checkweighman	Trafalgar	Ruardean 1864
Enos Taylor	Checkweighman	Foxes Bridge	Cinderford 1862
Martin Perkins	Checkweighman	Lightmoor	Cinderford 1857
William Morgan	Timber Man	Eastern United	Soudley 1871
James Clement		Norchard	Bream 1885
John Pritchard		Princess Royal	Bream 1864
Albert Wilding		Parkend	Whitecroft 1883
Jesse Hodges (Snr)		Crump Meadow	Cinderford 1881

Name	Role	Colliery	Home and year of birth
Amos James		Wallsend	Blakeney Hill 1872
Wallace Watkins		Crown	Yorkley 1888
Charles Mason		Cannop	Brierley 1889
Frank Matthews from 29/11/19		Cannop	Broadwell 1879
William Hatton		New Fancy	

The FDMA Executive Committee In 1921

Name	Role	Colliery	Home and year of birth
Elected district officials			
David Organ	President and Checkweighman	Norchard	Oldcroft 1876
Albert Wilding	Vice President	Parkend	Parkend 1882
Thomas Etheridge	Financial Secretary	FDMA Employee	Cinderford 1897
Horace Jones	Finance Committee and Checkweighman	Parkend /New Fancy	Yorkley 1874
Samuel Cooke	Finance Committee		Whitecroft 1866
Gilbert Jones	Finance Committee		Yorkley 1897
Richard Kear	Auditor and Checkweighman	New Fancy	Oldcroft 1876
Ambrose Adams	Auditor and Checkweighman	Crump Meadow	Ruspidge 1859

Name	Role	Colliery	Home and year of birth
Charles Luker	Political Committee	Crown	Whitecroft 1886
William Howells	Political Committee		Yorkley 1863
Ivor Brain	Political Committee		Drybrook 1884
Albert James	Political Committee		Pillowell 1877
Charles Beach	Political Committee		Cinderford 1889
Delegates from pit lodge			
Jesse Hodges (Snr)	Checkweighman	Crump Meadow	Cinderford 1881
William Bradley	Checkweighman	Trafalgar	Ruardean 1864
Enos Taylor	Checkweighman	Foxes Bridge	Cinderford 1862
Martin Perkins	Checkweighman	Lightmoor	Cinderford 1857
John Harper		Waterloo	Ruardean 1867
William Morgan		Eastern United	Soudley 1868
James Clement		Norchard	Bream 1885
Reuben James		Princess Royal	Pillowell 1870
William Vedmore		Parkend	Parkend 1876
Amos James		Wallsend	Blakeney 1871
Frank Matthews		Cannop	Mile End 1878
George Banstone		Small Collieries	

Appendix Three: MFGB Executive Committees

The Executive Committee of the MFGB in July 1919. [1]

Robert Smillie	Scotland (President)
Frank Hodges	South Wales (Secretary)
Herbert Smith	Yorkshire (Vice-President)
James Robson	Durham (Treasurer)
James Cook	Scotland
William Webb	Scotland
Joseph Batey	Durham
Thomas Trotter	Durham
William Straker	Northumberland
Edward Hughes	North Wales
John Hoskin	Yorkshire
Samuel Roebuck	Yorkshire
John Tinker	Lancashire and Cheshire
Frank Hall	Derbyshire
George Spencer	Nottinghamshire
John Baker	Midlands
Herbert Booth	Forest of Dean
William Brace	South Wales
Vernon Hartshorne	South Wales
George Barker	South Wales

1 *Western Mail* 19 July 1919.

The Executive Committee of the MFGB at the time of the 1921 Lockout.[2]

Herbert Smith	Yorkshire (President)
Frank Hodges	South Wales (Secretary)
James Robson	Durham (Treasurer)
Duncan Graham	Scotland
William Richardson	Durham
William Whiteley	Durham
John Potts	Yorkshire
Samuel Roebeck	Yorkshire
John McGurk	Lancashire and Cheshire
Gordon MacDonald	Lancashire and Cheshire
Frank Hall	Derbyshire
Frank Varley	Nottinghamshire
Samuel Finney	Midlands
W Latham	Midlands
James Winstone	South Wales
Thomas Richards	South Wales
Noah Ablett	South Wales
Arthur Cook	South Wales
Levi Lovett	Leicestershire
William Whitefield	Bristol
Robert Shirkie	Representative of Enginemen

2 Arnot, *The Miners*, 311.

Appendix Four: Forest of Dean Colliery Companies[3]

Henry Crawshay & Co. Ltd.

In the nineteenth century Henry Crawshay (1812-1879), whose family had built their empire out of iron making in South Wales, invested heavily in iron and coal in the Forest of Dean. In August 1889, Henry Crawshay & Co. Ltd. was formed with directors William Crawshay (Henry's son), Tudor Crawshay (Henry's nephew), Colonel Augustus Arthur Kilner Brasier Creagh, from Creagh Castle, County Cork (married to Henry's daughter Catherine) and Sir Gabriel Goldney and Frederick Hastings Goldney who were wealthy landowners from Corsham in Wiltshire.

As the Crawshay family's wealth grew, they built extensive country mansions on the edges of the Forest and grew to regard the Forest of Dean as their fiefdom. Henry Crawshay's first residence in the Forest was Abbotswood House on the Abbotswood Estate in Ruspidge. He then moved to Oaklands near Newnham. William Crawshay *(1845-1910)* built Riverdale mansion in Newnham and another son, Edwin Crawshay (1836-1902), built Blaisdon Hall on his Blaisdon estate.[4]

In the twentieth century another Forest family, headed by the Crawshay's accountant George Morgan (1814-1912), gradually became influential within the Company. George Morgan's children Henry, George (Jnr), Edwin, Eliza and Arthur all became part of the Crawshay business empire. In the 1890s, George Morgan (Jnr) bailed out Edwin Crawshay who had got into financial difficulty and, as a result, gained a stake in the Company. The Morgans already held extensive business interests in the Forest, particularly in the coal factor trade.[5] Edwin Morgan (1862-1919) took over the role of company Secretary from his brother George in 1912. Arthur Morgan started work for the company as a clerk in about 1880.

In January 1919, the Company owned Lightmoor and Eastern United collieries and had interests in Foxes Bridge colliery. At this time, the

---

3 This account of ownership of the Forest of Dean collieries during this period provides a very rough summary of what was, in reality, a very complex web of shifting directorships, share dealings, take-overs and investments. A full account can be found in Ian Pope, Bob How and Paul Karau, *Severn and Wye Railway, Forest of Dean*, Volumes 1, 2, 3 and 4, (Bucklebury: Wild Swan Publications, 1983–2009).
4 M. M. Beech, "Henry Crawshay & Co. Ltd., the Man and his Colliery", *New Regard*, No. 11, (Forest of Dean Local History Society) 5-25.
5 A coal factor is a coal merchant.

company's Managing Director was Edwin Morgan and the Chairman was Tudor Crawshay. Other members of the board included Arthur Morgan, John Washington Brasier-Creagh (Augustus Creagh's nephew), Richard Crawshay Heyworth (Henry's grandson) and Alfred Billings, a property developer from Cheltenham.[6] In November 1919, the company bought the Trafalgar Colliery from Sir Francis Brain for £10,000 and, in December 1919, bought a substantial interest in Howbeach colliery.[7]

In December 1919, Arthur Morgan was elected as Managing Director after the death of Edwin Morgan. The other Directors, mainly from the Crawshay dynasty, lived a life of leisure which included fishing, hunting, painting and writing. In May 1921, Brasier-Creagh was elected Chairman of the Company after the death of Tudor Crawshay. At the same time Leonard Corfield Bucknall, who was also a member of the Crawshay dynasty, was elected to the board.[8] Other main shareholders included Sir John Goldney, Frank Washbourn and various members of the Morgan family.

Lydney and Crump Meadow Collieries Ltd.

Joseph Hale (1836–1928) was Managing Director of Lydney and Crump Meadow Collieries Ltd, which owned Waterloo Colliery and Crump Meadow Colliery. The company was registered in 1884, with Hale as Managing Director, and he remained in that role for over 40 years.[9] In the 1920s, he shared responsibility for running the company with his sons, Charles and Eustace, who were also directors of the company. The relationship Hale had with his men is reflected in this statement from Elsie Olivey when speaking about her father who worked for Hale:

> Father had attended Wesley. Since he was already working at Crump Meadow Pit, he would have attended Wesley. If you worked at Joseph Hale's pits, you went to Wesley, if you knew what was good for you. If any of Hale's men were not in their accustomed place in Chapel on a Sunday, Joseph Hale would

6 Board Minute Book of Henry Crawshay & Co. Ltd. Ltd (O) 1919-1921. Richard Crawshay Heyworth (1862-1942) was born at the Crawshay manor house at Oaklands. His mother, Emily Crawshay, was the daughter of Henry Crawshay & Co. Ltd. He lived at Hamilton House in Cheltenham

7 The main motivation for these purchases was to maintain pumping operations to keep their other pits free from water.

8 Major Leonard Corfield Bucknall (1874-1944) was born in Kent, the son of a steamship owner. He married Dorothy Crawshay who was the granddaughter of Henry Crawshay.

9 Obituary in *Gloucester Citizen* 6 January 1928.

want to know the reason why. If you wanted to get or keep a job you attended the Chapel of the pit owner's choice.[10]

Parkend Deep Navigation Collieries Company Ltd.

In 1921, Thomas Deakin (1850-1935) was the Managing Director of Parkend Deep Navigation Collieries Company Ltd, although his son Thomas Carlyle Deakin had by now begun to take more responsibility. The company owned New Fancy, Parkend Royal and Crown collieries. Deakin was an ardent Wesleyan Methodist and lay preacher.[11] He became the unofficial squire in the village of Parkend where he lived. People were expected to doff their caps or curtsey when he passed in the village.[12]

Princess Royal Company Ltd.

Sir William Henry Marling (1835-1919) was the principal shareholder of the Princess Royal Co. Ltd. when it was formed in 1890 to mine the deep steam-coal seams in West Dean. Marling owned the huge Sedbury Park Estate, with its mansion house which dominated the Chepstow skyline.[13] In 1916, Flour Mill colliery and Park Gutter colliery were connected underground to improve ventilation and safety, and to permit larger-scale production from the deep seams which could be up to six foot thick. The colliery then became known as Princess Royal. In April 1920, after Marling's death, a new board of directors took over the management of the Company. The Chairman was Philip Berrill from Bristol whose family held extensive shipping and coal trade interests. The Managing Director was Percy Moore from Chapel Hill House in Aylburton.

Cannop Coal Company Ltd.

In 1906, a group of businessmen from the North East led by Montague Francis Maclean (1871-1951) invested in the Cannop Coal Company Ltd which operated the Cannop colliery. Montague Maclean was the son of Sir Francis Maclean, a London barrister who went on to be Liberal MP

---

10 Phelps, *Forest Voices*, 30.
11 Obituary in *Gloucestershire Echo*, 02 August 1935.
12 Forest of Dean Family History Trust.
13 At the time the estate covered 5,887 acres and included 25 farms in Tidenham, Woolaston, and Hewelsfield and most of the land between Sedbury and Hewelsfield.

for Woodstock and later Chief Justice for Bengal. Montague Maclean was educated at Eton and Cambridge University and became Managing Director of Cannop colliery after gaining some experience managing Broomhill Collieries in Durham.

Park Colliery Ltd.

In 1911, Norchard colliery was bought by the Park Colliery Limited, whose Chairman was Charles Bathurst (from October 1918, Lord Bledisloe) from Lydney Park Estate. In 1910, Bathurst entered parliament representing the Conservative Party as MP for South Wiltshire. The other main directors were Robert Rawnsley Bowles who was a wealthy landowner from Priors Mesne, William Jones who owned business at Lydney docks and Brigadier General A. M. Tyler from Clanna, Alvington.

Appendix Five: Forest of Dean Collieries employing less than 120 men in 1918[14]

Owner	Name of Mine	Situation	Manager	Men
Adams Brothers, Joyford Hill.	Never Fear No.2	Coleford		10
Frank Baynham & Henry Brown, Wynols Hill, Coleford	New Speedwell	Berry Hill		10
Bixlade Colliery Co., c/o B H Taylor, Forest House, Coleford	Bixslade No.2	Bixlade Valley		9
ditto	Hopewell	Speech House Road		8
Brown and Ellis, Laburnum House, Broadwell.	Foundry Gate	ditto		20
AW Brown, Broadwell.	Valletts Level No.1	Coleford		23
ditto	Trenchard No.2 (Abandoned)	ditto		
ditto	New Pot Lid	ditto	Not worked separately. Coal raised at Valletts	
James & Thomas Collins, Yorkley.	Bailey Hill	Yorkley		33
Cooper & Taylor, Forest View, Lydbrook	True Blue and Newnham Bottom	Ruardean		6

14 https://home.rootsweb.com/

Owner	Name of Mine	Situation	Manager	Men
Dean Forest Central Collieries Ltd., 109, Victoria St., London	Moseley Green	Parkend	P Y D Trotter	41
C Elsmore & Sons, Ellwood.	Darkhill Endeavour	Ellwood Green	(Not worked in 1918)	
ditto	Tile Quarry	ditto		5
Henry Goodwin, Belle View, Berry Hill.	Lonk Level	Coleford	Henry Goodwin	105
Grove Engine Colliery Co., Whitecroft.	Grove Engine	Lydney	E A Worthy	21
Gwilliam Brothers, Arles Level Colliery, Shortstanding.	Arles Level	Shortstanding	J W Gwilliam	16
ditto	Mapleford	Bixslade		8
Executors of late Thomas Gwilliam, English Bicknor.	Farmers Folly	Joyford		13
Gwilliams & Hawkins, Society Colliery, Joyford.	Society	Joyford Hill	Thomas. Gwilliam (Jnr).	5
Hamblin Brothers & Co., Broadwell.	New Roberts Folly Gale No.2	Cinderford	Closed during 1917	
Harrow Hill Colliery Co., Drybrook	Harrow Hill	Nailbridge	Albert Jones	58
Healey and Co., Cinderford	Mount Pleasant No.2	Nofold Green	Not worked in 1918	
ditto	Gorbrook Gale	Cinderford	Ditto	

Owner	Name of Mine	Situation	Manager	Men
SG & G Hughes, Hillersland Colliery, Hillersland.	Hillersland	Coleford		10
Fred James, Pillowell.	New Engine Ditch	Moseley Green	Not worked in 1918	
F Jeffries, 26, Nicholas St., Bristol	Cross Knave	Woodgate	W Miles	17
George Jones & P S Taylor, Boxbrush Rd., Coleford	Hollow Meadow	Moseley Green	Abandoned	
Mrs E Lathom, Poolway Villa, Gloucester Rd., Coleford	Lydbrook Deep Level	ditto	AR Buffrey	31
Lydney, Tile, Brick and Sanitary Pipe Co., Ltd., Lydney	Allastone	Lydney		14
F Matthews, Pendleton, Manchester	Fire Engine No.1	Cinderford		7
ditto	ditto No.2			17
Meadow Cliff Colliery Co. Ltd., Cinderford	Meadow Cliff	Cinderford	PKD Trotter	59
GW Morgan, Barn Hill Lodge, Coleford	Morgans Trenchard	Fetter Hill		
ditto	Worcester No.2	Speech House Road		6
Frank Pardoe, Abbotsford, Mellish Rd., Walsall, Staffs	Drybrook Folly No.2	Drybrook		27

Owner	Name of Mine	Situation	Manager	Men
George & William Pegler, High St., Cinderford	Heywood	East Dean		9
Thomas Pegler, Mill Hill, Bream.	Clements Tump (Lass of the Mill)	Coleford		25
ditto	Darkhill	Ellwood	Not worked in 1918	
ditto	Wavers Pitching No. Gale	Woodside, Bream	Ditto	
C M Phipps and Co., Chapel Hill, Whitecroft.	Whitecroft	Lydney		18
George Powell, Berry Hill.	Well Level	Coleford		4
ditto	ditto No.2	ditto		7
ditto	Whitehall No.2	Berry Hill	(Commenced Aug. 1917)	5
Alfred J Smith Ltd., 9 Queen Sq., Bristol	Glyncarn	Coleford	Thomas. R Jenkins	9
Smith Brothers, Coalway.	Gentleman Collieries, No.3	Coalway	Not worked in 1918	
ditto	Prosper Gate	ditto		10
Success Colliery Co., Fetter Hill.	Success	Fetter Hill	Arthur Brown	30
Sulla Colliery Co. Lydney, Simeon James, Parkend.	Sulla	Lydney	S James	26
ditto	Bailey Hill	Yorkley		

Owner	Name of Mine	Situation	Manager	Men
Arthur Taylor, Valley Rd., Cinderford	New Regulator	Cinderford		29
P S Taylor, Berry Hill Farm, Coleford	Morgans Trenchard No.2	Coleford		
Tom Teague, Marion Lane, Berry Hill.	Mailscot Gale	Berry Hill		7
J H Walby Lower High St., Cinderford	Addishill	Cinderford		8
J Wheatstone, The Vention, Lydbrook	Worral Hill	Lydbrook		5
Woodgate Colliery Co. Ltd., Mile End.	Woodgate	Woodgate	W Miles	

New Regulator Colliery.

Appendix Six: The Government

David Lloyd George	Liberal	Prime Minister	December 1916–October 1922
Winston Churchill	Liberal	Secretary of State for War	January 1919–February 1921
Winston Churchill	Liberal	Secretary of State for the Colonies	February 1921–October 1922
Andrew Bonar Law	Tory	Leader of the Tory Party	December 1916–May 1923
Andrew Bonar Law	Tory	Chancellor of the Exchequer	December 1916–January 1919
Andrew Bonar Law	Tory	Leader of the House	December 1916–March 1921
Robert Horne	Unionist	Minister of Labour	January 1919–March 1920
Robert Horne	Unionist	President of the Board of Trade	March 1920–April 1921
Robert Horne	Unionist	Chancellor of the Exchequer	April 1921–October 1922
Thomas MacNamara	Liberal	Minister of Labour	March 1920–October 1922
Eric Geddes	Tory	Minister of Transport	May 1919–November 1921
Auckland Geddes	Unionist	President of the Board of Trade	May 1919–March 1920
Stanley Baldwin	Tory	President of the Board of Trade	April 1921–October 1922
Austen Chamberlain	Tory	Chancellor of the Exchequer	January 1919–April 1921

Appendix Seven: Booth in Nottingham

On his return to Nottingham in the Spring of 1922, Booth was elected as a checkweighman at Annesley Colliery. The miners in Nottingham were not so severely hit by the defeat following the lockout compared to other areas as they were able to negotiate better terms because of higher productivity. However, they were very demoralised, and this allowed the colliery owners to extend the butty system and introduce company unionism. In Nottingham, the butty system was operating on a different scale to that in the Forest of Dean. The buttymen often employed large numbers of daymen and sometimes did little work in the pit themselves. Tom Mosley, writing of his pit, reported:

> before the stoppage of 1921, Gedling was one of the best-organised collieries in Notts. Of three thousand men who worked at this pit a relative few were non-members of the NMA. After the 1921 debacle, no colliery suffered more from disorganisation and demoralisation. Many and varied factors brought this about ... (including) a return of a vicious form of bullying ... while after the return to work the branch committee was dominated by a 'caucus club' that ... stood for a positively immoral system of "sub-contracting" which meant a few exploiting the many.[15]

Despite this, the left still had a strong presence within the NMA and had its own organisational base around Mansfield. However, the butties had their organisation as well and with the backing of the colliery owners met with a measure of success in re-establishing the butty system. It was this which allowed Spencer to form a nucleus of miners who would become a base for a non-political union which would oppose strikes and consolidate the butty system. In 1924, Booth wrote an article called 'The Butty System in Notts' for *The Mineworker* in which he said: "the proportion of daymen to butties was now any number from one to twenty", in other words, the buttymen were employing teams of up to twenty men and boys which was significantly different from the Forest of Dean.

Consequently, the conflict between those who supported MFGB policy, like Booth, and those who supported Spencer continued over the next couple of years, particularly over the threat to use industrial action to

15 Barry Johnson, *Who Dips in the Tin, Who Dips in the Tin? The Butty System in the Nottinghamshire Coalfield* (Nottingham and Derbyshire Labour History Society, Occasional Pamphlet, March 2015) 1–2.

impose a new national agreement in 1924. Booth remained part of the left wing and in 1924 joined the National Minority Movement set up in 1923 with the aim of building a national rank and file organisation. However, Booth soon left when he discovered that it was tightly controlled by the Communist Party and there was little democracy.[16]

When the inevitable conflict over wage reductions came in 1926, Spencer made it clear he was against any stoppage. The General Strike started on 1 May 1926 but only lasted two weeks and was followed by the Miners lockout which lasted the rest of the year. On 5 October, Spencer negotiated a return to work deal with the local colliery owners at the Digby pit near Eastwood. However, this brought him into conflict with Booth and the MFGB, who wished to maintain unity. Unhappy with the influence of the MFGB, Spencer, supported by moderates, led a breakaway union from the NMA and set up the Nottinghamshire and District Miners' Industrial Union (NMIU). The breakaway union was strongest in those pits where the butty system operated and where the buttymen dominated the union. Of the 1926 miners' lockout, Les Ellis, who after the Second World War became Nottinghamshire Area treasurer of the National Union of Mineworkers, wrote that:

> the coal owners, desperate towards the end of the struggle, carefully analysed Notts. and came to the conclusion that a break in the miners' ranks could be affected, (1) because the long-established butty system lent itself to this purpose and (2) because of the spineless nature of the leadership of Spencer, Varley and Co.[17]

In December 1926, an anonymous miner stated:

> the cause of the breakaway in this county I put down first of all to the butty system. This only prevails in the Midlands, and it was in the Midlands that breakaway first took place. The first breakaway took place at one of the Bolsover pits—Clipstone, where the butty system is at its worst.[18]

Booth remained loyal to the NMA and MFGB and continued to

16 Griffin, *The Miners of Nottinghamshire*, 1914–1944, 143.
17 Johnson, *Who Dips in the Tin*, 1.
18 Ibid. Note that Clipstone is in Nottinghamshire, though the pit was owned by the Bolsover Colliery Company.

oppose the butty system and was elected NMA Vice-President in 1926. In a ballot in 1928, the Nottingham miners voted 9 to 1 in favour of the NMA (with 32,277 for the NMA and 2,533 for the NMIU).[19] Booth was aware that the employers would exploit the existence of the NMIU and spent the next ten years arguing for reunification even when this brought him into conflict with some of the more hard-line members of the NMA, such as William Bayliss, who was President from 1929–1930. Val Coleman, who was President from 1930 – 1932, generally supported Bayliss but was willing at least to meet with Spencer.[20]

The butty system had now become more widespread in the Midlands coalfields and was associated with the rise of other company unions. As a result, the first resolution presented to the MFGB conference at Weston-Super-Mare in August 1930 proposed that:

> The Miners' Federation of Great Britain Committee take the necessary steps to make the butty system illegal.[21]

Herbert Booth proposed the resolution and described the system as one that created a cleavage between the men, not only in the pits but in social life. Williams from the Forest of Dean backed Booth and said:

> only districts that had experienced the system had any idea what an abominable thing it was. Not only did it corrupt the relation of men with employers, but it corrupted the relations of workmen with one another. As a rule, a butty was a man who was a sort of boss without the status of one. He was a driver and a forcer and a man who often did little work himself. It was usual as a rule to find that where the system worked there was a low membership. At one colliery where the system works in my district, the average membership is less than 50 per cent. In a neighbouring colliery a mile away, where the system does not work, the membership, over the same period, is in the neighbourhood of 75 per cent.[22]

The resolution was seconded by Val Colman and carried unanimously.

In 1932, changes in the union's leadership led to a series of elections. Booth stood unsuccessfully for the posts of General Secretary

19 Griffin, *The Miners of Nottinghamshire*, 1914–1944, 224.
20 Griffin, *The Miners of Nottinghamshire*, 1914–1944, Chapter 14.
21 *Western Daily Press* 14 August 1930.
22 Ibid.

and Financial Secretary, before being elected President. Coleman was elected General Secretary and Bayliss as Financial Secretary and agent. However, by this time, the NMA, which was run by a hardcore of loyal supporters, was struggling to maintain its credibility as the employers would only negotiate with the NMIU. Despite this, nearly one in five of Nottinghamshire miners remained loyal to the NMA. In response, Booth continued to argue for reunification with the rival NMIU. This policy was unpopular with some NMA activists but was supported by Arthur Cook and the MFGB Executive. [23]

As predicted, the employers took full advantage of the split with increasing victimisation and arbitrary sacking of workers. It was clear to some miners that the NMIU was not providing trade union protection and had failed to increase wages or improve work conditions. At the same time Booth, Bayliss and Coleman worked together to rebuild the NMA, and by 1935 its membership reached 10,000 which was about one-third of the miners working in the coalfield.

Things came to a head in 1936 at Harworth Colliery where the NMA members were increasingly victimised. After a ballot organised by the MFGB, in December 1936, the NMA members at Harworth came out on strike for trade union recognition. Against this background, talks started between the MFGB and the NMIU on the possibilities of reconciliation. In January 1937, a meeting of the NMA heard a report from the MFGB setting out a strategy to fuse the two organisations, but this found little support among the NMA delegates. As a result, Booth vacated the chair, resigned the presidency and left the meeting.[24]

The MFGB launched a nationwide campaign in support of the Harworth strikers, and this heralded the increasing isolation of the NMIU which was growing steadily weaker regarding members and influence.[25] In April 1937, the MFGB voted in favour of a national strike in support of the recognition of the NMA in the Nottingham coalfield and in particular against victimisation of the men at Harworth Colliery. This motion was supported by the majority of the Forest of Dean miners who voted 2,973 in favour of a strike in support of the Harworth men and 336 against.[26]

By the end of May, the Harworth strike had been going for over six months, but with the threat of a national strike, a compromise was reached,

23 Griffin, *The Miners of Nottinghamshire*, 1914–1944, Chapter 14.
24 Bernard Taylor (Lord Taylor), *Up Hill All the Way, A Miners' Struggle*, (London: Sidgwick Jackson, 1972) 78.
25 Griffin, *The Miners of Nottinghamshire*, 1914–1944, Chapter 15.
26 R. Page Arnot, *The Miners in Crisis and War*, (London: George Allen and Unwin, 1961) 221.

resulting in the fusion of the two organisations. During the six months of the strike, the Harworth miners and their families endured arrest, police harassment, evictions, owners' intimidation and imprisonment with hard labour.[27]

The Nottinghamshire Miners' Federated Union (NMFU), affiliated to the MFGB, came into existence on 1 September 1937 with Spencer as President and Coleman as General Secretary. The Executive was made up of an equal number of representatives from each of the unions. Booth and Bayliss were appointed as full-time NMFU agents.[28]

In 1944, the NMFU became the Nottinghamshire Area of the National Union of Mineworkers. At the end of 1945 Spencer and Coleman retired and subsequently Booth was elected as General Secretary and Bayliss was elected as President. The two new agents, Dai Ley and Harry Straw, were members of the Communist Party. Booth was able to oversee the final removal of the butty system from all the Nottingham pits and the introduction of the public ownership of the mines in 1947. Nationalisation also allowed the NUM to negotiate more egalitarian wage structures based on a series of national agreements which sought to establish a uniform system of payment which was not dependent on the conditions in each district, pit or seam. Booth retired a few years later in 1950 and died in 1978.[29] The spectre of Spencerism reared its head again in Nottinghamshire during the 1984/85 miners' strike with the formation of the breakaway Union of Democratic Miners whose leadership opposed the NUM and the strike.

27 Ibid.
28 Ibid.
29 Griffin, *The Miners of Nottinghamshire*, Volume 2, 39.

Appendix Eight: Labour Unrest in the 1919 Miners' Strike

Labour unrest: coal miners' strike, 1919
Catalogue reference: HO 144/1534/387000/11

**SPECIAL INTELLIGENCE BRANCH.
THE COAL SITUATION.
SPECIAL DAILY REPORT.
11.a.m. - 24th July, 1919.**

**PART ONE.
SUMMARY OF POSITION TO MIDNIGHT 23rd July 1919.**

YORKSHIRE

Position in both West and South Yorkshire is reported quiet with no prospect of disturbance or riot at present. In the bulk of the pits in both districts the work of pumping is being carried on by volunteers (such as colliery officials) and naval ratings. Sir Eric Geddes is arranging to meet Mr. Herbert Smith to discuss the return of the proper pump hands to duty; and winding enginemen and pump-men of three colleries (sic) have resumed work today. The total number of naval ratings now employed is 158; and it is reported that winding enginemen and pump-men are contemplating a return to work in several districts to prevent naval ratings being sent. Six pits are flooded, and it is expected that four others will be flooded in the course of to-day. The hardship caused by the Coal Strike is increased by a Strike of the Co-operative Shop Employees which has extended to Barnsley, Doncaster, Rotherham and Sheffield.

DERBYSHIRE

The number now on strike (sic) is variously estimated at 25,000 (DAILY HERALD and DAILY TELEGRAPH) and 45,000 (DAILY EXPRESS). The Miners' leaders have appealed to the men to resume work. All the pits in South Derbyshire are still working. Pumping has been stopped at two pits and naval ratings have been sent.

NOTTINGHAMSHIRE.

The total number on strike in the county is stated to be about 20,000 including 15,000 in the Mansfield area. Pits were closed yesterday at Sherwood, Babbington, Wollston, and Bradford involving a further 3750 men.

STAFFORDSHIRE

Men are out at the Midland Coal, Coke and Iron Company's pits, also at Silverdale New Hem Heath and Parahouse; and further trouble is expected. Three pits are idle at Cannock Chase through insufficient surface-men turning up to work. Men have also been brought out at Bignall Hill. But safety men are being allowed to remain at work.

NORTHUMBERLAND and DURHAM

Dinnington and Stobswood and Allendale Collieries and in Northumberland have been standing idle since morning on a dispute as to the application of the Sankey Award on Hours. In county Durham following collieries idle on similar dispute: - Mainforth, Bear Park, Claravale, Westpelton, Alma Twisell, Handon, Holt, Craghead, Dandon, Adelaide and Langley Park.

LANCASHIRE and CHESHIRE and NORTH WALES

8,000 are idle owing to piece-rate dispute. 1,000 are on strike in the Bolton area. All pits in Cheshire and North Wales are working.

SOUTH WALES

Nine collieries are idle owing to a dispute as to alteration of hours; involving 6,920 men. Two Lewis Merthyr pits are stopped over reinstatement of a roadmen (sic), involving 3,900 men. Two pits are on strike as protest against intervention in Russia; one pit as a protest against the 6/- increase; and one pit owing to shortage of wagons. Total idle in the coalfield – 11,870 Later: – All pits have resumed work except Lewis Merthyr and one other (Acorn).

KENT

The strike at three pits continues, but the threat to call out the pumpmen has not been carried out. The owners are making enquiries about naval ratings in case of necessity.

SCOTLAND

The majority of the collieries are working normally. This week is an annual holiday in most of the Districts; but 2700 men are on strike in Fife on the seven hours question.

Bibliography

Allsop, D. and Wray D., 'The Rise and Fall of Autonomous Group Working in the British Coal Mining Industry', *Employee Responsibilities and Rights Journal,* September 2012, volume 24, Issue 3

Anstis, R., *Blood on Coal, The 1926 General Strike and the Miners' Lockout in the Forest of Dean* (Lydney: Black Dwarf, 1999)

Arnot, R. P., *The Miners: Years of Struggle* (London: Allen and Unwin, 1953)

Arnot, R. P., *South Wales Miners, Glowyr de Cymru: A History of the South Wales Miners' Federation (1914–1926)* (Cardiff: Cymric Federation Press, 1975)

Arnot, R. P., *The Miners in Crisis and War* (London: George Allen and Unwin, 1961)

Bagwell, P., *The History of the National Union of Railwaymen* (London: George Allen and Unwin, 1963)

Beech, M. M., 'Henry Crawshay, the Man and his Colliery', *New Regard*, No. 11, Forest of Dean Local History Society

Bevan, A., *In Place of Fear* (Great Britain: Simon and Schuster, 1952)

Bell, G., *Hesitant Comrades, The Irish Revolution and the British Labour Movement* (London: Pluto Press, 2016)

Bowley, A. L. *Prices and Wages in the UK 1914–1920* (London: Clarendon Press, 1921)

Boyce, R., *British Capitalism at the Crossroads, 1919–1932: A Study in Politics, Economics, and International Relations* (Cambridge: Cambridge University Press, 2011)

Bruley, S., *The Women and Men of 1926* (Cardiff: University of Wales Press, 2011)

Clegg, H. A., *A History of British Trade Unions since 1889 Vol. 2, 1911-1933* (Oxford: Clarendon Press, 1987)

Cole, G. D. H., *Labour in the Coal Mining Industry* (Oxford: Clarendon Press, 1923)

Cole, M. (Ed), *Beatrice Webb's Diaries, 1912-1924* (London: Longmans, 1952)

Coombes, B. L., *These Poor Hands, the autobiography of a miner working in South Wales* (Cardiff: University of Wales, 2002)

Craik, W.W., *Central Labour College, A Chapter in the History of Adult Working-class Education* (London: Lawrence and Wishart, 1964)

Dallas G. and Gill D., *The Unknown Army, Mutinies in the British Army in World War One* (London: Verso, 1985)

Desmarais, R. H., 'The British Government's Strikebreaking Organization and Black Friday', *Journal of Contemporary History*, Vol. 6, No. 2, (1971)

Douglass, D., 'The Durham Pitman', in *Miners, Quarrymen and Saltworkers*, Raphael Samuel (Ed), History Workshop Series (London: Routledge and Kegan Paul, 1977)

Englander, D., 'The National Union of Ex-Servicemen and the Labour Movement, 1918-1920', *History* (1991)

Field, G., *A Look Back at Norchard* (Self-Published: Cinderford, 1978)

Fisher, C., 'The Little Buttymen in the Forest of Dean', *International Review of Social History,* 25 (1980).

Fisher, C., *Custom, Work and Market Capitalism, The Forest of Dean Colliers, 1788-1888* (London: Breviary, 2016)

Foley, W., *Full Hearts and Empty Bellies* (London: Abacus, 1974)

Foot, M., *Aneurin Bevan* (London: Victor Gollancz, 1997)

Francis, H. and Smith D., *The Fed* (London: Lawrence and Wishart, 1980)

Fraser, W. H., *A History of British Trade Unionism 1700–1998* (London: Macmillan Press, 1999)

Glynn, S. and Oxborrow J., *Interwar Britain* (Allen and Unwin, 1976)

Griffin, A. R., *The History of the Nottingham Miners 1881–1914* (Nottingham: Nottingham Printers Limited)

Griffin, A. R., *The Miners of Nottinghamshire 1914–1944* (London: George Allen and Unwin, 1962)

Harrison, R. (Ed), *The Independent Collier, The Coal Miners as Archetypal Proletarian Reconsidered* (Sussex: Harvester Press, 1978)

Hart, C., *The Free Miners of the Royal Forest of Dean and Hundred of St Briavels* (Lydney: Lightmoor, 2002)

Hart, C., *The Industrial History of Dean* (Newton Abbott: David and Charles, 1971)

Hinton, J., *Labour and Socialism, A History of the British Labour Movement 1867-1974* (Brighton: Wheatsheaf Books, 1983)

Hodges, F., *My Adventures as a Labour Leader* (London: George Newnes, 1925)

Ives, M., *Reform, Revolution and Direct Action amongst British Miners* (Chicago: Haymarket, 2017)

John, A. V. (Ed), *Our Mothers' Land: Chapters in Welsh Women's History, 1830-1939* (Cardiff: University of Wales Press, 2011)

Johnson, B., *Who Dips in the Tin? The Butty System in the Nottinghamshire Coalfield* (Nottingham and Derbyshire Labour History Society, Occasional Pamphlet, March 2015)

Joynes, J. S., 'Description of seams and methods of working in the Forest of Dean', *British Society of Mining Students Journal,* XI (1889)

Kear A., *Bermuda Dick* (Lydney: Lightmoor Press, 2002)

Kendall, W., *The Revolutionary Movement in Britain 1900-1921* (London: Weidenfeld and Nicolson, 1969)

Kirby, M.W., *The British Coal Mining Industry, 1870 -1946* (London: Macmillan, 1977)

Lawson J. J., *The Man in the Cap: The Life of Herbert Smith* (London: Methuen, 1941)

Lovell, J., *Stevedores and Dockers* (London, 1969)

Marfell, A., *Forest Miner, A Forest of Dean Collier remembers life underground during the 1920s* (Coleford: Douglas McLean Publishing, 2010)

May, E., *A Question of Control: Social and Industrial Relations in the South Wales Coalfield and the Crisis of Post-War Reconstruction, 1914-1921*, A thesis presented to the School of Historical and Archaeological Studies, submitted in fulfilment of the regulations for the degree of Doctor of Philosophy in the University of Wales (Cardiff, 1995)

McCormick, B. J., *Industrial Relations in the Coal Industry* (London: Macmillan Press, 1979)

McIlroy, J., Campbell A. and Gildart K. (Eds), *Industrial Politics and the 1926 Mining Lockout: The Struggle for Dignity* (Cardiff: University of Wales, 2009)

Milliband, R., *Parliamentary Socialism* (Merlin Press, 2009)

Millman, B., *Managing Dissent in First World War Britain* (London: Frank Cass, 2000)

Mitchell, D., 'Ghost of Chance: British Revolutionaries in 1919', *History Today* (November 1970)

Morgan, K., *Wales, Rebirth of a Nation 1880-1980* (Oxford: Oxford University Press, 1982)

Mowat, C. L., *Britain Between the Wars, 1918–1940* (Methuen, 1955)

Murphy, J. T., *Preparing for Power* (London, 1972)

Oldham, T., *The Mines of the Forest of Dean* (Self-Published)

Organ, David M., *The Life and Times of David Richard Organ, Leading the Forest Miners' Struggle* (Cheltenham: Apex, 2011)

Orr, N. G., 'Keep the Home Fires Burning: Peace Day in Luton', *Family & Community History* (2:1, 1999)

People of Pillowell, *Pillowell* (Yorkley: Yorkley A&E, 2017)

Phelps, H., *Forest Voices* (Stroud: Chalford, 1996)

Pope, I., How B. and Karau P., *Severn and Wye Railway, Forest of Dean,* Volumes 1, 2, 3 and 4 (Wild Swan Publications, 1983–2009)

Renshaw, P., 'Black Friday, 1921', *History Today* (June 1971)

Renshaw, P., *The General Strike* (London: Eyre Methuen, 1975)

Roberts, H., *Memoirs* (Gage Library)

Roberts, H., *The Tar Castle* (Gage Library)

Roberts, H., *Cinderford, a Town Built on Coal* (Gage Library)

Rosenberg, C., *1919, Britain on the Brink of Revolution* (London: Bookmarks,1987)

Rothstein, A., *The Soldiers' Strikes of 1919* (London: Macmillan, 1980)

Rowe, J. W. F., *Wages in the Coal Industry* (London: King and Son, 1923)

Scotland, N., *Agricultural Trade Unionism in Gloucestershire, 1872–1950* (Cheltenham and Gloucester College of Higher Education, 1991)

Sherry, D., *Empire and Revolution* (London: Bookmarks, 2014)

Stubbs, J. O., 'Lord Milner and Patriotic Labour, 1914–18', *English Historical Review*, 87/345 (1972)

Supple, B., *The History of the British Coal Industry, Volume 4* (Oxford: Clarendon, 1987)

Taylor, B., *Up Hill All the Way, A Miners' Struggle* (London: Sidgwick Jackson, 1972)

Thomas, G., *The Sky of Our Lives* (London: Hutchinson, 1972)

Thomas, J., *The Miners' Conflict with the Mineowners* (London: Forgotten Books)

Tuffley, D., *Mining and Quarry Fatalities in the Forest of Dean*, CD (Forest of Dean: Forest of Dean History Society, 2006)

Turnbull, R., *Climbing Mount Sinai: Noah Ablett 1883-1935* (Socialist History Occasional Publication 40, 2017)

Ward, S. R., 'Intelligence Surveillance of British Ex-Servicemen, 1918-1920', *The Historical Journal* (1973).

Webb, S., *1919, Britain's Year of Revolution* (Barnsley: Pen and Sword, 2016)

White, C. and Williams, S. R. (Eds), *Struggle or Starve, Women's Lives in the South Wales valleys between the two World Wars* (Powys: Honno, 2002)

Williams, C., *Capitalism, Community and Conflict, The South Wales Coalfield* (Cardiff: University of Wales Press, 1998)

Winter, J. M. *Socialism and the Challenge of War* (London: Routledge, 1974)

Woodhouse, M. G., 'Mines for the Nation or Mines for the Miners? Alternative Perspectives on Industrial Democracy, 1919-1921', *Llafur* (1978)

Wright, I., *Walter Virgo and the Blakeney Gang* (Bristol: Bristol Radical History Group, 2013)

Wright, I., *Coal on One Hand, Men on the Other, The Forest of Dean Miners and the First World War 1910 – 1922* (Bristol: Bristol Radical History Group, 2nd Edition, 2017)

Newspapers

Bath Chronicle and Weekly Gazette
Daily Herald
Dean Forest Mercury
Gloucestershire Echo
Gloucester Citizen
Gloucester Journal
Gloucestershire Chronicle
Labour Gazette
Merthyr Pioneer
Northern Whig
Rhondda Leader
South Wales Daily Post
The Times,
Sheffield Daily Telegraph
Western Mail
Western Morning News
Western Daily Press

Minutes

FDMA minutes 1919—1921, Richard Burton Archives, SWCC/MNA/ NUM/3/8/20a-h.

Board Minute Book of Henry Crawshay & Co. Ltd. (O) 1919-1921, October 1919 Accounts, Gloucestershire Archives, D8729/1/1/15.

Websites

Ralph Darlington, *Syndicalism and strikes, leadership and influence: Britain, Ireland, France, Italy, Spain and the United States* (University of Salford, 2017) usir.salford.ac.uk/id/eprint/31003/

Jeroen Sprenger, *The Triple Alliance,* London School of Economics and Political Science (1975-1976)
www.jeroensprenger.nl/Triple%20Alliance/the-1919-railway-strike.html

Oxford Dictionary of National Biography www.oxforddnb.com/

Warwick Digital Collections
contentdm.warwick.ac.uk/cdm/ref/collection/tav/id/2357

www.pillowellsilverband.com/band-history.html

List of mines in Great Britain and the Isle of Man, 1918 ancestry.com

Ancestry www.ancestry.co.uk

British Newspaper Archive www.britishnewspaperarchive.co.uk

Hansard hansard.parliament.uk

Forest of Dean Family History Trust www.forest-of-dean.net

Interviews or Memoirs

The Gage Library, Dean Heritage Centre, Soudley, Forest of Dean.

Harry Barton

Jesse Hodges (Jnr)

Molly Curtis

Caroline Nicholls

Fred Warren

Erik Warren

Alan Drew

Albert Meek

Amy Adams

Harry Toomer